Praise for *Make a Difference*

"In this interesting book, Gary MacDougal goes well beyond analysis and theory. His story takes you directly to the people and communities involved, and it actually provides practical answers to some of our most difficult welfare problems. The whole country can learn from this timely and engaging new book."

—William Julius Wilson, Harvard University

"At UPS we've been lucky to hire sixty thousand former welfare recipients and we're a better company because of them. *Make a Difference* is a lively, example-filled story that shows how this works—a fascinating read for anyone."

—Mike Eskew, CEO, UPS

GARY MacDOUGAL

Make a Difference

A SPECTACULAR BREAKTHROUGH

IN THE FIGHT AGAINST

POVERTY

The New, Updated 2005 Edition

TRUMAN TALLEY BOOKS
ST. MARTIN'S GRIFFIN
NEW YORK

To Harvey W. Branigar (1913–1993)

A great, compassionate man

and a

wonderful mentor

www.stmartins.com

ISBN 0-312-34726-X
EAN 978-0312-34726-0

Second Edition: May 2005

10   9   8   7   6   5   4   3   2   1

Contents

Contents

Prologue

This book is about how a dramatically changed government in Illinois helps disadvantaged people become self-sufficient, and about how Illinois can be a model for the nation. But the story starts over ten years before and also far away, measured in distance, about ten thousand miles away; in time zones, twelve—in other words just about halfway around the world from Illinois. I was in Nepal. Both my job and my marriage had ended, and I was on a solitary trek in the Himalayas. I was on my way to gaze at the very top of the earth, Mount Everest, with my own eyes. I can't explain why that was important to me, it just was. More important, I wanted to think about what to do with the rest of my life.

The story ends in a far different place—in Illinois, with people on welfare. I have logged many hours over the intervening years as "the only white guy in the room," and additional hours over those same years in the halls and back rooms of the capital with legislators. The Governor's Task Force for Human Services Reform that I led for 3½ years, bureaucrats, union leaders, self-interested state contractors, trapped caseworkers, and the governor fill out the picture.

There wasn't a straight line from Nepal to the end of the Governor's Task Force. Along the way I helped out with George Bush's campaign for the presidency, came close to running for the U.S. Senate from Illinois, and learned some things about the problems of poor people by serving as a trustee of several foundations. And I had to flag down Governor Edgar of Illinois and persuade him to get the task force process underway.

Over most of the intervening years, the task force led the way in highlighting the mess, typical of all big states, that was the welfare and human services systems. At the end of our work, most human services in Illinois had been combined into a single organization, managed in a way that delivers rational, seamless "one stop" services to individuals and families temporarily in need. According to experts, Illinois now leads the nation in truly fundamental reform.

To anyone who looks at the state's organization chart, the task force's result was consolidating all or parts of six agencies into one. But more important, the task force began a process of involving communities in decision-making about how to deliver services, and helped inspire a statewide system that measured real self-sufficiency results.

Perhaps the most valuable lesson, one that I can't prove but that I know is right: the overwhelming majority of people still on the welfare rolls, even in the roughest inner city neighborhoods, would work if they had the opportunity, usually inspired by the desire to help their children. Another crucial lesson learned is that *we know the answers* to helping even the toughest longtime inner city welfare recipients become self-sufficient, and applying the answers *won't cost any more* than we are now spending. We're poised at a unique moment in time to really *make a difference,* a permanent difference.

Like anything worthwhile, lots of people played a role in the transformation. I learned at least as much from "the ladies in the backyard," a group of hardcore women on welfare that included a prostitute and a convicted felon who came together to talk to me about their lives, as I did from the many foundation meetings and policy books. I learned about "swimming around in oatmeal," a bureaucratic skill, and how to set things up so that politicians can keep moving forward with a minimum of political risk. I met some "poverty pimps," people who need poverty as a business and who worry more about what change will do to themselves than they worry about poor people. Getting the task force reform enshrined in law put me in a weird dance with some remarkable characters. Throughout the adventure some real heroes emerged in unlikely places, people without whom reform would not have happened. You start meeting them in the first chapter.

Introduction

Rarely a day goes by without a major article on some aspect of welfare reform or the seemingly intractable problem of poverty. We as a nation spend about $520[1] billion for a myriad of welfare and related human services each year, largely on the 36 million[2] Americans below the poverty line—about $14,500 per person in poverty. This compares with the poverty line in the U.S. at $18,850 per year[3] *for a family of four.* Yet this so-called river of money somehow rarely reaches poor people in a way that helps them escape dependency.

This book shows the way out of this morass. It will show—based on the experience in one important state, Illinois—how straightforward bipartisan principles can be developed and implemented which can dramatically improve the chances of those on welfare becoming self-sufficient. It will describe how a special Governor's Task Force, which I led, set up successful test sites in vastly different communities (African-American, heavily Hispanic, rural, small city, and suburb) to prove the soundness of the principles, and then built a new statewide system from the bottom up, incorporating all that was learned.

The results, as we will see, were *spectacular*—a real breakthrough in our understanding of what it takes to solve this problem that so many thought could not be solved. From the summer of 1996, when Illinois legislation initiating what Governor Edgar called "the biggest reorganization of state government since 1900" was signed, and when federal welfare reform was enacted, the Illinois rolls declined from 642,644 recipients to 92,667—an amazing 86 percent.[4] Post-reform (leaver) studies showed that most who left the rolls were working and, on average, earning above the minimum wage. This placed Illinois ahead of all "big city" states, second only to Wyoming among all states. Nine county human services offices had *no welfare recipients*!

Three basic ingredients underlie the Illinois reform effort, and some of them, to some degree, have contributed to progress in other states. First, the myriad federal and state programs on the front lines (e.g., welfare, mental health, child care, transportation, job training and placement, and substance abuse) must be combined in a single organization, managed in a way to allow rational, seamless "one stop" services to individuals temporarily in need, taking into consideration their whole families. Second, effectively connecting these government and government-financed services to communities (e.g., schools, businesses, churches, police, local governments, United Way) so that the overwhelming share of money directed to poor people by government can work with and be informed by the grass roots leaders and citizens who know the problems and resources of their community best. Third, measuring the outcomes—the real outcomes along the path to self-sufficiency—of the billions invested. We must know which taxpayer dollars are working, and which are not. True accountability in welfare/human services spending seems obvious but is really quite rare.

This is a story of a from-the-bottom discovery of what has been wrong with the current system nationwide, anchored by the views of actual welfare recipients, not ideologues or academics. The "ladies in the backyard," a group of welfare recipients an inner-city minister friend of mine assembled to help educate me, know what is wrong.

We either don't ask them, or don't listen when we do. I will describe how I persuaded the governor to set up a task force on human services reform and name me to chair it. I will explain how I formed it, set a strategy for developing the guiding principles, how we selected the test sites and got them started, how we broke down skepticism in the community about the state's commitment to change, how champions for change emerged within the huge bureaucracies, and how the initiation of the efforts in the test sites began to change people's lives—mostly by using existing taxpayer dollars better.

This book will also describe how the success of the five test sites became well-known statewide, attracted the interest of other communities and the public, and paved the way for legislation to reform the entire system and state. The whole effort became embroiled in a legislative battle that required me to cash in political chips in order to keep the reform from being destroyed. In addition, concerns of those who receive the billions of dollars in state human services contracts and payments for services as well as the unions needed to be managed. Special interests and entrenched bureaucracy gave new meaning to the term *passive resistance*. The story of this dramatic change is narrated in a way that highlights the thoughts and feelings of the wide array of people involved, but also it serves as a "how-to" guide for other states and for Washington, D.C. Numerous personal profiles and anecdotes from people at all levels have been utilized to illustrate the policy lessons and to give the reader a firsthand, grass roots flavor of what happens inside the welfare labyrinth. Along the way, lives and communities were changed, and the idea of creating what I call a "ladder of opportunity" for disadvantaged citizens to climb gained widespread acceptance. Helping people become self-sufficient became a bipartisan goal. All of this may sound simple, but making it happen was far more challenging than I ever dreamed.

Illinois now leads the nation in truly fundamental reform, and has shattered some dearly held biases of both liberals and conservatives. Conservatives need to know that large numbers of people really do want to work, but that the bottom rungs aren't there on the ladder they need to climb. Liberals will learn that the passage of the recent welfare reform legislation energized the entire system with its focus on work, that the one-way handouts really did sap incentive, and that much of the government money for programs, however well intended, wasn't working very well.

At the heart of all this are real people, people whom most of us, including policymakers, rarely get to know. I contend that the great majority of the individuals on welfare share the same desire to work and have the same personal aspirations for themselves and their families that most Americans hold. It's hard for most of us to appreciate just how tough the circumstances of many disadvantaged people really are and why they often don't behave in a way that makes sense to the rest of us. I became a believer that if most of us started out with the disadvantages I saw, we'd be stuck, too, unless we spotted some kind of "ladder of opportunity."

For example, you will meet and hear the success story of formerly chronically unemployed welfare recipient Janice McCrae, who was able to move into meaningful work, despite having spent thirteen years on welfare. Janice happened to live in the Grand Boulevard community of the south side of Chicago, an area some have called the most disadvantaged urban area in the country. As a result of the Illinois effort, when I talked to Janice she had now worked part-time with full benefits sorting packages at a United Parcel Service hub for over two years, and was being considered for promotion to full-time work. She was thirty-one years old, has sons nine and fourteen, and a twelve-year-old daughter. She lives in the notorious Robert Taylor Homes housing project, a half-hour bus ride from her job. With its drugs, gunfire, garbage, boarded-up windows, bad plumbing, and lack of reasonable access to any amenities such as grass or even a loaf of bread, it is hard to imagine any worse place in the whole world than Robert Taylor Homes. Janice told me she had seven sisters and six brothers with their own problems, primarily drugs. The siblings ranged in age from eighteen to forty-five, with, for example, a twenty-five-year-old sister with seven children "who is always high on drugs, can't read labels, and doesn't care," according to Janice.

Interviewed at work, Janice was very happy. She says: "I enjoy coming to work and learning different things . . . I really like my kids to know I work . . . This should have happened ten years ago . . . I believe many of my friends wouldn't do no drugs if they had a chance for a real job." After almost an hour of conversation Janice clearly trusts me, and starts to tell me the harder facts of her life. She tells me about the drug dealer father of her older son, having her tubes tied, and having to leave work to escort her kids home from school when the gangs are shooting. I remember often, in discussions with people like Janice, wishing that my affluent white friends could have the experience of listening to her. I feel very lucky that there is something about me, and something about her, that allows us to share our feelings, despite our origins in different worlds.

Stories like Janice's come from the cross-section of Illinois communities where the reform effort has been tested for over three years. A key theme of this reform is that one size does not fit all, because communities are so different. Top-down solutions from Washington or state capitals will continue to fail; the right thing to do will be different in the South Bronx than it is in Southern Illinois. We will see how high-minded intentions of legislators quickly lead to wasted human and financial resources, perverse incentives, and administrative nightmares.

A key myth that needs to be shattered is the sometimes-convenient idea that most people on welfare are lazy and don't want to work. I say convenient because it's easier to write people off with a clear conscience if you convince yourself that they are lazy and don't care about themselves. There are some that are lazy, but the overwhelming majority, over 70 percent in my observation, really want to work if given a chance. There is another group with mental and physical disabilities that may never be totally self-sufficient, most of whom would like to make a contribution. The relatively small remaining group who have both capability and opportunity but chose not to move toward self-sufficiency will need tough love.

These issues are crucial, since the 1996 welfare reform law devolves much of this seemingly intractable problem to the states. In the coming years, governors will be expected to produce better results with less money, or their states will face increased social problems and severe financial penalties, making "ending welfare as we know it" a failure. This book contends that since the states have long spent the overwhelming majority of both federal and state funds directed at welfare and poverty and since states are now empowered with greater flexibility, state system reform is a sine qua non in solving the welfare problem. When asked why he robbed banks, Willie Sutton answered, "Because that's where the money is." The states are not only where the money is, they are closer to the people who need help. All of this means that our country badly needs a strong, successful, and replicable state model. Though still a work in progress, Illinois is this model, and this book can serve as a blueprint for other states.

This book will describe, often in the words of enthusiastic former welfare recipients and others affected, how the massive change was accomplished. This reform required strong and institutionalized connections among the massive, multibillion-dollar state (and federal) human services/welfare systems, and between the system and communities (churches, schools, businesses, local government, community leaders, and ordinary citizens) throughout Illinois. Community collaboratives or "federations," as we came to call them, were formed in each of the five test sites, and these federations proved to be a community magnet, the "go-to" place for problem-solving. The federations also tapped a vast reservoir of community volunteers—people who wanted to make a difference.

Among other major changes, this reform integrates the myriad disconnected government programs built up over many years into "one stop shopping" for those in need. It's hard to get a job if you are running all over the city dealing with three or more bureaucracies, each with thick files on your case and often conflicting requirements. The program dollars from Washington and state capitals often pick out a single family member (e.g., a teen mother) and a single problem (e.g., drugs), and attempt to solve the problem in isolation, without considering the impact of family and other problems. However, the family (even a fragmented family) is often where answers (as well as other barriers) to self-sufficiency are found. Often the connection of human services to jobs is nonexistent, and the numerous human services departments don't (and sometimes can't by law) share data. The new Illinois system is backed up by an integrated management information system, a little-talked-about but crucial ingredient. Relevant public policy issues show up throughout as a sort of subtext, but care has been taken not to let them get in the way of the story of the people involved in the reform effort and how they came together to create this historic change.

No one, not the sharpest of state budget officers, the most thoughtful of Washington think tank gurus, not Mayors Daley or Giuliani, and certainly not a presidential candidate, can tell you how much federal, state, and city human services money goes into a given community (e.g., the South Bronx, Chicago's Grand Boulevard, or South Central L.A.), much less what the outcomes might be for those investments in a given community. The money flows in by program (Food Stamps, WIA [Workforce Investment Act], WIC [food for women, infants, and children], etc.) to armies of private providers, state workers, and direct recipients, most of whom operate largely unaware of the others' activities. Yet there is a river of money flowing into each poor community, for example more than $240[5] million per year is spent on Chicago's Grand Boulevard community alone. The management information systems don't speak to each other, and this bewildering array of well-intentioned and expensive programs operate largely independent of one another, even though they are intended to serve largely the same families. As shown in an Illinois newspaper political cartoon,[6] an organization chart of the human services systems is far more complicated than even Rube Goldberg could imagine.

It is obvious to the most casual observer that any sprawling, complex system that has been in disarray for decades (especially a government system), can't become truly effective in the relatively few years since the 1996 welfare reform act was passed. However, in what we might call the first phase of welfare reform, much *has* been accomplished. In particular, welfare reform has dramatically changed the direction of most state systems, establishing a powerful overarching focus on welfare recipients becoming self-sufficient, and on the now temporary nature of most welfare assistance—a hand up, not a hand-out.

Nationally, the nation's welfare rolls came down an amazing 60 percent in the seven years since welfare reform was enacted in the summer of 1996! As the following table from the Web site of the U.S. Department of Human Services (Figure 1) shows, the U.S. total number of recipients of Temporary Assistance for Needy Families (as welfare is now called) was 12,241,489 in August 1996, and declined to 4,955,479 by June 2003, a reduction of 7,286,010 recipients. This was achieved despite a sluggish economy in 2000. Though those who leave the rolls for work are often still below the poverty line, clearly a giant step has been made on the road to self-sufficiency. The table shows a wide variation in performance among states. Interesting questions arise—why should Indiana's number of recipients be about the same as before welfare reform was enacted, while neighbors Ohio and Illinois have reduced the rolls 66 percent and 86 percent respectively? This question and many others arise from these data and, to me, show that as a nation we have a tremendous opportunity to help millions more start moving from dependency to self-sufficiency.

With the reductions in number of clients, the individual case-worker's client loads are approaching more manageable levels, and there is greater value added in the form of breaking the pattern of dependency passed down for generations. Self-sufficiency role models are now starting to show up in the housing projects. I have interviewed numerous welfare recipients and caseworkers in the last few years, and among other things, I usually ask the question, "What percentage of your neighbors [or your caseload] would you guess use drugs?" Though, for understandable reasons, there are no hard data, the answer usually comes out well over 50 percent, often 70 percent. Though much of it is casual or recreational drug use, employer drug testing will often catch it, resulting in a lost job opportunity. The other question, "What percentage have criminal records?" Again no hard data, but it is a fair estimate that 20 percent of remaining welfare recipients have criminal records, usually felonies. The percentage of ex-offenders among fathers of children on welfare is undoubtedly

FIGURE 1. TEMPORARY ASSISTANCE FOR NEEDY FAMILIES
TOTAL NUMBER OF RECIPIENTS
PERCENT CHANGE FROM AUGUST 1996 TO JUNE 2003

State	Aug-96	June-03	(96-03)
Alabama	100,662	45,792	-55%
Alaska	35,544	15,358	-57%
Arizona	169,442	115,943	-32%
Arkansas	56,343	24,403	-57%
California	2,581,948	1,106,624	-57%
Colorado	95,788	37,364	-61%
Connecticut	159,246	43,153	-73%
Delaware	23,654	12,678	-46%
Dist. of Col.	69,292	43,113	-38%
Florida	533,801	115,510	-78%
Georgia	330,302	131,349	-60%
Guam	8,314	10,783	30%
Hawaii	66,482	24,994	-62%
Idaho	21,780	3,260	-85%
Illinois	**642,644**	**92,667**	**-86%**
Indiana	142,604	139,974	-2%
Iowa	86,146	52,349	-39%
Kansas	63,783	40,942	-36%
Kentucky	172,193	76,211	-56%
Louisiana	228,115	56,431	-75%
Maine	53,873	28,479	-47%
Maryland	194,127	60,916	-69%
Massachusetts	226,030	107,455	-52%
Michigan	502,354	202,584	-60%
Minnesota	169,744	95,755	-44%
Mississippi	123,828	45,152	-64%
Missouri	222,820	106,338	-52%
Montana	29,130	17,843	-39%
Nebraska	38,592	26,804	-31%
Nevada	34,261	24,312	-29%
New Hampshire	22,937	14,809	-35%
New Jersey	275,637	100,613	-63%
New Mexico	99,661	43,540	-56%
New York	1,143,962	333,522	-71%
North Carolina	267,326	82,312	-69%
North Dakota	13,146	8,735	-34%
Ohio	549,312	185,132	-66%
Oklahoma	96,201	36,040	-63%
Oregon	78,419	43,237	-45%
Pennsylvania	531,059	208,973	-61%
Puerto Rico	151,023	53,945	-64%
Rhode Island	56,560	34,547	-39%
South Carolina	114,273	46,346	-59%
South Dakota	15,896	6,197	-61%
Tennessee	254,818	184,253	-28%
Texas	649,018	335,906	-48%
Utah	39,073	22,032	-44%
Vermont	24,331	12,494	-49%
Virgin Islands	4,898	1,428	-71%
Virginia	152,845	69,928	-54%
Washington	268,927	135,887	-49%
West Virginia	89,039	40,585	-54%
Wisconsin	148,888	49,791	-67%
Wyoming	11,398	691	-94%
U.S. Total	**12,241,489**	**4,955,479**	**-60%**

Source: Department of Health and Human Services – Administration for Children and Families[7]

much higher. Prospective employers ask that the criminal record box be checked on the application form, and then the job disappears. The result is that someone, usually a young African-American male in the inner city, is sentenced to the street corner for the rest of life. These problems are manageable. As shown by successful programs at UPS and other places, *we know the answers.* Self-sufficiency is attainable for those deep in the pool, but it will take some time and vision to put some lower rungs on the ladder of opportunity so that it can be climbed. Once the ladder is there, we should have no qualms about a complete cutoff. A hungry stomach will get most people back on the ladder.

The President, governors, legislators, businessmen, journalists, state administrators, church leaders, and most of the rest of us can pick up the banner of self-sufficiency and march on to new high ground. We can all *really make a difference.* As in most states, we have lots of examples in Illinois of people who had been on welfare most of their adult lives, with extremely difficult circumstances, who are thrilled to be working and who have been on the job for over a year. They will tell you how proud they are to have their children see them go off to work, and tell you of their plans to take courses that will prepare them for promotion. Their questions are "Why didn't you make these changes a long time ago?" and "What can we do to help my neighbors who aren't working yet?" This is a win, win, win—states and companies need a larger entry-level labor pool to keep growing, poor people need jobs for a better life, and our political leaders need to show results.

Wouldn't it be exciting to be part of the team that brought our country to the point where *everyone* had a ladder of opportunity, so that it was just up to the individual to climb it? What a wonderful example to set for the world! As the nation with the biggest and strongest economy in the world, and as the world's only superpower, shouldn't this be our goal? Success in creating opportunity for everyone would remove the sole remaining criticism of democracy and capitalism—that we ignore people who are suffering, that they don't really have a chance. As a conservative Republican I'm talking about a decent *chance* to be self-sufficient—not a handout. And I continue to maintain we don't need to increase taxpayer spending—just use the present resources better.

Despite the success of the first phase of welfare reform, we must remember that almost 5 million[8] human beings are still on welfare. Welfare, for the most part, is given to mothers with children, so there is a very large group of men in our most disadvantaged communities who are also unemployed and not easily employable. Though not on welfare, this group is of particular importance, since a very large percentage of them are the fathers of those children who are on welfare. Right now many of them are getting federal food stamps, hanging out on street corners, and getting into trouble. We will talk more about them when we discuss future steps later in the book. They are a key part of the puzzle we are finally starting to solve.

It is a wonderful time to get something done, since a strong economy has created opportunities for people whose lack of work experience might have left them out in times when employers could be more selective. When welfare reform became law, many critics foresaw disaster, because they feared there would not be enough jobs. What they didn't appreciate was that the availability of a larger pool of job seekers can be a factor in encouraging employers to expand—available jobs are a moving target. Persistent pockets of unemployment in the face of overall strong demand for labor in recent years have highlighted the fact that there are barriers for people in distressed communities that keep them from working, even though there are employers needing help. We now know there are answers to this problem. When the economy takes its next downturn, welfare recipients will be affected disproportionately. An economic downturn, coupled with mistakes that will inevitably be made by some states, will produce pressure by critics to go back to the old ways—running the risk of throwing out the baby with the bathwater. This would be a tragic mistake. We have to build on our proven success, correcting mistakes as we continue to move forward.

There are those who will criticize my strong focus on entry-level jobs. Shouldn't we be worried about training people in the sophisticated skills needed by the American economy in the new millennium? Of course we should worry about this, but let's start at the beginning. What was your first job? Did it require sophisticated skills, and would it support a family of four? Was it on a direct track to a "well-paying" job? Most first jobs are not—mine was in a gas station, pumping gas and cleaning restrooms. For people in families where no one has worked for several generations, a regular entry-level job is a *huge* breakthrough, a place on the ladder, albeit on a very low rung. The barriers overcome, the work habits learned, the example set, and the beginning of a credible resume are very big steps forward.

Recent studies of what happens to workers at McDonald's[9] show that the popular dead-end image is often wrong. We have to start at the beginning, and we can't let the perfect be the enemy of the good. We have to have more faith in what is inside people, and what happens to their aspirations once they break out. Susanne Motley started sorting packages at UPS, took courses after work, and is now a licensed practical nurse. Many employers have tuition reimbursement plans—and a strong desire to upgrade the skills of their workforce. Let's get everybody up on the first rung of the ladder, and not let our worries about the working poor distract us from focusing on the millions who are worse off. Future efforts can address ways of helping community colleges become more relevant and effective and on the deployment of other public and private resources that can help the process of improving skills. As with the nurse who began at UPS, once the self-sufficiency process is started, individual responsibility begins to become more important than government responsibility.

My intense focus on getting the most intractable unemployed to work may also agitate another group of critics, who will say, "Doesn't he understand that education is the key to all of this?" Clearly, unless we fix the schools, particularly the inner-city schools in the most distressed areas, we're going to continue to generate a pool of difficult-to-employ people. Schools are a crucial part of the puzzle, but the welfare mothers, youths in prison, and others in the bottom half of the poverty ranks have, for the most part, already dropped out and aged out of school. They are already out there. It is these people who are learning, for the first time, the discipline of going to work every day, showing up on time, and doing the work. These successful first jobs change their outlook and reconnect them, paving the way for further education and training after work for those that want it.

Of course fixing the schools is going to greatly reduce the flow of additional people difficult to employ, the problem-filled people that this book focuses upon. Some of the principles in this book have already been used in turning around the Chicago school system in recent years. A strong requirement that outcomes be measured, involvement of parents and communities, and integrated after-school and summer school activities and requirements have pushed up test scores. Waste has been identified and resources redeployed. Running a big-city school system now looks more like a thoughtful management job than it used to—more MBA than EdD. Big-city schools still have a long way to go, but the $7,000 plus per capita spending in places like New York City, Chicago, and Washington, D.C., should be enough, especially when compared with the Catholic schools that spend about half that amount, but get dramatically better results. Education is very fixable when someone is really in charge and the political will is there to back it up. Aggressive governors in Florida and other states are embracing this challenge. But that is someone else's book.

The 60 percent[10] national reduction in welfare accomplished by 2003 happened in most places despite the fragmented mess that was most human services systems when the effort began. Those remaining on the rolls can be moved to self-sufficiency if each state, with flexibility from Washington, can fundamentally reform its human services systems in the manner of the Illinois model—integrating services for the whole family, connecting with communities, and measuring outcomes.

As a nation we're off to a good start, but we need to keep the momentum going and move to that new, higher ground. This book intends to show that we do, in fact, know the answers, and to advance some ideas on how we can all make a difference in the lives of our most disadvantaged citizens. This effort makes sense from many perspectives, whether as taxpayer, concerned citizen, or proud American. Many of us also add feelings of moral obligation, or religious conviction. There is an opportunity for each of us to get involved in an important and satisfying piece of this challenge.

1
Getting Involved

Traveler, there is no path; paths are made by walking.
—SPANISH SAYING

It was a cold, gray Chicago afternoon and I was headed to a meeting way down on the South Side in an area that clearly made my white cab driver uncomfortable. "Are you sure you know where you are going?" he said, observing my white face and middle-class attire. I had learned some time ago from my African-American friends that it wasn't wise to drive my Mercedes in the Grand Boulevard area because that car was much too inviting when stopped for a red light or a stop sign in front of clusters of young men loitering on the street corners. Once, when visiting a welfare office in Chicago's Austin community on the West Side, I walked the one short block to the CTA train, and a young black man raced across the street and grabbed my arm shouting, "Hey, white man, what are you doing down here? You're afraid of me, aren't you?" There was some combination of hatred and mocking in his eyes. Knowing the knives and other weapons that he and his friends surely possessed, I was *definitely* afraid. I remembered a friend of mine who was mugged and his arm slashed, cutting a nerve that caused him to lose the use of his thumb and fingers. I kept walking briskly, then sprinted up the stairs to the elevated train. It's hard to come to grips with the fact that a large number of people who don't even know you deeply resent you because of the color of your skin—and the privileges that color is thought to, and most assuredly does, bring with it.

This time I was headed for an afternoon discussion with a group of African-American women that the Reverend B. Herbert Martin and I came to call "the ladies in the backyard." I would be meeting with Maxine, a dour twenty-year-old felon and mother recently released from prison, and Lavon, a vivacious midtwenties mother and prostitute, among others. The Reverend Martin, a smart, handsome, charming man in his forties, had become a friend in the course of my work on the state's convoluted and problematic human services systems, and he was an important, though sometimes controversial, leader in Chicago's large African-American community. He became pastor of his church, Progressive Community, when it had only forty-two members, and in a dozen years had built it into a vibrant institution of over two thousand parishioners engaged in a wide range of activities, largely centered on outreach to the poverty-stricken Grand Boulevard community. His charisma was electric, and attending a service at Progressive is an unforgettable experience. B. Herbert, as he is often called, counted among his parishioners the legendary Harold Washington, Chicago's first black mayor—a man whose picture and memory are still omnipresent in Chicago's black community many years after his death.

My wife, Charlene, and I found his Sunday services inspirational and fascinating. At our first visit there, our white skins made us feel somewhat self-conscious, but the friendliness of the parishioners and the incredibly beautiful gospel singing of the huge choir soon dissipated our anxiety. The music soared in a very exciting way, and the end of each piece was followed by heartfelt exclamations of "Thank you, Lord!" from all parts of the congregation. I learned that this is part of the "talk-back" or "call and response" African-American religious tradition[1] that enriches the service from beginning to end, finding its roots in the Deep South. We couldn't help but be swept up in the spiritual electricity and the deep devotion that filled the lively church.

The Reverend Martin's preaching made full use of the long pause, always stimulating responses ranging from the grateful "Amen!" to "Hallelujah, praise the Lord!" There was a musicality to his homilies, which often addressed the problems of race, overcoming great obstacles, and the importance of family. Although I didn't agree with everything he said, this church was clearly an oasis of hope and values at Ground Zero in the struggle against poverty and crime. Like many inner-city church leaders, B. Herbert ran a regular food pantry and countless other programs serving the community—without any government money. The congregation consisted predominantly of women and younger children, a large number of them dressed beautifully in white, with white hats and white gloves. The few men present were usually honored with leadership roles, in part, I suspect, to encourage their attendance. The Reverend Martin always sought out good male role models to strengthen the congregation. The services were long—one Palm Sunday service we attended lasted from 10:30 A.M. to 2:00 P.M.! When we asked B. Herbert about the length of the service, he said, "We are providing therapy to people who can't afford therapists—and look at what they have to go back to when they leave the service."

Several weeks before this afternoon's scheduled meeting, I got a call from B. Herbert asking to get together. We ended up agreeing to meet for breakfast at his apartment on Grand Boulevard. The apartment building was rehabbed public housing, and he was the only male tenant, living there with his teenage son and daughter. He greeted me at the door on the third floor of the walk-up and ushered me in to a small but comfortable apartment where a lavish breakfast was laid out on the kitchen table. Southern food traditions show up everywhere in Chicago's black community, and the dizzying variety and heaping portions are hallmarks of this folk cuisine. When we sat down I eagerly picked up a fork, but he paused and announced that it was my turn to say grace. I apologized, mumbling something about the food looking so good that I had inexcusably overlooked grace. Saying grace one-on-one with a man whose prayerful oratory is beyond eloquent made me a little nervous, but I think I did a passable job.

After some interesting small talk, he got to the point. "Gary, you are the only white guy I've seen in the twenty-five years I've been here who has come to this area to help and who has stayed with it to really make a difference. We've seen well-meaning white people 'parachute in,' as we say, bringing an idea and good intentions. But they tend to disappear in reasonably short order. As you well know, Grand Boulevard is a very tough situation, and I don't want you to be disappointed. You and the governor need to really understand, at the grass roots, what you are up against."

He went on to tell me about a group of women who gathered most afternoons in the small backyard of his apartment building. He told of their drinking, swearing, and how they often shared their monthly welfare checks with their boyfriends. "The bottom line," he said, "is unless we can reach this group and do things that will result in a change in their behavior, we won't have succeeded in our reform efforts. You can change how the state does things and how it is organized, you can support the formation and operation of community groups, but until the ladies in the backyard change their behavior, you will not have success." I knew he was right. A rough analogy from my business world was the need to really get to know the customer. He ended by saying: "Gary, you are a great guy, I know you care a lot, but I don't want you to get hurt. You know this community and the human services systems well, probably better than any white guy I've ever met, but you may still be naive about what's going on here and how tough the challenge really is."

I was easily persuaded that there was much more to learn, and I was very happy when he agreed to attempt to arrange a meeting for me with the ladies in the backyard. He said it wouldn't be easy, given their natural suspicion of white people and people representing government. We would have to lean heavily on his credibility and persuade them that talking openly with me might do them some good and wouldn't come back to hurt them. Trust would have to be developed. My credentials for sitting with these ladies and having an open exchange must have seemed incredibly suspect. They might also wonder: why would I want to spend time like this? Meeting with the ladies in the backyard was another milestone in a journey that, much of it developing unconsciously, pointed inexorably to an intense commitment to do whatever I could to make a difference by helping to solve our country's welfare/poverty problem.

I had been the chairman of the Governor's Task Force on Human Services Reform for the state of Illinois since February 1993. For most of my career I was a businessman—a partner in McKinsey & Co., a large international management consulting firm, and CEO of Mark Controls Corporation, a company my management team and I built up from a small, marginal, money-losing valve manufacturing company into a Fortune 1000 electronic and process controls company. In 1987, the various divisions of Mark Controls were, in total, worth almost three times what the company's stock sold for on the New York Stock Exchange. I decided I should break it up by selling the pieces before some Wall Street raider decided to do it for me—our longtime investors deserved those gains. A *Chicago Tribune* headline said, "Firm Beating Raiders to the Punch, CEO Manages Himself Out of a Job."[2] The overall strategy worked well, with the stock becoming worth $160 per share, compared with $10 per share when I became CEO. After selling the major units, I turned the remainder over to a longtime partner and went trekking in Nepal by myself in an effort to think through my future. I was on a number of corporate, venture capital, and foundation boards. A special interest, though only part-time, was the United Parcel Service board of directors, which I had joined on the recommendation of some McKinsey friends. The company has wonderful people and a legendary culture, and was in the process of rolling its service across the country, around the world, and into the air. These activities were very stimulating, but something was missing, and I felt a need for a core activity that was quite different from my business activities.

When my two sons, my best friends, went away to school, I moved from our small farm to an apartment in Chicago and also bought a small apartment in New York for business convenience and to pursue my passion for the theater and other arts. My first wife, with an affinity for the wilderness and an intense dislike of cities, went off to Wyoming. Over the years we had developed and changed quite differently, and I was single for the first time in many years. This arduous adventure in Nepal seemed like a good way to survey the possibilities of how my life might unspool from that point forward.

Trekking for days, purposely without reading material, and accompanied by a Sherpa, a porter, a cook, a yakateer (a young fellow with a firm stick who keeps the yaks moving), and two yaks laden with our small tents, food, and cooking gear, we were a quiet, purposeful group. The entire menagerie cost $25 per day, apparently attractive work in a country where the average income is $160 per year. My companions spoke Nepali only, with the exception of the Sherpa, whose limited English restricted conversation to primitive operational details. I was on a verbal fast—thinking was the only available activity besides walking. We marched on for days in silence—quite remarkable for someone as naturally loquacious as I am. I was determined to see Mount Everest, the highest spot on the face of the earth, with my own eyes, but more important, to think clearly about what to do with my life.

I was extremely fortunate to be financially secure at age fifty-one, and to have many options. I really didn't have to do anything. However, though I always enjoy traveling to an interesting spot in the world, or playing tennis at a resort, I'm soon anxious to get back and do something that I think is meaningful. My sons tease me because I can usually be counted on to judge activities on the basis of whether or not they will have some kind of "impact" on the world. A director and member of the search committee of Conrail had asked me to consider becoming Conrail's chairman and chief executive officer, a former Illinois governor had asked me to consider being the Republican nominee for the upcoming U.S. Senate race, venture capital firms had expressed interest in my becoming a partner, and there was the prospect of buying a company and starting anew.

To me, there has always been something spiritual about tall, beautiful mountains, compelling the soul to look upwards, leading to a higher level of consciousness. Years earlier I had climbed the Matterhorn and the Grand Teton, experiencing intimately the beauty and magnetism of the Alps and the Rockies, but to me the Himalayas were more awesome, more beautiful, and more mysterious. Looking down, the "usual" sights were magical endless vistas, dotted with tiny villages. Buddhist prayer flags and a prayer wheel could be seen in each village, proclaiming hope, I thought. Looking ahead, above the next segment of trail, was always another jagged, steep mountain pass, often enticingly wreathed in a wispy fog.

In such an incredibly beautiful setting, it was natural to think about the big questions: why am I here on this earth? How much of my good fortune was the result of decades of hard work, and how much was just plain luck? How am I different now than when I cleaned gas station restrooms for $1 an hour, or when I graduated from business school in debt? What am I good at, and what are my weaknesses? Whose lives do I most admire? Where does God fit into all of this? What makes me happy?

Several thoughts emerged. Yes, I worked hard, but without overwhelming good fortune, I could have been one of the illiterate Nepalese struggling at least as hard for mere survival in a remote mountain village. Instead, I was born in the greatest country in the world, white, male, and with some abilities in math and conceptual thinking. I was born on the South Side of Chicago but for Depression-related job reasons, my family moved to New Jersey when I was four. My parents were not college graduates, and though not poor, I was aware that we lived on the south side of the tracks in the then-small New Jersey town of Westfield, and the kids whose families belonged to the country club lived in bigger houses on the north side. Getting to swim in a pool, instead of using yard sprinklers, was an exciting event. It happened once or twice a summer when I was invited by a school friend to join him at the country club. My friends and I played baseball and football in the street almost every day after school and in the summers. I was sure there wasn't enough money for college, so I worked hard to get admitted to the Naval Academy.

When I was fifteen, my stepfather was transferred to California as plant manager of a paint factory, and I ended up going to engineering school at UCLA, where the tuition was a bargain at $48 a semester. I won a navy scholarship and worked as a stress analyst in an aircraft company to pay for living expenses. The scholarship was for any of fifty top schools, including the Ivy League, but I was only dimly aware of what the Ivy League was. In any event, I knew I couldn't afford to travel to the East. Why engineering? Though I had never even met an engineer and had little idea what they did, somewhere along the way I had developed the impression that if a person was good at math, engineering could be a route to a decent middle-class living. However, I found working part-time in college as a stress analyst "B" calculating airplane safety factors for Douglas Aircraft very tedious. Fortunately, a chance meeting with a banker led me to an awareness of graduate business schools that, to my great surprise, would accept engineers with no business training. I pursued this thread, and it dramatically changed my life, opening doors I didn't even know existed. The chanciness of these life choices and their profound implications have stayed with me over the years. What about a person from neighborhoods where not only is advice on college unavailable, but where no one in the family, building, or neighborhood *even works*.

When the rest of my family was transferred from California to Florida in 1955, I remember visiting Florida on a school break and seeing separate department store drinking fountains marked "white" and "colored." This made no sense to me at all, so I took great pleasure, one hot day, in switching the signs and watching everybody dutifully drinking from the "wrong" fountain. Suppose I had been born black, I thought. Clearly, I would not have been accepted in my fraternity, much less elected its president—a credential that helped me to be the only UCLA graduate admitted to my class at Harvard Business School. By the way, there were about ten women, all with specialized training, in my seven hundred-student business school class. There was only one African American, a man. My skin color, my ability to do well in math, my gender, those chance fragments of career advice—what luck! These issues did not come up in our family; in fact, to the extent they did come up, it was clear that my stepfather, who married my mother when I was four, was a racist. Though discussions of race didn't come up much since we were in an almost all-white town, occasional remarks about "colored people" let me know he thought that as a race they weren't as good as we were. Why was I sensitive to these fairness issues? Was it genetic in the same way some people seem naturally gregarious from an early age, while others are more reticent? Was it some sort of need to be different from my parents—to be better?

By the time I embarked on my Nepal trip, I had developed the rudiments of a political philosophy. From the navy I had learned of the incredible waste that occurs in large bureaucracies, and from my business experiences I came to appreciate the value of entrepreneurism, tenacity, hard work, and having a mentor. Lots of people with more initial advantages than I had not done as well, either personally or professionally. To me, this all added up to everyone deserving a reasonable chance, call it a "ladder of opportunity." But it is up to the individual to climb it. Life will never be completely fair, but it does make sense to try and level the playing field—not the final score.

Though not usually described this way in the press, I believe conservatives and liberals share the belief that it is not fair for children to start out life with bullets whizzing by on the way home from school, or to go to schools that don't teach the basics. It's also very tough to grow up with no productive role models—middle-class blacks have long since left the bullets and bad schools for the increasingly integrated suburbs. Rank-and-file conservatives tend to be underrepresented in the media and in academia and, with some exceptions, not very involved in the national debate. This, and their natural skepticism about bureaucracies, politicians, and the effectiveness of government programs leaves conservatives vulnerable to charges of not caring about the less fortunate. Extremists on both sides (liberals and conservatives are each saddled with a Jesse) help keep simplistic labeling of conservatives like me alive.

I'm unlikely to forget a benefit dinner for Voices for Illinois Children, an Illinois advocacy organization, where, seated at the prime table with the executive director and the guest of honor, I listened to speech after speech bashing Republicans and accusing them of not caring about children. I suppressed a strong urge to leap up and say, "We Republicans have children and love them very much. Because we know that birth circumstances are often very unfair, we help lots of nonprofit organizations and foundations that help others. Everyone deserves a good chance to help himself or herself, and many people do not get one. But we believe government has a job to do to demonstrate positive outcomes from the myriad of existing programs now spending billions without much to show for it, before we commit more taxpayer dollars." Some unthinking conservatives do believe that lack of character is the main reason people are on welfare, and some liberals don't look to character at all—thinking of all people on welfare as victims. Both views are, of course, narrow and wrong in most (but not all) cases, reflecting an intuitive lack of understanding of the much more complex reality.

During the many hours of climbing the trails up the Himalayas, my mentor and role model, Harvey Branigar, kept coming to mind. Harvey was about twenty-five years older than I, about the same age as both my father, whom I never saw, and my stepfather. I had spoken with Harvey, a former business partner and devout Christian Scientist, at least once a week on the phone for over twenty years. Harvey had taken over his father's bankrupt real estate company during the Depression, building it up into a major, high-quality development company. He sold the Branigar Organization for many millions when he was in his sixties, but stayed involved with other investments he had made, including my company, Mark Controls Corporation. He and his investment group gave me the opportunity to be the CEO of Mark Controls when I was thirty-three, despite my having had no corporate management experience. I had joined McKinsey & Co. right out of business school, and was doing well as a partner. However, after six years of consulting, the chance to have direct line responsibility was enticing. When we first met we had immediate mutual trust, the kind of chemistry that rarely occurs. This led to a wonderful yet stress-tested relationship that survived two periods of near bankruptcy but ended with a sixteenfold increase in the value of Mark Controls stock.

During the rough times, Harvey was always there: "If anyone can do it, you can," he would say one way or the other. Because I sensed that he meant it, and because I didn't want to let him down, this was a powerful message. He had a marvelous ability to inspire, to create in people the ability to see themselves at their full potential. Among many other roles, Harvey was always pushing me to not be too busy to develop my spiritual life. I remember when I was in grade school, my stepfather dropping me off at the local Episcopal church to sing in the choir. This was a remedial effort, since I had received a very poor grade in music in fourth grade. Sitting and singing through the services, I picked up some appreciation for what church was all about, but it never really took hold. For a long time I thought myself too busy running my international company and spending time with my two young sons, Gary and Mike, on their activities and other family activities to have time to get involved. Sunday morning was my only "free" time. Besides, I thought, I was doing a pretty good job following the Bible's teachings without the necessity of going to formal meetings. Perhaps sensing a lack in me, and once commenting tactfully on the lack of religious preparation given to Gary and Mike, Harvey suggested that I needed more, and he was right. I went back to church in 1985, after a thirty-five-year absence, and started to appreciate the importance and value to me of faith.

Harvey, though somewhat shy, was made of steel when it came to his unwavering personal convictions about right and wrong. He was just under six feet tall, of medium build, and with piercing but friendly bluest-of-blue eyes. His handsome, rugged face was usually deeply tanned from riding his favorite horse out on his Arizona ranch. When he talked with you, his head would be cocked and his eyes would sparkle in a quizzical way that expressed curiosity and real interest in what you were saying. He listened to every word. He could look through you, but his manner was so diffident that there was never any feeling of being threatened. He regarded humility as a great strength. Those of us who knew him well would compare notes on our efforts to get him to walk through a door before we did since he was invariably holding it for others. When Mark Controls Corporation grew and I was becoming successful and getting media attention, I received a carefully crafted letter from him warning me that humbleness was an asset more important than the visible trappings of success that were coming my way. I wasn't sure whether he had noticed signs of arrogant behavior or just felt it was a risk that came with success. I felt terrible that I might be letting him down, and made sure that I did not.

Harvey's caring for people came through in everything he did. He was a director of Mark Controls, and after the first few years we had an annual ritual: he would offer to retire and I would insist that he stay. I would then persuade him to give a talk at our annual management conference, when our one hundred top managers would assemble from around the world. In a featured talk at the conference, Harvey would tell stories about people, especially those in the factories, and their importance to our success. One poignant story about an after-hours farewell talk he had with an elderly, heavyset African-American cleaning woman at his real estate company brought some of us to tears. Harvey was retiring, and she wanted to (and did) hug him for taking a personal interest in her and her family, and for his kindness. He told the story in his usual, extremely modest way, explaining that his interest in and helpfulness to her was just the normal response of one human being to another, but it doesn't happen as often as it should. The younger Mark Controls managers, seeing a highly successful (and, of course, quite wealthy) entrepreneur in front of them placing people values at the top of the list was a powerful message. Get good people, inculcate those people with values, and you will be successful personally (most important) as well as professionally.

Harvey put most of his money in a foundation to provide scholarships for the disadvantaged—dealing personally with each individual. He would get letters from far and wide, and read most of them personally. In choosing recipients, he would look primarily for qualities of character, especially determination, as well as degree of hardship. Though possessed of incredibly good instincts and judgment, he didn't consider himself smart or particularly good with numbers. His scholarship selections favored tenacity and tough circumstances over test scores, and many lives were dramatically changed by his generosity. Every so often, I would get an envelope full of letters he found particularly interesting. Since he maintained correspondence with his recipients during and after the scholarship, the impact on people's lives could be felt. A mother of two who had spent time in prison before matriculating, with Harvey's help, at MIT was one I remember quite well. Trekking in the Himalayas provided great inspiration and space for reflections, and Harvey kept appearing in my thoughts.

As I trekked across the Himalayas I also often found myself thinking about God. Looking out at the incomparable vistas, and at the staggering image of Mount Everest, the case for His existence was overwhelming. What I was seeing with my own eyes each day transcended what most of us can even imagine. I reflected on what I read about top men of science returning to church and their explanations of how their scientific knowledge moved them toward belief in God, not away from it. I had made my own important leap of faith a few years ago, when Harvey inspired my return as a regular churchgoer. I usually found the once-a-week opportunity to listen to a story from the Old Testament, New Testament, and the Gospel very interesting and often helpful to me in my daily life. The discipline of sitting still and listening to the larger thoughts of life for an hour and a half most weeks was clearly helping to change me, moving me more outside myself. This preparation gave me a base to draw upon as the seemingly endless hours and days went by in Nepal. My trek was strengthening my belief that God is working in all of our lives. The phrase "we are all God's children" kept coming to mind as I wound my way up into these amazing mountains, passing incredibly poor Nepalese villages. The average per capita income in Nepal is *less than 50 cents a day*! This connected in my mind to the Canadian nurse who sat next to me on the flight from New Delhi into Katmandu who, turned down in her efforts to adopt a child in her own country because she was single, planned to come up into one of the villages to "arrange for the adoption," in effect, to purchase, a child from a poor Nepalese family. Imagine!

These larger thoughts came together with some others: the remembrance of the shock I experienced as a young naval officer when I volunteered to deliver a Christmas basket to a family in the slums of Charleston, South Carolina, and saw the pitiful living conditions—three beds in the one room, rickety stairs, no screens, a broken-down stove, and ragged, unhappy-looking people. I remembered my outrage at the segregated restrooms on the U.S. Naval base in Charleston, and the threatening response from the local congressman, L. Mendel Rivers, to my letter to him alerting him to this immoral and illegal condition. Congressman Rivers wrote me an angry response saying that if I had a problem with "alleged discrimination" I should write President Kennedy. At age twenty-three, I was jarred to learn that not only wasn't the congressman interested in ensuring that the law against discrimination on government bases was being carried out, but the thought crossed my mind that, as the powerful chairman of the House Armed Services Committee, his anger could show up in the form of a letter to the Pentagon delaying my scheduled release from the navy the following June. Later, I came to learn it was Mendel Rivers who caused most of those ships to be based in Charleston in the first place. If a powerful national leader with tremendous influence over our armed forces took this kind of position about segregated restrooms, what kind of influence must he have in other areas, such as employment and housing?

While in the Himalayas I also thought back on my embarrassment during a trip to Moscow in the Iron Curtain days when, on Moscow television, I saw homeless Americans sleeping in doorways in the inner city. The gist of the message was, "This is capitalism—you don't want it." I was affected by that message, because I didn't want the "Evil Empire" to have *any* rationale, and I was worried that the Soviets might have had a point. I came to believe that the message worked quite well, as subsequent conversations with educated Eastern Europeans, after the wall came down, revealed a genuine fear of capitalism that clouded their embrace of freedom. They wondered if they might be sleeping in doorways, without a caring "Big Brother" to plan their lives.

Now that the "Evil Empire" is gone there is an arguably more important need to show the world that the United States, as the paramount example of a free society, can have something approaching a level playing field for all of its citizens. A crass, but to me meaningful, rough test of success as a society would be to be able to walk by someone asking for a handout, knowing that the odds are overwhelming that the person has a decent "ladder of opportunity" to climb, and refuse to contribute. That is the tough love needed to push him or her to take advantage of the opportunity that awaits. Without really being conscious of it, I had been developing a personal philosophy about disadvantaged people over a number of years, and trekking in Nepal gave me the opportunity to start pulling the various threads together.

I had always taken great pride in the organizations that were an important part of my life (UCLA, Harvard, Mark Controls, UPS, McKinsey, and the navy) and I wanted to be just as proud of my country. Clearly, some things had to be fixed if I was going to be as proud of my country as I would like to be. We Americans had things right for 90 percent of our people, but we had some tough work to do to level the playing field for the remaining 10 percent. What could I do? I began with a self-assessment. I'm good at large-scale organization change. I enjoy people of all types—from cab drivers to factory workers to professors. I'm good at picturing how things ought to be—and how to get there.

I also knew I had an acute need for the intellectual stimulation of taking on new challenges—especially something that no one had done before. Undergirding the intellectual aspect of my Nepal thinking was my longtime service on the board of trustees of the Russell Sage Foundation, the largest foundation in the country devoted solely to social science research. At the time of my Nepal trip, I was chairman of the board, and because of economic globalization and other trends, we had steered the foundation to a primary focus on poverty research. We met with and supported most of the leading poverty researchers in the country, and I had learned a lot in the process.

I remember vividly a Russell Sage trustees' weekend retreat at the famous Meyer mansion, now a conference center, in Seven Springs, New York. Mr. Meyer was the owner of the *Washington Post* among other properties, and his daughter, Katherine Graham, the publisher of the *Post*, grew up in the sylvan surroundings. As an odd contrast, the focus of the retreat was poverty, and we were joined by half a dozen leading poverty research grantees.

I had recently experienced a day teaching remedial algebra and meeting with students at the Lucy Flower Vocational High School in Chicago's inner city. Lucy Flower was one of those high schools where the dropout rate and pregnancy rate were both about 50 percent and the average ACT score was 8, the lowest in the entire city and less than half the score needed to get into an average college. I arrived the day after an incident in the schoolyard where a student had brought a loaded gun to school and had been threatening other children. Lucy Flower is an all black school, and a bitter white teacher who seemed to be counting her days to retirement escorted me around. When we arrived in the cafeteria it was quite rowdy, much like my memory of lunch period at my own high school. She turned to me and said, in all seriousness, "The only real answer to all of this is castration." Unbelievable, I thought—their teacher! The rest of the day was filled with stunning revelations—a code in each teacher's record book showing mental and physical disabilities and other problems diagnosed for each child, with more than half the children on each roster marked with one or more of these problems; the locked computer room full of computers donated by a manufacturer, idle due to lack of connecting cables and qualified teachers; the incredible noise level in each classroom, including the one I tried to teach; teachers in the faculty lunchroom telling of visits from the downtown bureaucracy where inspector/observers came to the school briefly, disappeared, and then filed reports that showed no understanding of the situation whatsoever; paint peeling off the walls and ceilings; and, finally, the principal who, I was told, spent much of her time in her office watching television. At one point I asked the kids what they would do if they were the principal. They said, among other things, "paint the classroom." By this time I *really* wanted to help, and turning to the teacher I said, "I'll buy the paint. Why don't we come in on Saturday and paint the classroom?" After discussion with the teachers

I was told it wouldn't be possible—security would be required, we'd have to pay overtime to open the door for the building engineer who reported to his own separate downtown bureaucracy, and we'd have union problems for doing work normally done by unionized workers. It appeared that the actual work of painting would be a small fraction of the total time and expense required to make this simple idea happen. I was beginning to understand why it is so hard to fix a big city school system. In the meantime I found out that the very good Catholic schools in Chicago were shrinking in size due to lack of students, with tuition levels at about one-third the per capita cost of the public schools. But school choice is another complex subject for someone else's book.

After dinner at the Russell Sage retreat, as we were sitting in the beautiful living room of the famous Meyer mansion while brandy was served, I told the Lucy Flower story. I then asked the poverty researchers and trustees how many had visited one of these inner-city schools. To my great surprise, no one had. I then offered to arrange a visit, and no one expressed interest. Based on this and many other experiences, I've become convinced that, with rare exceptions, most poverty researchers are interested in the intellectual stimulation of manipulating data sets, writing articles, attending seminars, and occasionally designing top-down policy recommendations and new programs. This was the business equivalent of designing new products in the executive suite, without going out into the field and talking to customers—the Edsel and the "new Coke." No wonder we've spent billions for years without really finding a handle to this problem!

In addition to Russell Sage I had also become a trustee of the Annie E. Casey Foundation, a foundation with a primary focus on the problems of disadvantaged children, with assets well over $3 billion. Jim Casey, the legendary founder of UPS, left a large portion of his estate to this foundation, named for his mother. Jim, a lifelong bachelor, founded UPS as a bicycle messenger service in Seattle in 1907 and led its growth to a multibillion dollar giant with over 120,000 employees at the time of his death in 1983 at the age of ninety-six.

One of the great privileges of my life was serving on the UPS board with Jim for about ten years. He had great vision, and, like Harvey, humility and a tremendous caring for people from all walks of life. This caring was manifested in the egalitarian culture that was built into the UPS organization which has since grown to 380,000 employees. Nobody has a private secretary, offices are plain and utilitarian, there are no limousines, everybody's on a first-name basis, and even the CEO answers his own phone. At the regular directors' meeting dinners we are seated at tables that include drivers, clerks, and janitors as well as front line and middle managers. Meetings are rotated around the country, and I vividly remember sitting next to a thirty-year janitor in Colorado who told me proudly of putting his three children through college and his pride in keeping his part of the package-sorting hub clean. His words are imprinted on me permanently: "You bring dignity to the job, the job doesn't bring dignity to you." Jim was also responsible for the strong company commitment to helping the communities in which it operates and for the remarkable fact that today, control of this huge company is vested in its employees and retirees with over 100,000 employee stockholders at all levels. Jim was a remarkable man, known well by almost every UPS employee, and virtually unknown outside the company.

As a UPS director, I saw helping shape the strategy of the emerging Casey Foundation as a great opportunity to contribute and to learn, so I volunteered for the board when Jim died. The early board sessions involved many hours listening to experts describe what is going on around the country in poor communities in the areas of education, teen pregnancy, mental health, drugs, and the like as background for developing a strategy to maximize the leverage of the foundation dollars in helping others. I noticed that the experts tended to see more money for their particular field as a primary solution to the problems. Given the billions already being spent, and the narrow focus of the experts, this didn't feel right to me.

Jim Casey, long interested in kids who were, in his words, "orphans," had also started a foster care organization called Casey Family Services, which became part of the foundation. I immediately started worrying that this was a high cost "Cadillac" operation that was not replicable on a wider basis. If we could get a sharper focus on the economics we could do more. It was great to help a few hundred kids, but we were the largest foundation in the country focused solely on disadvantaged children and their families. Therefore, in my view, we had a huge responsibility to leverage our efforts to change the country.

My interest grew—someone needed to get in there and make a difference, to really understand and help solve our country's welfare/poverty problem in a thoughtful, cohesive way. A leading conservative, Paul Weyrich, called this problem the "Achilles heel of capitalism," those Americans who are not part of our system as we know it. I don't worry about people who are capable but lazy. If someone is not mentally or physically disabled; has some kind of reasonable opportunity accessible to him or her; and some exposure as a child to a caring adult, mentor, or role model, then the rest is up to them. These individuals should not be denied the valuable and instructive consequences of individual failure.

An important problem with the ongoing welfare debate is the assumption that one size fits all. Yes, there are significant numbers of people who cheat the systems and some who have made a conscious decision that welfare is easier than working. However, I believe that there is a larger number of people who never had a real choice, whose life chances from their day of birth were overwhelmingly negative, and for them there is an important role for both government and private charities. I knew that every year many billions of dollars were being spent on welfare and related human services, most of it intended to help those in poverty. A whole industry of thousands of charity and government employees had been at work for years, yet the problem seemed to be getting worse. This was a problem I connected with emotionally and spiritually, and a tremendous challenge. I didn't know it, but my life was clearly moving toward the ladies in the backyard. I came back from Nepal determined to get involved, in one way or another, to make a difference for those whose life chances were really tough.

The first step, shortly after my return, turned out to be a commitment to work full-time as a volunteer in Washington in the 1988 Bush campaign, focusing on policy and speeches in the area of families and children's issues. Why not start at what might be the top? I had some credibility on domestic issues in the eyes of the campaign leadership from my position as chair at Russell Sage and as a Casey trustee.

My experience as a CEO was not particularly helpful in the campaign policy area, since in that role I had very little contact with unemployed or poor people. The hiring at our various factories and other facilities around the world went on at the local level, and obtaining qualified workers was normally not a problem. I typically met and interacted with workers *after* they were hired, and there were eventually about five thousand of them. However, I was subconsciously applying managerial thought to what I had learned so far in the human services area—thoughts such as accountability, listening to the customer, establishing principles and a strategy, redeploying funds, and organizing effectively.

To get introduced at the top of the campaign, I used some business connections, including one that resulted in a long chat with then Vice President Bush at a cocktail party. It was early in the primary season, before the Iowa and New Hampshire primaries, and George Bush was battling Bob Dole and Pat Robertson, among others, for the Republican nomination. At our first meeting the two of us ended up talking off to the side, and I decided it would be helpful to him and that I had nothing to lose if I told him how poorly he came across on TV. I speculated that the staffers on his payroll might not be so direct, and he needed to hear an unvarnished reaction. Now was the time, I told him, to invest the time in whatever training it took to develop the necessary skills. I speculated that he was likely to smile and figure out a way to start talking to someone else. Instead, he listened carefully and suggested that I look at a tape of his recent David Frost interview and let him know my thoughts. He also wondered if I knew Roger Ailes, who had been trying to help him in this area. I was impressed by his openness, and shortly after that meeting I volunteered to go to work for him. Here was a chance to connect with the ideas that started to emerge in Nepal, and at a level much higher than I might have dreamed.

After George Bush won the primary, I was convinced that welfare reform could be an effective Republican issue in the general election against Michael Dukakis. The polls in 1988 were starting to show welfare reform as an emerging voter concern, and this would be a chance to show voters that Republicans had a heart. At one point, polls showed it fourth in importance. I wrote position papers, argued the case at the top levels and contributed to a few speeches and events, but crime, defense, and the economy got most of the airtime. I remember my excitement when I had contributed a few lines on families and children to a speech George Bush was to give in Seattle. On the day of the speech I eagerly turned on the ten o'clock evening news in my hotel room, hopeful to hear my eloquent, persuasive prose come out of his mouth and into the national debate. Alas, when the CBS newscaster switched to the campaign coverage, there was George Bush attempting to give his speech at Seattle University while facing shouting pro-abortion protesters. The entire campaign news clip that day was the protest, with no mention of the speech content. Making a difference sometimes isn't so easy!

When the campaign was in trouble—down seventeen points in June 1988—I was asked by Campaign Manager Lee Atwater to become assistant campaign manager for management. Lee called me in to his office and said, "Most CEOs are assholes, but you seem to be different. My people like you, and I think you can be a big help. We are in trouble, everybody's fighting, speeches aren't getting done on time, scheduling is a mess, the White House Office of the Vice President is at war with the campaign, and we don't agree on strategy. You're the only one around here who's ever been a real manager. I'd like your help in managing the campaign as assistant campaign manager for management." I protested that my real interest was policy for families and children, and he said I could continue with that if I wanted, but that my policy work wouldn't matter if we weren't organized to win. He sent me over to see Vice President Bush, who repeated the request, and so I began the extensive interviewing of key players, including Mary Matalin, Roger Ailes, Bob Teeter, George Bush, and the vice president's son, later Texas governor and now President George W. Bush. I developed recommendations for Vice President Bush and Treasury Secretary Jim Baker, and then helped implement a restructuring of the campaign. Among a long list of changes, I became a sort of glue for a seven-thirty meeting each morning with Campaign Manager Lee Atwater, Chief of Staff Craig Fuller, Senior Adviser Bob Teeter, communications guru Roger Ailes, Vice President Bush (when he was not on the road), and myself.[3] I prepared an agenda to force decisions on scheduling, the message of the week, and other elements of the rapidly changing campaign. Discussion often focused on projecting the candidate's image on television.

Once, when the vice president was in our meeting, Roger Ailes (now head of the highly successful Fox News Channel) told him he needed to look warmer, and that he should put his arm around Barbara in public as Michael Dukakis did with his wife, Kitty. Bush bristled and said, "*You* go tell Bar. We've been married over forty years and getting along fine, changing things now is ridiculous." At another point Roger confided in me, "It's really hard to make him seem like a regular guy—he's the kind who thinks it's not proper to take a leak in the shower." Roger knows how to make a point graphically! I was learning a lot about campaigning. I took the decisions made in the morning meeting and passed them on to the rest of the campaign staff as the other attendees ran off to their frenetic personal schedules, talk shows, and the like. From my new leadership position in the campaign I pushed on the family and children's issues with limited success, quickly learning in the process the huge difference between campaigning and governing.

In later reflection on the campaign, my mind goes back to a meeting my wife-to-be, Charlene Gehm, and I had in 1990 with Yitzhak Rabin in his small Knesset office when Saddam Hussein had his missiles trained on Jerusalem just prior to the Gulf War. We had booked a trip to Israel before the Kuwait threat emerged, and I had help in arranging the trip from my longtime friend Harold Tanner, a leading New York fund-raiser for Jewish causes. The arrangers in Jerusalem learned of my background as a U.N. delegate, and we ended up in a series of meetings with Rabin, then–Deputy Foreign Minister Benjamin Netanyahu, and Jerusalem's mayor Teddy Kolleck. Most visitors to Israel had postponed their trips—there were very few in the King David Hotel—and these leaders seemed glad that we had made it. Commenting on the Seven Days War, which he had led heroically, Rabin said, "When you start a war you never know what is going to happen." Plans and intentions can quickly become irrelevant. Political campaigns are like wars, and the 1988 campaign twisted and turned in bizarre ways. Who would have guessed that the issues that would come to decide the campaign would be a questionable prisoner release program in Massachusetts symbolized by the murderer Willie Horton, the then–heavily polluted Boston Harbor, and Michael Dukakis's ill-advised photo op where he was riding in a tank looking goofy in a helmet and appearing to be the last person in the world a voter would want as commander-in-chief?

The closest we got to my interest in disadvantaged families and children were Peggy Noonan's memorable phrases in George Bush's convention acceptance speech that described a "thousand points of light" leading to a "kinder, gentler nation." Bob Teeter later told me that Peggy threatened anyone who tried to change those phrases (together with the infamous "read my lips—no new taxes") with her "scissors through their heart." She later told me that "the men who ran the campaign terrified" her. I knew that they, in turn, viewed her as a true genius with words, but impossible to manage. I give her credit as the only effective voice in the campaign even touching on the issues important to me.

Despite investing a year of my life in the campaign without pay, mostly living (at my own expense) in Washington's infamous Jefferson Hotel, I figure that I had somewhere between negligible and minimal impact raising the issues relating to disadvantaged families and children. I had to face it: in 1988 you didn't have to say much about children's and family issues in order to win a presidential campaign. However, it was a fascinating experience that helped, in unexpected ways, move me toward the meetings with the ladies in the backyard.

Upon Bush winning, I was asked what I wanted to do, and I decided that the job of Health and Human Services (HHS) secretary had the potential for incredible impact on the problems important to me. What a chance to use my management background to help make effective the billions of dollars already being spent! This was an opportunity to make a real difference in the lives of disadvantaged people—a shot at the "kinder, gentler nation."

The search for executives proceeds far differently in an American presidential transition than in the corporate world. There is no search firm retained to identify all the possible candidates, and there are no fixed prerequisites. What is required is to be on the lists that get put together by those who have the President-elect's ear. I did my best to be sure I was on those lists, and I soon became the leading candidate for HHS secretary, with mentions in many of the major newspapers. I was helped by the fact that nobody else who fought in the campaign trenches was interested in HHS, and Jim Baker, the President-elect's closest advisor and friend, told me he would support me for the job. My Nepal vision was taking shape in a very important and exciting way!

Then one day when I was in the transition team offices, George W. Bush informed me that I had a "pigmentation problem" since the cabinet was short of African-Americans. In a thoughtful and friendly way he stated the importance of diversity in a President's cabinet, and did it in a way that made it clear to me he didn't have an ounce of racism in him. I was very disappointed, but I had to respect the need to have the cabinet reflect the electorate. Maybe it was a good lesson to experience discrimination against me because of the color of my skin on something I wanted very much. However, I wished they hadn't used up most of the other slots with white males. My consolation prize was a long column in the *Wall Street Journal* by Paul Gigot called "Perils of Tokenism[4] . . ." citing me as the front runner pushed aside for tokenism and questioning whether, four years from now, we really would have a "kinder, gentler nation." Well, we didn't, and Bill Clinton adroitly exploited that weakness, along with an economic slowdown, to end George Bush's presidency.

I then went on, with the urging of Lee Atwater, who by then was chairman of the Republican National Committee, and with the earlier strong support of former Illinois governor Dick Ogilvie, to become a candidate for the Republican U.S. Senate nomination in Illinois, with the idea of having an impact on the reform of welfare and human services in the Senate. Dick died unexpectedly in the spring of 1988, but he had previously shown me how to build a network with Illinois party leaders, and had enlisted a number of them to support me. The Democrats had Pat Moynihan as their point person on poverty and the issues of the disadvantaged; maybe I could make a difference in the Senate since there was no clear Republican counterpart to elevate the understanding and work to really make a difference.

I set up a small "MacDougal for U.S. Senate" office on LaSalle Street in Chicago, and began running up and down the state, speaking at Lincoln Day dinners, raising money, and learning how to relate to the media. This was initially great fun, but soon became very hard work. Most county Republican organizations have Lincoln Day dinners, and there are 102 counties! One evening I finished a speech downstate in Effingham at 10:30 P.M., and had a 7:30 A.M. fund-raising breakfast with a group of Arthur Andersen partners the next morning in Chicago—a four-hour ride across the cornfields. Those nights were not fun.

I was fortunate that the top Republican business leaders in Illinois joined my finance committee. The committee was chaired by Bill Sanders, the savvy billionaire real estate mogul, and Larry Fuller, CEO of Amoco, the biggest company in the state. Soon hundreds of thousands of dollars came in. I became the leading candidate for the Republican nomination, with growing name recognition. I kept in regular touch with my Bush campaign boss Lee Atwater, who was a regular presence in the Oval Office. Lee assured me that I had his backing, and that rumors of Representative Lynn Martin's interest in running were nothing to worry about. "She is running for a House leadership post and doesn't want to make the Senate run—and besides, if she acts like she's thinking about running, I'll talk her out of it, because she'll lose." I campaigned vigorously for about six months, quite confident that the nomination was mine, and that I had the support of Lee as well as President Bush.

Quite unexpectedly, I was summoned to the Oval Office. The President and I each sat in one of those two wing chairs I had seen so often in pictures and John Sununu, his chief of staff, and Lee sat facing us on a couch. After some small talk and a few photographs, it was clear right away President Bush wanted me to step aside for Lynn Martin. Lynn had lost the House leadership race, and according to Lee, she had gone to the White House without Lee's knowledge to ask President Bush to help get me out of the race. As a congresswoman she had supported Bush in the early eighties, giving him much-needed credibility, leading to his selection as Reagan's running mate. She had been national cochair of his presidential campaign. George Bush is loyal to a fault. After hearing about my campaign and our progress and the reasons why Lynn Martin would lose, he put his head in his hands and said he had "screwed this one up." But it was clear he had given his word, and to me it was unthinkable that he would go back on his commitment. Picturing *Air Force One* coming in to raise money for my opponent, and wanting to be a good team player, I agreed to talk to her about supporting her, which I did. She lost by a very wide margin. I should have respectfully told the President that I was staying in the race because I would win—I was just too new in politics back then to oppose the President in the Oval Office.

In the course of the Oval Office discussion, after I agreed to pull out of the race, the President said he'd like me to stay on the team, and inquired if there was a job in the administration I might like. Knowing that I faced a press conference after the meeting, and figuring I would be asked what I "got" for stepping aside, I told him I thought it would be better if I could say that I made the decision because it was the right thing to do. Somehow, at that moment, a job offer seemed like bribery, although in retrospect I may have missed a chance to advance my Nepal agenda. Some time later, at a meeting in John Sununu's office, John asked me what I might be interested in doing. He rattled off a couple of top jobs that had not been filled, including SEC Chairman, and I told him I wasn't interested, reminding him of my desire to help on social issues. "I'd be very interested in setting up and chairing a commission on the homeless or children and families," I said. I pointed out that something like this would demonstrate that the President cared about people, which he did, and that we could come up with some worthwhile ideas. John replied, "One-third of the homeless have a drug problem, another third mental illness, and the rest are in and out with housing problems. There really is no homeless problem when you break it up." The way he spoke made it clear to me he had no interest or appreciation for my agenda. I began to understand the widespread take on him: "When you're in a room with John Sununu, it is clear he thinks there is only one smart person in the room, and it's not you." He later called asking if I would be interested in running the Social Security Administration, and after a Florida hurricane he asked if I would head the Federal Emergency Management Agency. These were important jobs that met John's needs at the moment, but not mine. However, while regrouping and planning my next move, I did sign on for a brief tour as a U.S. delegate to the United Nations. Among other duties, I was responsible for relations at the U.N. with East Bloc countries during their time of change, as well as for economic development for Third World nations. It was fun to see the Communists eagerly picking my brain on how capitalist businesses worked. I enjoyed being the first to lecture on American business and management at Karl Marx University in Bulgaria, and its counterpart in Prague. It was a tremendous experience, but I was anxious to get back to my main quest.

As an unsolicited bonus I was invited one day to ride with President Bush on *Air Force One* from Washington to Chicago—something to tell my mother about. The President wandered through the big living room–like main cabin, bantering in his usual friendly way. He greeted me enthusiastically and said he'd like me to come up to his private cabin after we were up in the air for a bit. My mind raced with possibilities—did he want some help on a domestic policy issue? After a while I was summoned to the presidential cabin where I found the President and Sam Skinner, then Transportation secretary, looking out the window trying to guess which steel mill or town in Ohio or Indiana we were flying over. I joined in, but couldn't contribute much. We discussed Illinois politics for a while, and that was it. The time wasn't right to try and change the nation's agenda. When we arrived I got another consolation prize—a mention in his speech to a huge crowd as a "great Illinoisian" that he was "pleased to fly in with." How could I use this newfound credibility and these experiences to move my Nepal agenda forward?

I had certainly fired some good shots in the twenty-four months since I had made my commitment in Nepal. The Bush presidential campaign, a strong HHS secretary candidacy, the U.S. Senate candidacy, and the Bush/Sununu ideas all had great potential, but none of it worked. I hadn't helped a single disadvantaged human being. Fortunately, things started to change, the tenacity Harvey always talked about would start to pay off, and the Washington experiences would be helpful.

I was back in Illinois and starting to look deeper at human services from a state level perspective. I had come to know Secretary of State Jim Edgar on the campaign circuit, and knew him as a decent, caring, honest person. I offered to help him in the policy area in his 1990 campaign for governor, and use that opportunity to get to know the huge state human services system. Out of that work I decided a massive overhaul was needed, and we needed to get all the key players, and some knowledgeable outsiders, around the table. I needed to persuade Governor Edgar to let me form a task force to work on the problem and to change things for the better.

This approach had the promise of being an even more meaningful hands-on experience than some of the Washington possibilities, with a real chance of making a major difference in people's lives. Here was an opportunity to draw upon my policy, political, business, and foundation backgrounds to lead the change in one major state with an extremely difficult city. In addition, the huge river of money, that famous $520 billion per year, was being managed in large part by the states, and at the state level you are closer to the real action. Success in Illinois, and especially Chicago, would make a real difference, and could be a model for the nation.

So there I was, in a cab on my way to the meeting the Reverend Martin had arranged for me with the ladies in the backyard. Knowing what was going on in their world was, in my mind, a crucial element in the major challenge of connecting the big policy ideas and the big dollars in a way that could create a ladder of opportunity for those willing to climb it. As chairman of the Governor's Task Force on Human Services Reform, I had become deeply enmeshed in my Nepal issues, and it was important to strengthen my understanding of the disadvantaged people who were the object of all the political rhetoric and the billions in spending, as well as to take Reverend Martin's advice.

2

The Ladies in
the Backyard

Poverty is the parent of revolution and crime.
—ARISTOTLE

When I arrived at the address on Chicago's South Michigan Avenue, I paid the cab driver, and he sped off. I looked around and saw the signature rubble-strewn lots with broken glass and trash across the street. In a very short period of time I had traveled across a huge cultural and economic divide.

Michigan Avenue starts at Lake Michigan, Chicago's "inland sea." As it goes south in a straight line, it is first the "Magnificent Mile," the most glitzy shopping district in the city, ranking with Rodeo Drive in Beverly Hills and Madison Avenue in New York as a mecca for affluent shoppers. Michigan Avenue then crosses the Chicago River, moving past high rise buildings filled with big law firms, advertising agencies, and corporate offices. In a few more blocks the view to the east opens up to the expanse of Grant Park, the Art Institute, and the beautiful Buckingham fountain, with the lake beyond. As Michigan Avenue continues south, its straightness takes it further and further from the eastern meandering of the lake's edge. After passing Mc-Cormick Place, the huge convention hall complex that is the anchor of Chicago's place as the leading meeting and convention destination in the country, the landscape becomes lower and more open. For a while you have a sense of the openness of the prairie. Once a prairie, then densely populated, the area has become open again. Where once there were solid rows of townhouses, many are now missing, like the spaces between the teeth of someone who needs dentures. South Michigan Avenue was a different world.

Standing on the broken sidewalk, I was relieved not to see the usual menacing loiterers marking gang borders or just hanging out. I figured this was because I was in a relatively sparsely populated residential area with four-floor walk-up apartments, and the "action" tends to be around the huge public housing projects and along the half-boarded-up shopping streets, like nearby Forty-seventh Street. I was still tense and uncomfortable—very much out of place. A scary thought raced across my mind. What if I copied down the wrong number in the address?

The Reverend Martin and I had been together many times at his church and elsewhere, but I had only been to his apartment once before and there are many blocks of similar apartments. Copying down the wrong number could have serious consequences. Though I was in the heart of the city, only twenty minutes from the Loop, there were no cruising taxi cabs—no escape. How could I get directed to the right apartment or make a phone call? It is always unwise in a big city for a stranger to knock unannounced on someone's door. With the heavy drug activity and associated violence on the South Side, I saw myself as a made-to-order target. I might as well have had a big "mug-me" sign painted on my back.

Perhaps I was more wary than some, because a few years earlier I *was* mugged by three young African-American men around the corner from my New York apartment. It's an experience you never forget, and from it you learn to be vigilant, looking around you all the time whenever you are in a big city. My mugging occurred in broad daylight at about 6:30 P.M. just off Central Park West on Sixty-eighth Street, one of the nicest, highest-income areas of the city. Walking along with heavy bags of groceries hanging from each arm, I was lost in my thoughts. Suddenly a hard object, perhaps a piece of pipe, hit me on the back of the head. I instinctively turned around, and a fist hit me in the face, bloodying my nose and knocking my glasses to the sidewalk. I dropped the groceries from shock, and they scattered out into the street. Most of us aren't really prepared for this type of experience, and hindsight is always wiser. Adrenaline surged through my body, probably from fear, and I became a wild man, swinging, hitting, and yelling. I felt, then saw, a black hand pushing into my left side pocket where I had my money clip. I grabbed the wrist with both hands and more strength than I had ever known and twisted intensely, yelling all the time for help from passersby. Suddenly the muggers ran off, probably having decided that I was more trouble than I was worth and that the robbery was taking too long. I looked around and saw a fragile-looking doorman and an elderly couple who had been watching. Someone called the police and the requisite reports were filled out, with no real hope of catching the attackers. The only damage was the bloody nose, a lump on my head, and a broken jar of pickles. After I stopped shaking, I realized how lucky I was that my aggressive resistance had not been repaid by a knife in the stomach. I was extremely fortunate that these three young men were probably not very experienced muggers. As a conservative I wanted them caught and punished, but I also was pretty sure their free market chances to get that $100 they were after were not what mine were at their age. But more on this more important kind of conflict, the conflict of ideas, later.

I walked over to the brick walk-up, found the apartment number, and was relieved to hear the Reverend Martin's voice, "Good afternoon, Gary. Welcome. Come on up." Because it was a damp and chilly day, Reverend Martin had decided we would meet in his small living room instead of the backyard. There was a tempting selection of food laid out—grapes, cheese, and cookies, but the ladies were nowhere to be seen.

"B. Herbert, do you think they will come?"

"I certainly hope so, but I can't say for sure. They're probably anxious as to what's going on—meeting with this guy who works with the governor. I can hear them now. 'Why would he want to meet *us?'"* Undoubtedly their previous experiences with authorities had rarely been positive. Could they lose their benefits?

About five minutes after the appointed hour, an obviously curious and somewhat apprehensive woman showed up. She came into the room, but would not sit down. She looked to be in her midtwenties, with a nice smile and bright eyes, and the Reverend Martin introduced her as Lavon. After some initial small talk and a few laughs, she turned abruptly and walked out of the room. What would happen next? How was I ever going to find out what was really going on in the lives of these women? I felt an urgent need to get beyond the mountains of academic studies, policy papers, and political rhetoric to find out what can make a difference with people living on welfare. How realistic was it for them to work? Did they want to work? Would anybody hire them? What were the barriers? What about paternity, education, childcare, drugs? In July 1997, the monthly welfare check in Illinois was $278[1] per month for a mother and one child, $377 for three (mother and two children), $414 for four, and $485 for five. Food stamps were additional ($360 per month for a family of three, for example). How do they make ends meet when there is clearly a gap between the absolute minimum cost of survival in a big city and the value of welfare payments and food stamps?

From my poverty research work with the Russell Sage and Casey foundations and as an avid reader of social policy studies, I was familiar with all these issues, but I knew from my business experience that you don't *really understand* until you've spent meaningful time face-to-face with the "customers." An important backdrop for all of this was the fact that Reverend Martin warned me that the Governor's Task Force could not be successful without firsthand understanding of the people.

Fortunately, Lavon came back followed by three women who seemed very shy and uncomfortable, but curious. I had been told that these women were all single mothers living primarily on welfare checks and food stamps. Everybody sat down, and Reverend Martin in his most pastoral voice thanked them for coming and introduced me as a friend who was working hard to try and make things better for people in the Grand Boulevard community. He pointed out that the governor was a friend of mine and that we needed to know more about their challenges in order to help. He encouraged them to be open, and we both promised that I would not use the information in any way that would hurt them. I talked a bit about how hard it was to sit in Springfield and figure out what to do, and how valuable their help would be. Then I leaped in. "If you were the governor, what would you do to make things better for people in Grand Boulevard?" After some giggles at the idea of being the governor, the talk began to flow.

"He needs to find us a job."

"Get rid o' them gang bangers."

They seemed to be getting reasonably comfortable. Lavon, clearly the leader, said, "I'm more fortunate than my friends here, because I'm not in as bad shape financially. I've fixed up my apartment and I can buy some toys for my daughter." She hinted, with a half wink, that some men had been helpful to her. "Where are people like us going to get a job?" Lavon turned to Maxine who has been sitting quietly in the chair next to me on the right.

Maxine was quite thin and looked like a teenager, though she later said she was twenty. Maxine said, "I done apply for jobs, but they always wantin' work experience. How I gon' get work experience if I can't get no job?" It turned out Maxine has another problem—she was just released from prison just a few weeks ago. I resisted the temptation to ask her why she was in prison, but the assumption in the room was drug-related crime. She kept talking: "At Decatur [Women's Correctional Center] I had lotsa talks and I'm goin' straight—doin' it for my kids." She had a son and a daughter, ages four and three. Her facial expression and body language reflected a determination to do better, but a frustration as to how to pull it off.

As a former employer, no matter how badly we needed to fill an opening, even at the lowest levels, there was *the* question: Have you ever been convicted of a felony offense? Checking the yes box meant we moved on to the next applicant. Bingo! Now here was an issue that didn't get talked about much in Springfield or nationally that really belonged on my list of problems to be solved. It is a reasonable estimate that up to 20 percent of the women remaining on welfare have felony records, and among the fathers of these children, knowledgeable estimates are above 50 percent. An amazing 37 percent of *all* African-American men between the ages of eighteen and thirty-four are under the supervision of the judicial system.[2] This obviously is a huge barrier. Connections to the prison system are present in most families in tough communities like Grand Boulevard. The impact of the justice system is part of everyday life in a poor community, just as it popped up in Reverend Martin's living room that day. What would I do if I were in her shoes? Maxine clearly made mistakes and, as we conservatives would wish, she was sent to prison. Also, as we conservatives would wish, she came out determined not to get in trouble again, with a big motive being the desire to do better for her children.

And yet here she was sitting in this living room facing a world that she knew did not want to hire her—a felon with no work experience, two kids, and like all but one of the women in the room, a high school dropout. A depressing thought went through my mind. She's probably got fifty years ahead of her. Should this felony, for which she has paid her dues, keep her from legitimate work for the rest of her life? What will this example do to her kids? Government has given her a welfare check, food stamps, and probably drug treatment. Government is also spending billions on job training and placement (over $700 million[3] in Illinois alone), but these well-intended taxpayers' millions aren't connected and, if they were, they still aren't focused enough and flexible enough to help Maxine. I have voraciously read the literature on welfare and poverty, and this huge issue rarely shows up, much less with any reasonable ideas on what to do about it. Illinois taxpayers were spending about $10 billion[4] per year on the approximately 1.3 million[5] people in poverty in the state, and almost nothing addressed this huge barrier standing in the way of the welfare-to-work effort. Yet this is a problem faced by a very large segment of the people we are talking about. It's like a business designing a product that clearly does not help the customer, then wondering why it's not selling.

The conversation turned to their kids. Shirley, on my left, was only sixteen, and she had a two-year-old daughter. I raised the question: Where was her dad?

Shirley replied, "I see him around, but I ain't doin' no drugs, an' I don't want him near my daughter."

"Is he recorded as your daughter's father?" I asked.

"No," she replied. "He said he ain't goin' to no hospital to sign up 'cause he don't want no state chasin' him for child support."

Wow, I think—I've never really dug deeply enough into the paternity establishment process to understand how it works. The idea that it's so easy for the father to escape responsibility shocks me. I later learn that paternity was established for only about 50 percent[6] of children of unwed mothers in Illinois. All the talk about reuniting families and bringing fathers back into the families, yet escaping paternity is so easy? As the discussion continued, a number of women revealed that they had a reasonably positive relationship with the fathers of their children, but for those with more than one child, each child often had a different father—a very policy-relevant point. A number of them said that the fathers of their children *did* come to the hospital and sign the birth certificate—a hopeful initial indicator of some feeling of attachment and responsibility.

As I listened to those women talk about their families, I learned two more things I felt were important. First, for child support purposes, signing the birth certificate is *not enough*. A further step involving additional paperwork was required, a step that often didn't happen. Second, even if paternity is established, there is a strong and understandable motivation to conceal any child support payment from the Department of Public Aid, since these payments became a deduction from the monthly welfare check, and the welfare check wasn't enough to live on. "I ain't going to give that money back to the state—my baby needs that money." In listening to them it became clear to me that the motivation for father and mother to conspire to manipulate the system is high, and overloaded caseworkers haven't much chance to figure it out. There is an important financial disincentive here. If the mother cooperates with the state to pressure the fathers of her children to pay child support, she gets the first $50 and all the rest goes to the state. Most often her cooperation is essential. Are the economic incentives sensible here? Clearly paternity establishment and child support are crucial to the strength of families for powerful cultural values reasons as well as financial reasons. The economic incentives should be pulling families together, not keeping them apart. If there is a feeling on the part of fathers for their children, and I believe that most of the time there is, then contributing child support should be rewarded by seeing the child better off as a result of that willingness and effort. I filed these concepts away as big problems, but solvable with smarter policies—the incentives and penalties needed to be aligned, so that establishing paternity and paying child support made sense to all.

Paternity establishment for unwed mothers in Illinois recently shot up to about 50 percent from about 30 percent, primarily as a result of simplifying the process, but there still is a long way to go. Child support requirements, though often an attempt to get blood from a stone, have the potential of paying a substantial portion of family support needs nationwide, if thoughtful procedures and mutual incentives are implemented. At the moment, due to weak systems and procedures and sometimes perverse incentives, the national percentage of welfare payments recovered through child support collections is only about 15 percent.[7] As I listened to these women I kept thinking how all of these issues seemed to be coming back to simple, understandable basics of human behavior—something the government has lost touch with over the years.

I also noticed the absence of any caring adult in the lives of these women. Most of us found a mentor, parental or otherwise, somewhere along the road as we were growing up. In the entire afternoon, no one was mentioned as a source of help or guidance. In listening to the ladies in the backyard, and to many others like them in the course of my work, when other adults come up, it turns out that they too are overwhelmed and aren't helpful with answers. It's hard to learn about work and self-sufficiency when no one in your family has a job and, further, none of your friends, neighbors, or even anyone in your building has a job. Potential role models and mentors who somehow got through school and got a job have long since escaped the violence and bad schools and moved to the now more integrated suburbs— understandable self-interest transcending the need for good examples in the ghetto left behind. Elimination of racist bias in housing is, of course, essential, but those left behind have suffered tremendously. Middle class black flight has also reduced local job opportunities as their businesses, professions, and buying power moved with them. Communities need not only jobs and economic capital, they need social capital to survive and become healthy.

I brought up the subject of welfare reform and asked about their thoughts. Shirley said she worried about who would take care of her daughter. I asked about her mother, and she said her mother was sick and couldn't do it. Then I turned to the others in the room and said, "What about you? If your friend here got a job, wouldn't you help her out by looking after her daughter?"

"Hell, no," Lavon replied. "I don't do nuthin' that don't pay me."

The Reverend Martin smiled. They were all aware that the state had a friends and relatives child care program that paid $1 per hour per child, but one said, "That ain't enough, and besides the check don't come for months."

My sense was that, though not ideal, there was competent child care capacity in that room—a good start anyway. While we might prefer that friends help each other for free, a longer-term solution can be found in paid care provided by friends and relatives who are also on welfare. The "twofer" value to this approach would be for the potential child care providers in the room to consider child care a starter job to get badly needed extra cash and, of course, the checks should arrive sooner. Some advocates are upset that this means getting along without a licensed child care provider offering education along with care, but sitting there with those women, it was easy to get excited about getting *something* going that was on the road to work. Also, providers in the licensed, center-based child care business would like to have a monopoly. But these special interests usually do not deal with the problem of how Shirley, with no car, would get her daughter to the child care center and back, nor do they consider the need of her relatives and friends for the income. Shirley loves her daughter and is unlikely to leave her with someone she doesn't trust. Unfortunately, the ladies in the backyard are not represented in the child care licensing debates in Springfield, while the pro-licensing crowd has the lobbyists. Of course, any incident where a child in unlicensed care is hurt becomes a marketing tool for those in the child care business, often producing laws relying more on state inspectors than on a mother's judgment. We can't let the perfect be the enemy of the good. I remembered the many hours I spent as a baby-sitter for neighbors—my first paid work, along with mowing lawns.

Sitting to Lavon's right, Kathy, in her midthirties, was the oldest of the group. She was somewhat heavyset, and seemed very calm and thoughtful. She had dropped out of high school in the eleventh grade, but had made the effort to complete her GED, or high school equivalency exam a few years ago. She was one of eleven children, and had, in her words "three wonderful young men," ages fifteen, ten, and five. She sang in Reverend Martin's choir, believing that the "uplifting spirit" of God kept her going. Unlike the others, she had some work experience, both domestic work, and for a brief period, work in an office. I asked why the office job didn't work out. "The job was out in the suburbs—Des Plaines. A friend helped me get it. To get there I had to take a bus up into the Loop and then wait for a train for Des Plaines. Then I had to arrange to be picked up or take a cab from the train to the office building. It took me over two hours each way, and it was expensive. With a car I could have done it in about an hour, but I can't afford a car. Traveling close to five hours a day, and with three kids, I just couldn't do it."

My mind flashed back to a discussion we had at one of our Governor's Task Force meetings. A professor and task force member from Northwestern University emphasized the problem of the job growth being in the suburbs, with a large core of the welfare population concentrated in the inner city. Of course this wasn't a new thought; in fact, naive attempts had been made in the past to lure factories back into the depressed areas. Security and the difficulty of attracting managers to the area, among other problems, made this impractical. If I had tried to move one of my factories to the south side of Chicago from the suburbs, my fellow managers and directors would have thought I was crazy, tax incentives or not. Over the long term, retail, service, and other businesses that serve the local population can be reestablished in the depressed areas, but local buying power must increase first. Jobs and self-sufficiency will start the snowball down the hill.

Eventually, the wide range of businesses that serve Chicago's downtown area can be lured to the disadvantaged areas when these areas become safe, because the low rent costs and proximity are attractive. These businesses will, in turn, be an important source of jobs for local residents in the future. But Kathy and the other ladies needed jobs now. The professor did consulting work with the Regional Transit Authority and pointed out that the schedules for the RTA's commuter trains were designed "To get the guys in the suits from the 'burbs to their offices in the Loop." The schedules were not designed for entry level people to get from the inner city to the suburbs where the jobs are.

"Why not work with the RTA to come up with better schedules to meet this need and design a transit rate package that entry level workers can afford?" A great idea. I tried to get the professor to see what he could do with the mayor and the RTA on that idea, but it remained on the Phase II things-to-do list. Transportation kept reappearing as an integral part of the self-sufficiency challenge.

One of the interesting aspects of Kathy's story was that she had helped make herself employable by completing her GED sometime in the past, and appeared to be a reasonable candidate for a variety of jobs. In Illinois a whopping 20 percent[8] of the caseload were not high school graduates, had no GED, and had no work experience. Another 28 percent were without a high school diploma or GED but had some work experience, bringing to almost half the proportion of those on welfare who were not at the high school graduate level.

I turned to Maxine, who had dropped out of high school in the ninth grade to take care of her son. "Have you thought about getting a GED?" I asked.

Maxine looked thoughtful, and replied, "The only GED course is at night up at Dawson [Community College on Fifty-fifth Street] and it ain't safe. They rapes us up there."

Wow! I could just picture some community college administrator, sitting in a high-rise office in downtown Chicago wondering why, given the overwhelming need, more people didn't sign up for the GED course. Another thought kept crossing my mind: What would I do if I were Maxine? She wants to turn her life around, but the barriers are huge. Where is her ladder of opportunity? The problem of violence was to show up at many points in the human services reform and welfare to work efforts, one woman telling me that the gang gunfire is so bad near her local grammar school that she regularly keeps her son home, in effect choosing illiteracy over death.

The time went by quickly, and the discussion had gone on for almost two hours. I didn't want to overstay my welcome, but I wanted some more feedback on work ideas. I knew that the Progressive Community Church did lots of work in the neighborhood. There was a food pantry, day care, community meetings, the cleanup of vacant lots in the neighborhood, and housing rehab work, among other activities. I said to the group: "What if you worked twenty-five hours a week at the church and, until you got another job, you got a work credit voucher that would be accepted at the local welfare office and entitle you to a check? You'd get some work experience, and a good reference from the Reverend Martin."

Shirley thought that was a great idea.

However, for the first time Lavon started squirming, and clearly looked uncomfortable. "I ain't goin' no church."

"Why not?" I countered.

"I just don't want to go to no church." The look on her face let us know that she was embarrassed, and we took the conversation elsewhere.

The meeting ended with my thanking them for their efforts to try to make me and Governor Edgar smarter about what needed to be done. They each smiled as we shook hands, and as I said good-bye to each of them I couldn't help but think that, but for the luck of the draw, it could have been me in their shoes.

After they left, with a smile, the Reverend Martin said to me that Lavon obviously hadn't heard the well-known Bible story of Mary Magdalene, the prostitute blessed by Jesus who became a saint. Further discussion of work possibilities at the church and elsewhere left me with the feeling that, like the rest of us, most of these women would rather be doing something beyond sitting around the backyard. They also left me with the strong feeling that a principle motivation was their desire to provide better lives for their children. They didn't want their children to fall into the same traps that snared them, but the formidable barriers—violence, finding an employer who would hire them, transportation, lack of job experience, a criminal record, child care, etc.—were overwhelming in their minds. Each barrier alone could prevent a successful outcome. If a ladder of opportunity is to be created, it can't have any missing rungs if we expect these women to climb it. Just getting on the bottom rung will require connecting welfare, transportation, alcohol and substance abuse treatment, job training and placement, child care, and probably other services in a way accessible to these women and their families. I was also struck by the need for some kind of mentor or role model to help connect them to the world the rest of us grew up in.

From a very personal perspective, this meeting deepened my commitment to do whatever I could do to eliminate the dysfunctionalities of the system and connect the big dollars flowing through the system to the communities and people that need a path out of poverty. For reasons I still don't fully understand, this is very interesting and important to me. These women had kids out of wedlock at too young an age, but at this point the number of kids was still manageable. Contrary to popular impressions, the overall demographic data shows that the average number of kids per family in the Illinois welfare population is now at about 2.1.[9] Forty percent have only one child. National numbers are similar. Work is realistic.

They also have something to offer an employer. Lavon, the prostitute, was very bright, and clearly showed leadership qualities. I could easily imagine her as a department head at Mark Controls or UPS. Many feelings and thoughts raced around my head as I listened to them talk: she's very smart and not at all lazy, how can the system be so stupid, we can change that, and there but for the grace of God go I. Once you are born in a place like Grand Boulevard, the odds are high your life will be deep in the hole before you even get started—and think of Lavon, Shirley, Kathy, and Maxine's children. What kind of life chances do they face? Suppose I was one of those children? Yes, they shouldn't have had them, but they did, and it's hard to blame the children. If we connect these women with a job and help them retain that job, the odds of the children sitting around a backyard drinking and swearing fifteen years from now are greatly reduced.

In this session and subsequent sessions arranged by Reverend Martin and others, I felt privileged that these people would confide in me in a very personal way, given the enormous racial and economic chasm that divided us—two different planets. I learned a great deal of valuable information, and the experiences changed me. Empathy and determination grew some more. I knew I was on the right track.

It took me a while to recognize the fact that when we read and talk about welfare in most states we are really talking almost exclusively about younger women with children and, with the exception of state programs in some states, men do *not* get welfare checks. However, in distressed communities men are important players—fathering the babies, initiating most of the violence, selling drugs, and filling up the prisons. If we are really going to achieve a goal of *family* self-sufficiency and understand what it takes, we must put ourselves in the shoes of some of the men, in addition to the ladies in the backyard.

One day I was visiting the Austin human services office on the West Side of Chicago to see how the reform effort was coming along on the front lines. I spent half of that day sitting in a cubicle with Mary, a very pleasant and experienced heavyset African-American "intake" caseworker. It turns out we had met at one of the information sessions in connection with the reform effort, and she was very anxious to help. Her job was to interview people who came to the office seeking benefits, with the initial objective of directing them to the kind of help that would connect each visitor with the job market as quickly as possible. Mary's three o'clock appointment, Julius, a slender twenty-year-old

African-American man dressed in baggy jeans and a sweatshirt, was ushered into the cubicle. Julius shuffled in with his head down, glancing at me somewhat warily, wondering, I suspect, what this white man was doing sitting in the corner of the cubicle and whether or not I was a problem for him. Mary introduced me with the usual "someone from the governor's office that wants to learn what's going on in order to help make things better." As Julius slumped down in the chair next to Mary's desk, he put his elbow on the table. I noticed that his right hand and wrist were grotesquely deformed, so that they connected to his forearm at an odd angle—as though they were badly broken and never set properly. Julius wanted food stamps, a federal benefit amounting to the equivalent of $50 per month[10] that states administer but which comes from the Department of Agriculture in Washington. Mary asked the basic questions and entered the information into her ancient computer. As always she had to leave to Xerox some document for the file, giving me an opportunity to talk with him.

I asked Julius if he'd had any work experience. He said, "I done work for a temporary place over not far from here."

"What happened?"

"I done work two weeks cleanin' up stuff, but when the paycheck come it was only about twenty dollars—it just ain't worth it," he said with a sort of shrug.

"It sounds like you were cheated. What did your boss say?"

"Nuttin' much—somethin' about 'ductions."

"Do you remember the name of the place?"

"No," he answered with the kind of resigned air that told me that he felt anything we tried to do was unlikely to help him.

I persisted, trying to display my warmest, most unthreatening face. "Would you like a job?"

"Yeah, but no one goin' give me no job."

"Why not?"

"The record," he answered. Further discussion revealed that he had been in prison or some form of detention for most of the time since he as fourteen. He said he'd only spent two summers outside prison since then. What happened?

"Gang bangin' and drugs," he answered. He told me his mother didn't want him in a gang, but he didn't have a choice. In the public housing project where he lived you either join the gang that controls your building or you get beaten up, starting at about age twelve. He was badly beaten a few times and he finally relented and agreed to join. Once in the gang he was expected to help carry his share of gang activities—fights with rival gangs, robberies, and drug dealing. Control of buildings and turf for drug dealing was the primary source of gang income. I had learned to spot the drug sentries marking the turf on my trips into Chicago's inner city. Julius lifted up one of the pant legs on his jeans to show me his bullet wounds. He said he had six, including his shattered wrist.

My mind flashed back to when I was twelve growing up in New Jersey. Many summer hours were spent playing catch in the street with the neighborhood kids and talking about the Yankees, Giants, and Dodgers. As a teenager, summer jobs were available, and I worked as a junior camp counselor and as a bag boy in a grocery store. Peer pressure was important then as now, but the worst that happened was that some older kids talked me into lighting a "campfire" and a whole field burned, bringing out the fire trucks. I don't believe my parents ever found out that I did it. The desire to impress my peers resulted in my periodically walking along center attic peak roof beams of houses under construction, where there was a free fall all the way through to the basement. Most of us know that the need to be part of some sort of group combined with undeveloped judgment often makes for difficult teen years. Imagine in your youth walking out the door each day into an intense gang environment each morning where you've had to pick a side, and the stakes are life itself. Most of the fathers are gone, and the mothers can offer only limited help. There are no mentors leading the way toward opportunity, and only rarely a competent adult who cares. The police are feared for good reason, and some of your young friends have been *murdered*. If I were Julius's mentor back then, what would I tell him to do? Julius's situation is worth thinking about, I believe, because as I listened to him I guessed that the odds were good that he would spend the rest of his life, perhaps fifty years, shuttling between street corner and prison, unless he met a violent end earlier.[11]

If I were a young black teenager in the housing projects, where the choices are much more limited, would I have been in a gang? It seems highly likely that I would. Julius was me. Mary had come back as Julius and I were talking, she finished up her work, told him he would hear shortly about the food stamps, and we said good-bye.

On the way home to my Lake Point Tower apartment I reflected on the session with Julius. If I were Julius, what could I do to break out? Could I do it myself? I decided I'd probably need some help. Julius needed a job—and a ladder to climb. With some coaching, I believe that a large majority of the Juliuses would make the climb, but some employer would have to give him a chance. But under what circumstance would hiring Julius be a reasonable business risk for an employer? This is an important question, because of the very large proportion of inner city African-American males (probably well over 50 percent) who are either in prison, have been in prison, or are in some way caught up in the justice system. It was Julius who was likely to mug you or rob your house. How could Julius get a real job? More on this later.

Large numbers of inner-city women ("ladies in the backyard") are directly affected by the fact that the fathers of their children are either in prison or have served their time but can't get a job if they honestly check the have-you-ever-been-convicted-of-a-felony box on the employment application. In Illinois there are, at any one time, close to 45,000 men and women in prison. The imprisoned men, of course, represent a large proportion of the fathers of the children on welfare. The Governor's Task Force principles identify the *whole family* as the entity that must become self-sufficient, yet a large number of the non-custodial parents are in prison.

In an effort to understand this phenomenon better, I arranged an interesting all-day visit for my wife, Charlene, and me to the famous Stateville prison, a maximum security prison, complete with lethal injection chamber, in Joliet, Illinois, about an hour west of Chicago. Charlene is very interested in my work in human services, and whenever I can include her, I do. The whole idea of spending a day inside the prison walls, where we were told 60 percent of the population was convicted murderers, made us more than a little bit nervous. We started out in Warden Davis's office, where we were welcomed and shown a gruesome display of weapons confiscated from prisoners, including some ingeniously fashioned from light bulb sockets, bed springs, and other available materials, and were introduced to Major Evans, who was to be our guide. In the course of the day we visited most of the cell blocks and facilities and were provided the opportunity to talk with prisoners. The typical dialogue:

"Hi, I'm Gary MacDougal; what is your name?" looking at each other through the bars.

"I'm Emmanuel Jones."

You don't ask them how they are, because you know. "How long have you been here?"

"Seven years" is the reply.

"What got you here?" I usually asked.

Typical response: "Messin' with drugs."

"How much longer?" I'd ask.

The answer to that would be either "a long time" for the lifers, or a specific number of years. There were almost always law books in each cell, representing hope, the major said, even though the law books rarely led to a successful appeal. I was surprised to see a television set in most cells, and comfortable, apartmentlike decoration. The environment was more comfortable than I expected for a maximum security prison. This masked a leitmotif of danger, and my adrenaline really pumped when a group of about fifty prisoners coming back from a movie was inadvertently let out into the passageway where the three of us were walking. We talked earnestly to the also-nervous major, pretending to ignore them as they walked by. The vast majority of all the prisoners at Stateville (and in the statewide prison system) are black, and the major estimated the breakdown at 85 percent African American, 10 percent Hispanic, and less than 5 percent white. He guessed that the average educational level was eighth grade, and the average IQ about eighty-five. The majority in Stateville, and statewide, were from Chicago/Cook County.

One of the many fascinating insights that emerged during the day was a discussion I had with four inmates who were seated around a table in the prison library. The library was a nice, large L-shaped room with books, almost all of them legal books, in the short side of the L. It was a popular place, with most of the numerous tables occupied. I walked up to one of the tables, the four seated prisoners looked up, and I introduced myself. Three of them seemed to be in their twenties, with one older fellow who later introduced himself as Charles, in his late thirties. They volunteered that they were trying to find a way to help one of their number, an attractive young fellow from Rockford, get out. The conversation progressed in a way that made it clear that two of them, Billy and Tom (the fellow from Rockford), were in for a "long time," i.e., they were lifers; a third, Richie, had ten more years; and the fourth, Charles, fifteen more years.

"Why are you here," I ventured, perhaps naively.

Tom took my question the right way and said, "I really screwed up. I had it made. I was a basketball star in a good private school. My parents were okay, but I wanted too much too fast. I wanted a fancy car and all that, and the fast track to that was drugs. I really messed up."

I asked, "Do you have any kids?"

"I have two, and that's the really bad part. Now they've got no father." He was thoughtful and articulate, taking full responsibility for his actions, which probably included murder.

Charles said his situation was typical. He has a younger brother and a sister, there was no man in the house, and his mother was trying to raise them on welfare in a tough Chicago neighborhood. "My friends were what I thought was important. When I'd do something bad, my mother would send me up to my room and I'd go out the back window. I wasn't afraid of her at all. I needed a man who could keep me in line. Now I've got three kids growing up without a father, and it's starting all over again. Think of how many kids have their fathers in this room." Richie listened thoughtfully, nodding periodically, but never did join the conversation.

Billy couldn't wait any longer, and blurted out some strong words: "Look at this room, everyone is black. There are some smart people in this room, but you white people are afraid, and want to keep us down. This is genocide. You are afraid of us." I was jolted, and Tom and Charles listened politely.

"Well," I said, "I was hopeful of getting your views, and I really appreciate your sharing them with me. I really thank you. I've probably kept the major waiting long enough."

I shook hands with Tom, Charles, and Richie, but when I got to Billy, he withheld his hand and said; "I don't shake hands with the enemy."

As we walked away, I asked the major, who had been standing within earshot and who is African American, what he thought. "You've just heard a good cross section. We try to make them see that they are responsible for their actions and not blame others. Billy hasn't done that and he's wrong. Charles came from a gang-dominated situation where the odds were against him, Tom had no excuse and to his credit, he admits it."

We went to the classroom area of the prison, which was empty. There weren't many classrooms, and the major acknowledged that the use was low, but he wasn't sure why. Part of the answer might be found in an interview that we had with Harold, an attractive fellow who looked to be in his midtwenties. Harold was in a corner cell on the second floor of the cellblock he shared with about 300 fellow inmates. We stood outside and talked through the bars. He seemed thoughtful and intelligent, and among other things, said he expected to be released in only three years. "Where are you from?" I asked. He said he was from Forty-seventh and Michigan in Chicago, an area notorious for young African Americans hanging out with nothing to do, and getting in trouble. "What are you going to do when you get out?"

"I dunno," he said. "Nobody goin' hire me 'cuz I got a record. I dunno."

"You got any friends that can help?" I asked hopefully.

"I don't think so—nobody's got no job." Again, no caring connected adult, much less mentor. What a gift my Harvey was! Would Harold be alternating between Forty-seventh and Michigan and prison for the next forty years? It costs us taxpayers over $38,000 per year[12] for each year that Harold is in prison. As a conservative I want Harold to pay his debt to society, but I also want lower taxes. As a conservative I want Harold to work when he gets out, but I don't want his first job to be coming into my home to fix the plumbing. How about demolition contracting, fixing cars, maintenance of parks? I file these thoughts away as we thank the major for a fascinating and valuable day.

A discussion one day with Rita, a forty-two-year-old woman with no children, helped to further fill out the picture of poverty in inner-city Chicago, a picture arguably representative of America's major cities. If you don't have children, you don't get a welfare check, but you still have big barriers to self-sufficiency. Rita took an emphatic position with me that she couldn't get a job until she had a decent apartment. She said she lived in a public housing unit infested with rats, and in a building where drugs were rampant. I asked what percentage of the people in her building used drugs, and she guessed 80 percent—in the range of percentages I usually hear. I said, innocently, "Why not get a job first, and use the additional money to get a better apartment?"

She responded, "If I'm off at work all day, som'un goin' break in my apartment an' steal all my stuff—I'd have nothing." This fit with a repeated pattern of housing crises we were experiencing in our efforts to keep some of our most distressed long-term welfare recipients in their first jobs. Housing emerged as an integral piece of the puzzle, yet it has historically been largely disconnected from the state's welfare caseworkers. The funds supporting and the regulations governing this troubled bureaucracy come down from Washington through the often nonresponsive, often corrupt HUD (Department of Housing and Urban Development) into the infamous Chicago Housing Authority (CHA). A visit inside a public housing apartment, like a visit to a prison, is absolutely essential to understand what is happening on the front lines of the battle to move people from dependency to self-sufficiency. About 125,000[13] Chicagoans lived in these public housing projects—a good-sized city by itself.

Merely driving by the gigantic Robert Taylor Homes projects is to feel apprehensive. Some windows were boarded up as a result of fire damage or other problems. Many of the ground floor apartments were boarded up for safety reasons, and people lived inside without sunlight. The "front yards" were dirt patches with refuse scattered about. Young men in hooded sweatshirts and baggy jeans were hanging out, looking about warily. Their principal purpose is to keep an eye on their turf borders, alert to encroachments from rival gangs, and to maintain their market share of the drug business in their buildings—the only economic activity they know. No one knows the percentage of residents in these projects that use drugs, but I've asked this question of many residents over the years, and the answer usually comes out 60 or 70 percent. Further questioning yields an estimate that most of these users are recreational, episodic users—parties on weekends and the like. I'm told that these users would gladly stop using drugs if the incentive of a real job was present. There would be a strong motivation to avoid flunking a job-related drug test.

My friends in the projects tell me that they estimate that about one quarter of the residents are seriously drug dependent and would require treatment before they would be employable. Unfortunately, most drug treatment programs are not directly connected to jobs upon completion, so recidivism is commonplace. Few drug treatment programs are even measured as to a self-sufficiency outcome, yet millions of taxpayer dollars are "invested" in drug treatment programs, and a multibillion dollar industry has grown up, providing lots of middle class jobs. As I watch the drug activity around the projects, I'm struck by its ubiquitousness as the country digs deeper into the welfare pool in the crucial welfare to work effort.

Not surprisingly, the incidence of domestic violence, rape, and other traumas has produced a high level of mental health problems in these terrible neighborhoods. A recent University of Michigan study of a census tract in Detroit's inner city showed serious mental health problems in approximately 25 percent of the residents.

For me, entering the Ida B. Wells public housing project was more uncomfortable than going inside Stateville prison. Undoubtedly the young men patrolling the yard had weapons, and I knew for many of them that whitey was the enemy that was keeping them down. I had been told by my African-American friends that they wouldn't go in the projects themselves unless accompanied by a friend who lived there, and not in the summer in any event—too much random gunfire. This was the fall season, and two high officials of the CHA accompanied me. Although, like many, I had read about the conditions, how could I understand enough to make a difference if I didn't experience housing conditions firsthand? We were eyed warily as we parked our nondescript car in the lot. There was plenty of space in the small lot, since most residents did not have cars. Of the dozen other cars in the lot, half looked inoperable. The building that we were visiting, one of many, was about fourteen stories high and contained about ten apartments on each floor. Rent was based on a sliding scale tied to income, among other things, and many residents paid no rent. No one knew for sure how many people lived there, but the guess was about four or five in each apartment or six hundred to seven hundred in the building.

We walked across the barren, rubble-strewn front yard, approaching a booth with a small window guarding a gate to the stairwell and the elevator. Somehow the "security" didn't feel secure. I found out later that young women in the projects fear attacks by the guards. The elevator looked banged up and uncertain, and the stairwell, covered with graffiti and smelling of urine, looked equally uninviting. We walked up a few flights and entered one of the caged outside walkways that ran across the front of the building on every floor and served as the entrance to each apartment. I was told that the wire fencing was for the safety of children. Mothers were understandably afraid to let their children go down the elevators and stairwells to the rubble-strewn and threatening front yard, so they played in the six-foot-wide caged walkways. It turned out my CHA escorts were not planning to show me inside an apartment, so no arrangements for this had been made. I felt a look inside was important, so I pushed them into knocking on a door and asking if we could come in for a brief visit. The woman who answered was assured that it was not a social worker inspection, just a look to get an idea of what we needed to do to help.

As we entered, I remember thinking how incredibly shabby and disorganized a scene we faced—rusty, exposed pipes, dangling wires, everything in disarray. A haggard woman, probably in her thirties, stood with three children looking to be from about three to eight years old. We entered next to a kitchen area on the right that connected to a living room in sort of an L. I would guess the kitchen was 8′ x 10′ and the living area 12′ x 12′. There was one small bedroom off the living room. I was taking this all in when I noticed movement behind the beaten-up refrigerator which jutted partway into the room. A sheepish man, looking to be in his forties gradually emerged and studiously edged into the background. It was clear he wasn't anxious to meet me, so I played my part by ignoring him. I suspected he was one of the fathers who did not want to be asked about child support or, more important, jeopardize the woman's single mother welfare check. Some welfare mothers undoubtedly remember the days when state workers would pay a surprise visit, looking for clothes or other evidence of a man's presence. Another possibility was that he was not one of the people on the lease, and his presence would be a lease violation. As one of the few people on the planet who has never even experimented with drugs, my observations on the subject are suspect. However, I remember thinking that if I were that woman an escape through drugs would be very tempting.

The objective of the visit was accomplished—the picture was vividly and permanently etched in by mind. As someone who travels a lot, I have visited many shacks in poor countries like India, Myanmar, and Papua New Guinea as well as dung huts in Kenya. The difference, it seems, is that in these places, and in poor rural areas of the U.S., people have access to the land. Walking out the door of a hut to play or go fishing, and having a small vegetable garden, chickens, pigs, or cows can convert a subsistence life into a tolerable life, albeit one with struggle. A choice between five years in Ida B. Wells and five years in Stateville requires careful consideration. In fact we met a Stateville prisoner who found life outside, though not at Ida B. Wells, so difficult that he committed a crime in order to get back in. His nicely decorated cell with books, TV, three healthy meals a day and a hobby woodshop looked better than the Ida B. Wells life. Freedom may not be worth much if you can't do anything with it.

We walked down the awful stairwell and out the metal door. Someone yelled something at us as we walked to our car. I just looked straight ahead and walked briskly. As we pulled out of the lot and headed down the street, I breathed a sigh of relief as I thanked my two escorts.

The stories these women and men on welfare and in poverty told gave me a richer understanding of the clients and circumstances encountered in the welfare and human services systems. My meetings with the ladies in the backyard and other close-up exposures as "the only white guy in the room" always remind me that there is a wide range of individual differences among the welfare population, just as in any other large group. One-size-fits-all thinking is usually a mistake. Some poor people are energetic, some lazy, some smart and some not so smart—just like the rest of us. Some have a reasonably clear path to get out of their predicament, and some not clear at all. Almost all started out facing very heavy odds against success through no fault of their own, with skin color only part of it. They all have the need for a ladder of opportunity that they can realistically climb, but it is up to them to climb it. When I get into a discussion of these issues with friends, I sometimes encounter the comment, "Nobody ever gave me anything. I worked hard for everything, worked my way through school, etc., etc." But then further discussion usually reveals no conflict with gangs and violence, a caring, connected adult somewhere along the line, a lucky break or two, transportation, access to housing and schools that were at least adequate if not great. The issues stand on their own without even adding the reduction in odds of success that has historically come along with being black and female.

The problem is incredibly complex, but it should be clear that it is, in fact, very tough for many clients, no matter how determined, to change their life circumstances under the present conditions. No one knows precisely what percentage of the people would, with some transition help, become self-sufficient, but I am convinced a good working number would be 70 percent, not just of those on welfare, but of the single men and women without children as well. In the remaining 30 percent we would find mental and physical handicaps, severe health problems, and some lazy bums. People with handicaps usually can and want to work, but may be able to become only partially self-sufficient. The small percentage of lazy bums may find that the need for food and warmth will change their attitude. We owe them nothing. Finally, whether we like it or not, were it not for the accident of birth we could be stuck with the ladies in the backyard or their contemporaries in the ghetto. We also saw that there are many pieces to the answer, starting with paternity and moving on through housing, mental health, alcohol and substance abuse, transportation, GED, child care and more. The need to have the various types of self-sufficient services work together is becoming quite clear. If any one of these pieces is awry a successful outcome is jeopardized.

In addition, in the course of this work I became increasingly convinced that most, but of course not all, of the people in these projects *would work if they had the chance*—all they needed was that ladder. One of the big incentives often expressed to me, among many others, is their desire to get out of the horrible housing. These are the kind of people Harvey cared about—people who wanted a chance for a good life, but needed some temporary help.

As we tour through the various pieces of the puzzle that got our country—the richest in the world—into the mess it is in with welfare and the poor, the next stop on the front lines are the caseworkers themselves. After the welfare recipients and other poor people we have already met it is important to understand those who come in contact with them regularly, usually trying to help. The caseworkers are on the front end of huge, sprawling organizations that dispense billions of dollars in taxpayer money each year. Who are they, and what do they think?

PRINCIPAL POINTS

1. The great majority of those on welfare would sincerely like to get a job and become self-sufficient.
2. Becoming self-sufficient would be extremely tough for *any of us* if we were at the same starting point and if we faced the same for-

midable barriers as those faced by the ladies in the backyard, Julius, and the others.

3. There are many pieces to the puzzle—housing, children, transportation, alcohol and substance abuse treatment, mental health treatment, a job—and if any one of these elements is missing a sucessful outcome is unlikely.

4. We can't responsibly generalize about the welfare population—one size does not fit all.

5. Everyone deserves a ladder of opportunity, but it's up to the individual to climb it.

3

If You Were
a Caseworker—Good People
Trapped in a Bad System

The chains of tormented mankind are made out of red tape.
—Franz Kafka

I was on a tour of the front lines of the human services bureaucracy, and one of my first stops was a large building on the South Side of Chicago filled with caseworkers and administrators from the Department of Children and Family Services, the agency that deals with child abuse and foster care, among other things. My tour guide, Jeanette Tomayo, had brought me to the office of Veronica, a heavyset African-American caseworker. After Jeanette made the introduction and set the stage for an open discussion I was left alone with Veronica. She sat at her desk, and I sat across from her on a hard, gray metal chair. I asked her how she was doing. "Well, I was doing great. I'm goin' on vacation next week, and I was getting all my work done when the phone rang. Now I got to go out and see a client." It was clear from her attitude that seeing this client was a real blight on her day. Further discussion reinforced the fact that she viewed her job as primarily a paperwork job, with client visits a distant second. She was evaluated on having mistake-free paperwork, not on helping people change their lives. Our discussion continued.

QUESTION: "How much of your day do you spend on paperwork?"

VERONICA: "I'd guess about 70 percent, on average."

QUESTION: "How much of that paperwork do you need to effectively serve your client?"

VERONICA: "Probably less than a third of it."

QUESTION: "Where does the rest go?"

VERONICA: "I really don't know—probably the feds require it.
I doubt *anyone* reads it."

Unfortunately this dialogue is a predictable one in almost any discussion with caseworkers, with the percentages only varying slightly
from meeting to meeting. I was getting excited about the potential of
system reform. If the paperwork could be cut 40 percent, the amount
of time spent with clients could be doubled! How much of this paperwork could be automated? Milton Friedman, the Nobel Laureate
economist, said it right when he wrote, "In a bureaucratic system,
useless work drives out useful work."

What better way to make a positive difference in peoples' lives
than to be a caseworker? Imagine spending each day face-to-face with
people who really need your help, with the ability to pass out im-
mense resources in addition to good advice? In Illinois, the approximately $10 billion in state human services spending is mostly parceled
out by an estimated five thousand caseworkers either employed by or
under contract with the state. With about 1.3 million people in
poverty in Illinois, that works out to about $7,700 per person in
poverty, or almost $31,000 per year for a family of four. The national
numbers are similar. Of course not all human services money goes to
the poor people, and a large portion is related to medical expenses,
but there is also additional money not in this total going to poor
people direct from the federal government (the source of public housing funds), the city of Chicago, and private charity.

A compassionate libertarian would say, "Don't bother with caseworkers, just take the amount of money, divide it by the number of
poor people and write a check to each person for that amount of

money. This would allow more money to flow directly to those in need, because the estimated ten to fifteen percent administrative expense would be greatly reduced." This argument has a certain logical appeal, but the result would clearly be chaos. Properly managed, motivated, and empowered, caseworkers can be heroes, not paperwork slaves and demons. In a logical system caseworkers have information that those who are served do not. They can link an individual to the services that will make it possible for that person to reach self-sufficiency. If they are trapped by the bureaucracy, they can be reduced to filling out forms and answering only the questions asked of them. We have to remember that this democracy we live in will always allocate taxpayers' money through a political process that requires someone to assign the resources in particular amounts to people in need, hoping for a result. Caseworkers are here to stay. The trick is to help them become effective.

I had the opportunity to begin spending time with caseworkers in 1990, when then–Secretary of State Jim Edgar was first running for governor. I had known Jim from my time on the campaign trail and, as I had with George Bush in 1988, I volunteered to help him with policy in the area of families, children, human services, and welfare reform. This was a good use of my time, I decided, because the action on welfare reform was shifting to the states, and the states were where the real implementation work went on. As in the presidential campaign, these issues didn't come up as much as I would like but we had to be prepared and I was interested. I arranged a front-line tour, visiting numerous local offices, intake centers for abused and neglected children, and other activities in a number of the human services departments. The experience was very valuable and left some vivid memories, such as a room filled with small, specially monitored crack cocaine babies who had been removed from their mothers. Another memory was of some volunteers going through the phone book making cold calls in a desperate attempt to find badly needed foster parents. Much of what I saw seemed poorly managed or on the edge of being out of control. I was determined to learn what was really going on.

I was assigned a bright-eyed, dark-haired staffer from one of the big departments to take me around. Jeanette Tomayo, an attorney and energetic mother of two, viewed our tour as a chance to get word back to a prospective governor that major changes were needed. Back in 1990, Jeanette was one of many good people trapped in a dysfunctional system. She was also one of a fairly large number of people I ran into over the years who knew what was wrong but felt powerless to do something about it. They are drawn into the work by the hope of helping other people, only to be disappointed by what they find on the inside. These thoughtful people almost never talked about needing more money, and almost always talked about a more rational organization, a management system that would allow them to do a better job. In fact, I thought Jeanette saw the larger picture so clearly, that before our ten-day tour was over, I asked her to make a pass at designing a new human services system organization structure. At the end of our first week touring the system, when I asked Jeanette how she would organize to manage the distribution of the billions, she had some excellent ideas. She sketched out some organization charts that combined the various services needed by a dysfunctional family in a way that most were accessible at a single office. She combined the key departments. I remembered how often, as a consultant with McKinsey & Co., doing work with a corporate client, many of the good ideas for change came from down-the-line employees. Often where we provided value was selling the ideas at the top and actually making change happen.

In this sort of introductory front-line review that Jeanette conducted for me, other surprises were in store. "Veronica, how does a client of yours get a welfare check?"

"Oh, that's not our department; they have to go over to the public aid office on Pershing Road to get the welfare check," she answered.

"That's quite a distance—how do they get there?" I asked.

"The bus, I guess; most of 'em don't have cars."

"What if they need drug treatment?"

Veronica responded, "That's another different department, DASA [Department of Alcohol and Substance Abuse]."

It turns out all or a large part of six different state agencies (Department of Public Aid, Department of Public Health, Department of Alcohol and Substance Abuse, Department of Mental Health and Developmental Disabilities, Department of Children and Family Services, and Department of Rehabilitation Services) play a major role with a largely overlapping population of poor clients. In addition, the Department of Commerce and Community Affairs and the Department of Employment Security have major responsibilities in the area of job training and placement. What a mess! A separate client file, sometimes a very thick file, is maintained by each of these departments. This means there are often many different files on a given client, endlessly repeating much of the same basic information. It also means multiple caseworkers for a given client, each with responsibility for a piece of the puzzle. Jeanette told me that coordination among departments was minimal, in fact there was frequently rivalry, with separate management structures and totally separate management information systems.

I subsequently learned in my work as a trustee of the Annie E. Casey Foundation that the fragmentation and other conditions I was discovering in Illinois were typical of almost all states. At the Casey Foundation we funded systems reform projects in many states, and were always on the lookout for efforts to integrate systems at the local level. However, almost a decade later, despite bipartisan agreement that systems integration and linkages make sense, only a few states other than Illinois have made much progress. Most of the organizational problems, both those created in response to Washington's demands and those created by the states themselves, still exist nationwide, even though many states have had success in getting their easiest-to-employ welfare recipients off the rolls.

As I was rather new to government in 1990, I was finding all of this unbelievable. I pressed on: "Veronica, there are a lot of private organizations in this part of the city that work with needy people, can you tell me where they fit in?"

"They do their thing and we do ours—I really don't know much about them," she answered.

I pushed it a bit. "Wouldn't it be great to have a community map on the wall over there that showed where the churches, Salvation Army, and other private organizations are so you could work together in helping families?"

"I suppose," came the answer.

How can the caseworker passing out the welfare check to someone in the Ida B. Wells public housing project encourage self-sufficiency when the necessary substance abuse treatment and job placement services are each from separate, unconnected organizations? What about housing issues? Child care? Transportation? The absence of any one of these elements can preclude self-sufficiency. I made a hopefully not too naive and idealistic mental note to explore the feasibility of "one-stop shopping."

Continuing my tour of the human services systems, I became acquainted with windy Miegs Field in downtown Chicago on Lake Michigan as the primary route to Springfield—the state capital and mother lode of most of the human services money. Springfield is a four-hour drive across the soybean and corn fields or a one-hour flight on an often bumpy, usually old, twenty-seat prop plane run by the marginal Great Lakes Airways. It felt like toy planes flying from a toy airport. As I ducked down to enter the little plane, I thought, "How badly do I really want to pursue my Nepal dreams and make a difference?" A very senior staffer to a previous governor smiled as I grumbled about running back and forth to Springfield on those planes from Miegs and said, "The thing that bothered me most about that commute was that I didn't want to die with a plane full of sleazeballs [read lobbyists and politicians—the majority of passengers]." Years later I came to think of that plane ride as an often useful place to connect with key people helpful in pursuing human services reform. Did I become one of *them*?

One of the stops arranged for me in Springfield was the local office of the Department of Children and Family Services. The office was a medium-sized stand-alone building in a relatively nice part of the city, with a nice, adjacent parking lot. I was ushered into a conference room which was already filled with about a dozen managers and caseworkers. They were told that a representative of one of the gubernatorial candidates was working on policy for families and children and wanted to learn about what they did and hear their ideas. We picked up coffee and soft drinks and sat down at a big conference table. I was a bit disappointed at the arrangement, because I always prefer one-on-one meetings as the best way of having an open discussion about what is really going on. In my experience, the larger the group—especially with the bosses present—the more likely the party line is presented, and the less likely problems will be raised.

This was different. "The next governor needs to change the rules," I was told. "We're prevented from doing what we know needs to be done," Carl, one of the administrators said. He went on: "We came into this work because we wanted to make a difference in people's lives, but we're so tied up in rules and regulations telling us what we can and can't do that we become ineffective. Gloria, tell him about the phone call you received this morning."

Gloria, one of the caseworkers, had just received a call from a distraught mother who was having serious problems with her drug-involved, early teen daughter. She said, "I had to tell the mother that regulations prevented us from helping—unless she locked her daughter out of the home so that abandonment could be demonstrated." The bureaucratic straightjacket in which she was forced to work provided dollars for abandonment, but not for prevention.

As the discussion went on and other examples were cited, I became deeply impressed with this Springfield office group. It was clear that most of them had embarked upon their career paths primarily because of a desire to help people. However, their frustration level was so high that to avoid bureaucratic constraints and be more effective, they said they would rather work for less money at the private agency across town. They described the private agency, noting that it involved some of the key people in town and that doctors and others donated their services to help out. Private agencies often contract with the state to provide case management functions and agree to certain guidelines, but also raise private money and use volunteer help, giving them greater flexibility. The key attraction was freedom from the myriad of bureaucratic constraints. "Are you sure you'd be willing to take a pay cut and get along with fewer fringe benefits to work over there?" I asked, surprised and perplexed. The agreement was clear. They weren't asking for more help or a bigger budget, they were asking for the freedom to be the kind of community resource that they thought they were capable of becoming.

That discussion made a real impression on me. With all the litigation—often from well-meaning advocates—and the extreme media attention that can accompany a child abuse case, for example, it's clear some guidelines are needed. But the value of local flexibility and freedom from bureaucratic constraints gets added to my list of reform needs. How can we get the people at the top of these systems to learn that one size does not fit all and to learn to appreciate the law of unintended consequences—two mantras that I adopted along the way and probably overused in the many speeches I gave during the course of the reform effort. I subsequently came to understand that the people at the top, especially those who wrote the regulations, were evaluated on reducing the agency's legal risk to an absolute minimum, satisfying the federal inspectors and avoiding embarrassment to the governor. Since real outcomes in the form of helping people change their lives and become self-sufficient are rarely measured, micromanagement and the pile of rules grow unrestrained.

The private agencies that I visited were more likely to see their mission as helping the client solve a problem, whereas government workers are usually restricted to providing a specific treatment to a specific demographically identified client, authorized and funded by law, and sharply defined by administrative regulations. A cheaper and more effective way of helping is normally not permitted (e.g., an emergency rent payment loan to prevent eviction), while a more expensive, less useful alternative is authorized (e.g., foster home placement). Before getting to know state caseworkers, I wondered if I would encounter people with a "post office" way of looking at their jobs—people who did the absolute minimum. There is some of that attitude, but I came away with the feeling that if I were a caseworker, I would have to do things much the way most of them did and I would probably feel much the way they felt.

There is an unfortunate logic to what I was learning. The *Chicago Tribune* or any newspaper in any city is more likely to run a story about mistakes than accomplishments, and the same is true for what will provoke a hearing in the state legislature. There are no bonuses for helping someone become self-sufficient, but termination is possible if mistakes are made or paperwork is consistently bad. It was clear that to change the system successfully, deep involvement of front-line caseworkers and their unions would be crucial, and their environment would have to change dramatically. Success would have to mean more than staying out of trouble.

As I was flying back to Chicago, I thought back to a time when I worked for a big bureaucracy with my life subject to thick manuals of rules and regulations—the U.S. Navy. I was the chief engineer of a very old destroyer, the USS *Stribling* (DD867), with responsibility for four big high-pressure, six hundred-pound-per-square-inch main propulsion boilers. The two manuals (probably five inches thick each, with small print) from the Bureau of Ships in Washington required that these boilers hold the six hundred-pound pressure for something like an hour in a test with cold water, with a pressure drop of no less than a pound per square inch during that time. In other words Washington expected all the welds and joints to be very tight—almost like new. The professionals in the shipyard had just overhauled the boilers, and I was asked to sign that the job was complete and satisfactory. I had been a destroyer chief engineer for several years, doing whatever was necessary to keep an old World War II ship moving through the water, all the time chafing under superficial bureaucratic inspections, regulations, and paperwork for Washington, and I was ready to go back to civilian life. The rules from on high came through as out of touch, and one of my cynical fellow officers said, "Those big manuals are to assure that, if something goes wrong, the admiral can point to us and avoid getting blamed himself." We all agreed it would be impossible to do everything by the book, but we did our best, balancing the regulations with the need to keep the ship operating.

I decided to make a point, refusing to approve the job, knowing that the fifteen-year-old boilers didn't (and probably never could) pass the pressure drop test. The commander who was captain of my ship agreed with me and wouldn't take the risk of signing off on the job. If the boilers exploded, a court of inquiry could find the ship's officers at fault. I also thought about the time when our squadron of four destroyers was ordered by the admiral and squadron commander to make an all-out, full-power run off Norfolk, Virginia, at a time when the fuel tanks were low and seas were heavy. The heavy seas and wild pitching caused five sailors to wash off the deck of a sister ship. We looked all night and never found them. Result? A young deck officer was found guilty of having lifeboats that did not open properly, and the admiral escaped responsibility. The captain who headed the shipyard sent a lieutenant commander over to try to persuade me to sign. I suggested we go to Admiral Mumma (yes, Mumma), who ran the Bureau of Ships in Washington and get him to acknowledge that the regulations didn't make sense for fifteen-year-old destroyers. The captain of the shipyard, probably believing that fixing the boilers so that they could pass the test was not possible, and probably not wanting to stir things up in Washington, backed down and we left without signing. It wouldn't surprise me if those regulations were still buried in those manuals.

These experiences were instructive to me in thinking about why the caseworkers did what they did. The human services caseworkers were also dealing with human lives and a lot of money. To take the sometimes necessary risks, they needed an organizational culture and environment that would support them. I began to think of them as *good people trapped in a bad system.*

Back in Chicago, I arranged to see a program called Project Chance that was designed in Springfield to get people on welfare into jobs. I sat in on classes where well-dressed instructors were explaining to not-so-well dressed, mostly African-American recipients how to look for a job in the newspaper, how to fill out employment applications, how to dress and put your best foot forward in an interview, and other job-seeking skills. The unfortunate feeling in the classrooms was one of going through the motions.

I asked one of the attendees why he was there. "Got to do this to get ma check; this is my second time."

"Do you think you'll be able to get a job?" I queried.

"Ain't no jobs 'round here no how," was the response.

At the end of the visit, I spent some time alone in his office with Fred Collins, MSW, the middle-aged, white program administrator responsible for this facility. Fred was a friendly, mild-mannered, conscientious-appearing fellow who had been with Public Aid for about fifteen years, commuting to this assignment from one of the nice suburbs north of the city. I asked what the Project Chance success rate was. "We don't keep track," was the response.

"What would you guess?" I persisted.

"I'd say maybe four percent get jobs," he said.

I then served up a question that grew to be one of my favorites: "Fred, what would you do if this were your money?"

The quick reply: "Heck, that's easy, I'd use the money to run a van from the Robert Taylor Homes where many of these people live out to Elk Grove Village where the jobs are." Onto the list went "outcome measurement." Imagine spending millions and now knowing what you are getting in return other than employment for instructors and MSWs (graduates holding a master's in social work). Also onto the list went "local flexibility." How could we try out his van idea?

In the course of touring the various human services departments and meeting caseworkers, I kept seeing the same problems: no connections with other needed pieces of the self-sufficiency puzzle, too much paper, limited flexibility, accountability for paperwork, not results. Jeanette assured me that what we were seeing was typical of most of the giant human services bureaucracies.

Further visits to local welfare offices filled out the picture for me. Entering a local office usually resulted in an immediate encounter with a security guard. "Why are you here?" If the answer had been to apply for benefits, I would have been asked join the twenty or thirty people camped out in the rows of plastic chairs arranged in straight lines in a large, stark, barnlike room. A model of clinical tastelessness, the room would sport a few official posters on the walls and that's it. The almost total absence of both color in the decor and energy in the people was striking. The atmosphere was one of a sort of evil banality, evoking for me the visits I made to factory offices housing Communist apparachiks while doing business in China and Bulgaria in the 1970s.

Those waiting seemed resigned to spending considerable time there, but no one read, and there was no magazine rack. I was conflicted: do we want welfare offices to be warm, welcoming places where people eagerly come for help? I remember a roundtable dinner discussion a number of years ago when I first met George Stigler, the famed conservative Chicago economist and Nobel Laureate. At just the proper point in a discussion about runaway youths he said, "Remember, the more shelters for runaways you build, and the nicer they are, the more runaways you will have." On the other hand, I found the public areas at Stateville prison nicer and more welcoming than most welfare offices. Maybe there is a middle ground.

Once admitted into the large office area, I saw that things got brighter. The intake (initial placement interview) workers had private cubicles for meeting prospective clients, and the usual family pictures and artifacts were carefully arranged in each area. In the larger open office area, caseworkers worked in long lines of desks with few separations. It looked like it wouldn't be easy to find private space to talk to a client in confidence. Around the edge were private offices with doors, the domains of supervisors. Scanning the large caseworker room, it was easy to get the impression that you'd stumbled into a time machine and been transported back to the 1950s: there was a sea of paper. Every desk was covered with paper piled high. Bulging file folders competed with myriad forms for desk space. Filing cabinets were everywhere, with many open drawers. A large forms room containing, I was told, five hundred different forms, was nearby. Numerous copy machines were very busy, but often several were broken down. Phones rang endlessly, as there was no voicemail. Voicemail, I was told, must be procured through CMS (Central Management Services, a separate bureaucracy that "serves" all state agencies), which marked up the cost substantially. The only clue that this was not the 1950s was the vintage Wang terminals on the desks. What kind of person would work in a place like this?

To begin to answer this question, I arranged to leave the office and go out to lunch with Roy Hobbes, a caseworker whose background, attitudes, and capabilities turned out to be reasonably representative. Roy was a forty-nine-year-old African American who was born in Alabama and brought to Chicago as a child. He remembers as a child his parents taking him along on Martin Luther King's historic Selma march. Roy is a nice-looking fellow, younger-looking than his age, very polite and soft-spoken. He dropped out of college (only about one-third of caseworkers in Illinois are college graduates) and worked in a warehouse and as a machine helper before he came to work for the state eighteen years ago in the Public Aid Department.

"Why Public Aid?" I asked.

"Frankly, I needed a job, but I did like the idea of helping people," he responded. Now, as an experienced caseworker, he made $37,000 per year. Roy believed he was being micromanaged, and would like more freedom to help people. Occasionally he would make a strong statement. On public housing: "Just because you are poor, you don't have to live like a rat." On the motivation of his clients: "If there was a ladder to self-sufficiency, seventy-five percent would climb it; ten percent would wait and see, then follow along; the remaining fifteen percent would need tough, tough love." On paperwork: "It takes seventy-five percent of my time, with about ten percent of it useful in helping the client. The rest goes into a file that I'm sure nobody reads." On overall vision: "It would take years, but if we did our job right, Stateway Gardens [a distressed public housing project] could look like North Lake Shore Drive [a high-quality residential area]." When we returned to the office I thanked him for his time, and watched with mixed emotions as he returned to his desk in the middle of the sea of paper and fellow workers.

Unlike Roy, who, according to his boss, was doing a very good job and who really cared about making a difference, there is a sizable minority of others like Martha Mae, a woman in her fifties, who burned out long ago from frustration. In our interview, Martha Mae seemed listless and uninterested, and had no suggestions as to how anything could be done better. Getting information or any kind of spark from her was like getting blood from a stone. It is quite likely that Martha Mae is the wrong person to be doing casework in the first place.

Without much education, she was on welfare herself, and eventually got a clerical job with the old Department of Public Aid. With rigid union seniority rules she moved up to caseworker, where for many years, with little training, she mostly did paperwork. Her almost-exclusive focus was determining whether people were eligible or ineligible for a government check. As with most caseworkers under the pre–welfare reform system, she was what I call a "gatekeeper to benefits," nothing more. For many years Martha Mae has done what she was told to do and therefore doesn't deserve to lose her weekly paycheck. The best answer for her is probably early retirement. I made a mental note to be mindful of the tremendous challenge it would be to sort out and train or retire what I was sure must be hundreds of Martha Maes working in state human services or, perhaps more likely, reassigning them to jobs consistent with their capabilities. It took thirty years to descend into the mess I was seeing, it's going to take more than a year or two to turn everything around. As a start, we've got to make sure we don't create any new Martha Mae caseworkers.

At one of the stops in the process of getting to know the front lines, I found myself sitting in the office of Ella Jones, one of the local office administrators (LOAs) with a responsibility for one of the larger Chicago offices serving some of the city's tougher communities. Ella was a heavyset, outgoing, maternal sort of woman whom I guessed to be in her midfifties. She had been around a long time, diligently working her way up from a clerk position to office administrator over twenty-five years, despite lacking a college degree. During our visit she seemed harassed and frustrated, and she complained that she was so busy fighting fires and preparing reports that she didn't have time to do the things she knew would make the office more effective.

As an example she showed me her monthly report—a tome about one-quarter to one-half inch thick that took several people several days each month to prepare and consumed two days of her own time each month. Ella said the report was "the way the head office has always wanted it." Among other topics, we also looked at the office organization charts, which showed a considerable number of people with only two people reporting to them, a red flag in most organizations, since a typical managerial span of control is normally six or more direct reports. Ella explained that the state's managerial department (Central Management Services or CMS) determined pay levels based on number of people supervised, so people are grouped that way to justify their pay. Ella struck me as having the potential to lead her office to a greater level of accomplishment, but she couldn't get there without some of the basic managerial tools and the management training to go along with it. Ella's world seemed untouched by the technology advances of the last twenty years or any managerial logic. She was like one of those Japanese soldiers found in a cave twenty years after the war had ended—insulated from all the dramatic changes that had occurred during that time. I couldn't help but think of the desks I'd seen over the years at all levels at UPS. There was very little paper, but a desktop computer could retrieve the data on the exact location of any one of the 13 million-plus packages going through the huge worldwide organization on any given day. At Mark Controls we were always streamlining reports to include only that information that led to action that would make a difference. Why should the taxpayers get any less?

As a businessman I wondered who was looking over the shoulders of the many caseworkers and other frontline administrators. Who was supervising people like Veronica, Fred, Roy, Ella, and the energetic group in Springfield? Wouldn't these managers, the higher-ups my interviewees referred to, also see the big barriers to effectiveness I was running across and be working to change things? I met many of these senior managers in the following five years that I spent working with Illinois human services, and came to appreciate that unfortunately, most (though not all) of the senior managers felt bound in the same cultural and regulatory straightjacket as their front-line troops. A good example is Leon Smith.

Before meeting with Leon, a region manager, I had visited several local welfare offices in his region and continued to hear the same complaints about drowning in paper, firefighting, and the like, often from the local office administrators who ran the offices. I was looking forward to my meeting with Leon at his downtown headquarters office, naively thinking he might jump at the chance to provide some relief to his troops on some of these problems. Leon was a somewhat stocky, pleasant, immaculately dressed African-American fellow of medium height about fifty years of age. Leon had twenty-four of the state's 128 welfare offices reporting to him (too *big* a span of control), and I asked him how high the stack of reports from all these offices measured each month. He gestured with his hand indicating a very big pile, then sat quietly. "Do you have time to read all of that?" I asked.

"No," he acknowledged. "I only use bits and pieces of it."

"Why not limit each office report to two pages, and ensure that only the most useful information is included?" I suggested.

His quick response: "I don't have the authority to change that—someone higher than me would have to do it."

"But Leon, you have about 3,000 people working for you, and these are reports to you that you don't pass on—can't you streamline them?" I asked in disbelief.

"No," he said.

"Have you asked your boss about it?"

No, came the answer.

Needless to say, the discussion with Leon of possibilities worth looking into to improve the organization of the local offices and increase their capacity lead nowhere as well. This inertia was displayed despite the fact that he agreed, without hesitation, that the changes would significantly improve the capabilities of the offices. Leon cited the genuine challenges of union contract restrictions and CMS involvement as reasons he couldn't do anything about the organizational structure of his offices. It was clear Leon viewed not making waves with CMS or the union or "higher management" as the key to lasting thirty-two years in state government.

In subsequent exposures to the front-line caseworkers and offices, some other facts emerged. The locations of the offices didn't fit very well with the location of the welfare clients they were hoping to help become self-sufficient. This is important, because most of the clients don't have cars. It's also important because locating the offices within the communities can give an economic boost to that community. It turns out that over the years state office buildings have typically been leased from politically well connected party benefactors, and it appears that the needs of these developers have taken precedence over the needs of disadvantaged families. One senior human services administrator said the "most politicized thing he had to deal with was building leases, and Central Management Services [CMS] was the real decision maker. I began to see the reason that CMS was often headed by one of the governor's most savvy political operatives. It's important to know who the good friends are, since there's always an upcoming campaign, and it's really tough to raise the necessary $10 million or more in campaign funds strictly from people who care about good government. Imagine trying to run Walmart under the condition that you could not decide where to put your stores!

As an example, the Grand Boulevard community, arguably one of the poorest census tracts in the country, has no welfare office, and is served from outside its borders. A scatter diagram showing clients in relation to welfare offices and the traditional Chicago communities highlights major mismatches (Figure 2). I make some more notes—let's develop a plan to relocate offices where the people are, so we're ready when each lease expires, then have the governor and the legislators tell their friends, "We'd be glad to do business with you, but you've got to put the offices where we need them." This one goes on the list, but it is not the right place to pick an early fight. However, it is important, and its time must come.

Another finding that was news to me, but long accepted in the "poverty business," is fact that in distressed communities the large majority of caseworkers and administrators don't live in, or often even near, the communities that they are paid to serve. This is also true of many private agency workers. The result is that many millions spent on behalf of poor people don't make it into their communities. In addition, if the workers actually enter the communities, the payroll dollars leave with the caseworker at the end of the workday, and add nothing to the economies of these poor communities.

Figure 2. Chicago's Communities: More Than Seventy Individual Identities

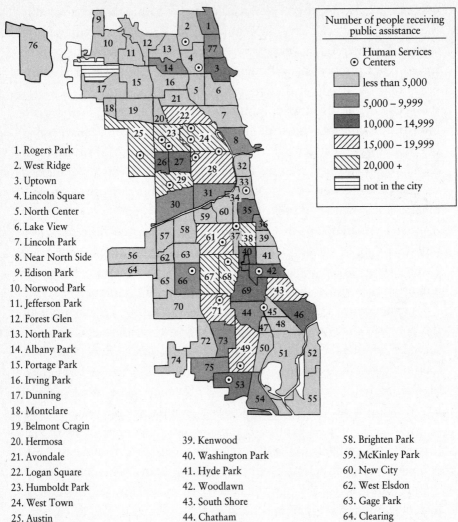

Number of people receiving public assistance

⊙ Human Services Centers

	less than 5,000
	5,000 – 9,999
	10,000 – 14,999
	15,000 – 19,999
	20,000 +
	not in the city

1. Rogers Park
2. West Ridge
3. Uptown
4. Lincoln Square
5. North Center
6. Lake View
7. Lincoln Park
8. Near North Side
9. Edison Park
10. Norwood Park
11. Jefferson Park
12. Forest Glen
13. North Park
14. Albany Park
15. Portage Park
16. Irving Park
17. Dunning
18. Montclare
19. Belmont Cragin
20. Hermosa
21. Avondale
22. Logan Square
23. Humboldt Park
24. West Town
25. Austin
26. West Garfield Park
27. East Garfield Park
28. Near West Side
29. North Lawndale
30. South Lawndale
31. Lower West Side
32. Loop
33. Near South Side
34. Armour Square
35. Douglas
36. Oakland
37. Fuller Park
38. Grand Boulevard

39. Kenwood
40. Washington Park
41. Hyde Park
42. Woodlawn
43. South Shore
44. Chatham
45. Avalon Park
46. South Chicago
47. Burnside
48. Calumet Heights
49. Roseland
50. Pullman
51. South Deering
52. East Side
53. West Pullman
54. Riverdale
55. Hegewisch
56. Garfield Ridge
57. Archer Heights

58. Brighten Park
59. McKinley Park
60. New City
62. West Elsdon
63. Gage Park
64. Clearing
65. West Lawn
66. Chicago Lawn
67. West Englewood
68. Englewood
69. Greater Grand Crossing
70. Ashburn
71. Auburn Gresham
72. Beverly
73. Washington Heights
74. Mount Greenwood
75. Morgan Park
76. O'Hare
77. Edgewater

Source: Geographic Information Study of the University of Illinois at Chicago

Early in the reform effort I remember sharing with the Reverend
Don Hallberg, the head of the giant Lutheran Social Services organization, my concern about the caseworkers not being part of the communities they were trying to help. Don, a gregarious, friendly, and
very open fellow responded: "Heck, Gary, it's dangerous down there.
We check our people in and out by cell phone when they make their
visits. Of course they don't live there." Interestingly, about 85 percent
of Hallberg's $21 million annual budget[1] is made up of government
contracts, primarily with the state of Illinois.

Regarding state workers, there is an understandable union problem. The jobs are decided on a bid system. When an opening occurs,
workers bid, and union rules say that the person with the most seniority gets it. The result is that the offices in the toughest neighborhoods tend to get the people with the least seniority. When openings
come up in more attractive neighborhoods, they go. The people most
capable of handling the toughest problems leave, and the incentive to
commit to a tough neighborhood isn't there. At the moment the system seems to be run for the convenience of those who work there, not
for the benefit of those who need to become self-sufficient. Business
solves these kinds of problems with some kind of premium pay incentive that makes up for work in tough locations—assignments that require living on offshore oil platforms or in Third World countries, for
instance. Another issue added to the growing list in my notebook.
More on this one later. I was beginning to see that establishing priorities was going to be crucial. We needed to have success with the easier
issues first, the "low-hanging fruit," then use the momentum to tackle
some of these other problems in a "Phase II."

In addition to their contact with clients, front-line caseworkers
and administrators are in a good position to see the various disconnected human services systems from the vantage point of the bottom
of the hierarchy. They look up to both the state bureaucracy and to
Washington, and see themselves as good people trapped in a bad system. They accurately view the systems as complicated, illogical, and
often unfair and unhelpful. The systems themselves often throw up
barriers to any goals the caseworkers may have for their clients to be-

come self-sufficient. Almost any review of human services systems in any state yields numerous caseworker stories with a common denominator: "Here is what I was required to do by the rules and regulations, and here is the logical approach I was prevented from following." Time and time again my front-line experiences in the communities with caseworkers and people in need brought home to me the futility of well-intentioned lawmakers, sitting in a Washington office, trying to design a program to fix some piece of the problem in Chicago's Grand Boulevard community or the Southern Seven (our rural poverty test site made up of the seven counties in the southern tip of Illinois).

As an example of the disconnect between Washington policymakers and the reality of Chicago's inner city, a Grand Boulevard site visit by Senator Bill Bradley, MIT economist Lester Thurow, political commentator Dave Gergen, former Harvard president Derek Bok, and other members of the Aspen Institute Urban Policy Group resulted in little real communication. They had heard about our work in connecting the Grand Boulevard community with government, and we showed up on their agenda. As one of the speakers I traveled around with them, and was fascinated to see how some opinion makers formed *their* opinions. I was sorry not to be involved in the planning, because during the visit they never really talked individually to people in poverty, visited a housing project, or had any other exposure that would help them understand how things really worked in Chicago's inner city. Instead they were in the nice neat offices of a well-connected private human services agency, being given presentations, complete with slides and brochures, by private agency people who viewed the visit as an opportunity to brag about their work and hopefully maintain or increase their government and private grants. The questions the visitors asked were often off the mark, or designed to fit some preconceived theory they brought with them. For example, a question to me from Lester Thurow: "Aren't the inner-city people you work with going to hold you responsible for the welfare cuts, since you represent government, and won't this hurt your effectiveness?" The patronizing assumption, of course, is that the people in poor neighborhoods with whom I build relationships are not smart enough to know that I'm not responsible for legislation in Washington. These national "opinion leaders" felt that they had made an informative field trip into the heart of the inner city and thought they were now prepared to offer solutions in op-eds, talking head TV programs, or books.

Also, on this visit Senator Bradley was interested in how the multi-billion dollar Empowerment Zone legislation (yet another separate organization and program!) which he had sponsored was being implemented in Chicago. This legislation was the biggest urban poverty initiative to come out of Washington in years. Senator Bradley was surprised to learn from the African-American community leaders on the South Side who helped design the proposal that they were struggling for their share of the $100 million Chicago award, which had become a political nightmare. They alleged that it was given predominantly to unrelated Hispanic groups that supported Mayor Daley. African Americans in Chicago often run a competing mayoral candidate, and therefore rewarding them with government dollars often makes less sense politically than some other options.

The Empowerment Zone became a political football, and it is unlikely that any permanent system change will result. When the money runs out, things will go back to the way they were until the next government grant comes along. I call this kind of government spending building castles in the sand—the certain result is the tide sweeping in and returning things to the way they were.

Senator Bradley discovered some of these things on his visit and, sitting across from him on the group's bus, I asked him how he felt. He had a worried look, and he said, "This is very discouraging. I wrote much of this legislation myself, knowing that we needed to avoid the mistakes that were made in the Great Society programs."

I said, "To me, what happened is to be expected. Like the law of gravity, the law of unintended consequences is the inevitable result of top-down Washington designed programs." Politicians and grant recipients know how to dress things up to make them look like neighborhood/community involvement is happening, but you have to be on the ground in the community to know if it is *really* happening.

In thinking further about why things have been such a mess at the caseworker level, it is helpful to touch on the role played by academics and think tank researchers, a number of whom were part of the visiting Aspen Institute entourage. They do valuable work in calling attention to the problems of poverty, mining census data and other sources to identify trends, and establishing correlations between and among the various factors relating to poverty. The most effective of the group shrewdly market their data to congressional staffers, political leaders, and the press in publications and conferences. Correlations between unemployment and poverty, minimum wage and poverty, income inequality among races and genders, and evaluations of individual programs and other, usually macro issues become fodder for the political process, driving political action, budgets, and new programs. Politicians and their staffers, looking for ways to make a difference and to show in their campaigns that they care, create these new programs and then move on to highway funding, defense spending, or whatever else is next on the agenda. Rules and regulations are then promulgated by back-office bureaucrats in various departments in Washington and passed on to the states, adding to the complexity of an already complex situation.

The rules and regulations that our caseworker friend Roy must follow are available at the side of the big room, mounted on a table, and measure almost *two feet* across the back of the spine! What is rarely talked about is how these programs will be implemented by the caseworkers on the front lines in the communities in a way that helps the ladies in the backyard. Fixing the front-line delivery systems has the disadvantage of being hard to describe, and fighting for dollars for caseworker training or a welfare office computer system is, correctly, not viewed as a way to attract swing voters.

Business analogies are sometimes (but not always) useful in gaining an understanding of what is happening, or not happening, in government. At the senior management and board level at UPS we spend a great deal of time developing a strategy for the company's future. As an example, delivering a package on time is a central element of that strategy. FedEx on-time performance for an important category recently was a very good 97 percent, and UPS was an even better 98 percent. Why shouldn't UPS use the government approach and just create a regulation that requires 99 percent on-time performance and put this in a manual with copies accessible to each of the company's 370,000 employees? Business managers know that to get a valuable result and make something happen requires a thoughtful organization structure, intensive training at all levels (especially on the front lines), first-rate technology, and more. Establishing a rule is, by itself, naive in the extreme. When I was a consultant, I shared with academics and think tank researchers the view that 90 percent of problem solving was knowing what to do, and 10 percent was implementation. After becoming a CEO, I realized that those percentages should be reversed!

Another important aspect of my review is clear—most government human services numbers are *not clear.* Numbers are collected, primarily by program and primarily for Washington, in order to keep the dollars flowing to the state. Normal businesslike analyses of effectiveness are doomed to frustration, compounded by antiquated management information systems. How can a manager understand how well or poorly an office is doing without knowing the level of employability of those in that office's client pool? Of those who get jobs, how many are still in those jobs ninety days later? Of course in 1990 there was very little worrying about jobs. The principal focus of federal inspectors visiting states were things like food stamp error rate and errors in completing welfare payment eligibility forms. How many were getting checks that should not be, or vice versa? Managerial data is tough to come by in government operations, and no state is immune from this problem. We'll return to the numbers later. Outcome measurement goes on my list.

From a personal point of view, time spent with front-line workers gave me great empathy for the difficulty of their job under present conditions. The caseloads were too big, the rules too restrictive, services too fragmented, and for the most part, essential ingredients for self-sufficiency and an exit from the systems (such as a connection to employers), were not present.

It was becoming increasingly clear to me that the system needed to be reinvented, starting from the bottom (clients, caseworkers, and communities) up and that, for the most part, it would be unwise to add more new top-down programs and dollars until we do. Reinvention would have to include putting all the organizational pieces together in a different way, so that caseworkers could really be held accountable for helping clients become self-sufficient. They would have to get out of their offices and enlist the help of their communities to find help in such things as transportation, child care, finding jobs, or whatever it takes. To do this we would have to create a process that could lead to the reinvention of human services in Illinois. While national level welfare reform was yet to come, it was clear that much could be done on the front lines in the communities and at the state level to reinvent the system. I knew that when a federal barrier stood in the way it was possible to get a waiver, so much could be done without getting bogged down in Washington. I thought back to the Bush campaign days and my exposure to HHS. I decided getting an important state like Illinois restructured from the bottom up could help set the direction for the nation.

PRINCIPAL POINTS

1. Caseworkers have a tough job to do, and they are drowning in paperwork and regulations limiting their effectiveness.
2. Caseworkers usually aren't connected to all of the pieces of the puzzle necessary for their clients to become self-sufficient, resulting in frustration and lack of success.
3. Adding more dollars and programs to the existing morass is likely to be ineffective and a waste of lives and taxpayers' money.
4. The system needs to be reinvented—a massive, from-the-bottom-up (clients, caseworkers, and communities) system overhaul is required. Some local flexibility is needed.
5. Outcomes/results from the huge taxpayer investment in human services need to be measured.

4

What Can Be Done About the Mess We Are In? There Is No Silver Bullet, But . . .

Whoever knocks persistently, ends by entering.
—MUSLIM SAYING, C. 650 A.D.

It was July 1997, and the setting was an elegant wood-paneled private dining room in the venerable Chicago Club overlooking Lake Michigan. The occasion was the final gathering of the Governor's Task Force on Human Services Reform, coming together to celebrate the successful completion of a daunting mission—a major overhaul of the state human services systems. Present were Governor Edgar, the members of the task force, and the task force staff, about twenty in all. Most of the task force members present had been part of the adventure since the beginning in 1993. Missing was task force member Vince Lane, the charismatic head of the Chicago Housing Authority. Vince was once talked about as a potential candidate for mayor, but it seems that several million dollars in CHA pension fund money disappeared on his watch. Vince stopped showing up for task force meetings. I was told by his office that they thought he was in Philadelphia, but no one seemed to have his phone number. A valuable addition for the last two years of the GTF activities was former Continental Bank chairman and CEO Tom Theobald, who was also a trustee of the huge MacArthur Foundation. Tom was especially helpful in bringing common sense business perspective to the deliberations. It was a purposefully eclectic group that was enormously helpful in driving the reform process, and I had a warm feeling as we enjoyed our lunch. I had purposely seated the chairs of two of the community federations, Margo Schreiber and Sokoni Karanja, next to the governor. Prior to passing out the small individually engraved keepsakes as tokens of gratitude, Governor Edgar stood up to make some remarks.

Jim Edgar was an enormously popular governor, holding a voter approval rating usually in the 70 percent range, quite a remarkable accomplishment for a Republican governor in a state with more Democrats than Republicans and two Democratic senators. Illinoisans accurately viewed him as a totally honest, totally reliable politician who truly cared about making things better. He was also given to incrementalism rather than bold change—with a strong aversion to political risk that goes right to the core of his being. Jim worked his way up through the political system in Illinois step by step with meticulous planning and hard work. He first experienced political success as student body president at Eastern Illinois University near his hometown of Charleston, a small downstate farming community. He then lost his first race for state representative. He worked on various state legislative staffs and eventually won election to the state house of representatives, where he established a reputation as hardworking and able. He then did a tour as popular Governor Jim Thompson's legislative liaison. Jim Edgar's big break came when Alan Dixon resigned as secretary of state to become a U.S. senator, and Governor Thompson appointed Jim to complete Dixon's term. The secretary of state in Illinois is responsible for driver's licenses and license plates and a few other relatively minor activities. However, with an army of about 3,600 workers spread all over the state, many of them patronage, the office is tantamount to command of perhaps the state's most potent political army, and Jim Edgar was its general for ten years. In addition, virtually every voter carried a driver's license bearing Jim Edgar's name in his pocket, saw Jim's name in large letters on state buildings and on important envelopes that regularly came to the homes of most voters. If there was one thing I learned during my forays into elective politics, name identification is the sine qua non of a political base, and it takes years to build. Jim Edgar used this base effectively and, as a Baptist teetotaler, mounted an anti–drunk driving campaign that became well known. In the meantime he worked tirelessly building awareness of Jim Edgar, out most nights of the week attending and speaking in most of Illinois's 102 counties at the ubiquitous Republican Lincoln Day dinners. Lincoln Day for Republicans in Illinois is almost any day of the year. He also paid his dues by working hard at an overwhelming number of county fairs and mind-boggling numbers of fund-raising events for candidates at the state, county, township, and local levels. When Governor Thompson decided fourteen years was enough in 1990, Jim Edgar was ready to go, and after a draining campaign during which he lost twenty pounds that he didn't need to lose, he became governor, defeating a shrewd but lackluster old-line Democratic pol.

Jim Edgar's first few years as governor were determined by the precarious condition of the state's economy. Revenues were stagnant, forcing budget cuts and an income tax surcharge. The state was way behind in paying bills, especially those due Medicaid and other human services providers. Policymaking was managing cash. For his reelection in 1994 he was aided by what my friend, longtime Republican strategist Bob Teeter, calls the first law of politics: have a bad opponent. He drew a very bright woman whose very liberal record was relatively easily sold to the voters as too extreme for a moderate state like Illinois. The economy had also improved, increasing state income tax revenues and giving him the chance to trumpet a fiscal turnaround.

On that summer day in the Chicago Club I had introduced Governor Edgar as a "courageous man who had taken a major political risk to push through the biggest reorganization of state government since 1900, consistent with the findings and recommendations of this task force."

Jim got up, looked at me, looked at the group sitting around the table, and started to speak: "I was trying to figure out how I would describe Gary MacDougal today, and I decided the right word was 'tenacious.' When I was running for governor back in 1990 he was a big help in lots of ways. When we won the election, I was very thankful for his help and thought that would be it. Well, he wouldn't go away. He kept coming around and talking about the need to reform welfare and human services, so finally I decided to let him go ahead and see what he could do." He added, in jest, "We formed the task force as much to get him off my back as anything else."

Much happened between Jim Edgar's 1990 election and that luncheon seven years later at the Chicago Club. The task force work had lasted four years—considerably longer than I might have guessed when we started. I knew we would move well beyond the standard "task force report to the governor," but I would not have guessed we would be the catalyst for the largest reorganization of Illinois state government since 1900. However, almost nothing happened on my dream of reforming the system for the first two years of Jim Edgar's term. During the gubernatorial transition between the November election and the January inauguration I worked hard polishing up the report that came out of my touring of the human services systems and my policy work. I presented it to key people in the new administration, competing with the myriad state issues demanding the new governor's attention—attracting industry, huge budgetary and tax pressures, roads, gambling and lotteries, a proposed new airport, thousands of job seekers, a state house controlled by the other party, etc., etc. Over thirty state departments or agencies report to the governor, not to mention oversight and/or appointment responsibilities for nearly three hundred boards, commissions, authorities, and other bodies—a managerial nightmare. Naively, I expected someone to call me and say, "Your ideas are great—let's get going." No one called—I was getting nowhere. I also got distracted while I was waiting.

All during this time I was talking with my friend and mentor Harvey every week, as I had been for over twenty years. Because we had restructured and stepped out of Mark Controls in 1987, I hadn't seen as much of him personally as when we came together regularly for meetings, but we both seemed to draw strength from our unfailing weekly communication. He would either be at his home in Scottsdale, or on his beautiful seventy-thousand-acre cattle ranch at the base of the majestic Santa Maria mountain range in northern Arizona, where he went on long rides astride Star, a peppy Arabian gelding that he loved. He would tell me of his work giving his money away to disadvantaged students through his foundation, and of long rides out in the open country where he always drew spiritual strength. Occasionally, but in hindsight not often enough, I would stop by and join him on one of the rides—an experience guaranteed to return me to earth thinking about things larger than myself. It's hard to figure out anything you can possibly do in return for a man like Harvey, and he expected nothing. However, one source of great happiness to me for many years was giving him a yearling Arabian colt born at my small farm and home outside Chicago. I had pulled the baby colt out of his mother's womb late one night, so Star was a very personal gift.

Harvey was a wonderful rider, but young Arabians are not easy to train and ride, especially in the rocky, rough terrain of northern Arizona—and Harvey was in his late sixties when the gift arrived. To my great joy, Harvey was thrilled. He had always loved Arabians, with their long beautiful necks, dished faces, wide-set eyes, and alert, flaglike tails, but his ranch, like most working Western ranches, was populated by the more sedate and practical quarter horses the cowboys prefer. Star, named for the white star on his bay face, became his constant companion, and I felt that part of me was with Harvey for the next ten years, even though I didn't get to Arizona as often as I would have liked.

In our weekly phone conversations Harvey would listen carefully to my descriptions of the work in Washington in the Bush '88 campaign, the possible Senate race, the welfare systems work with Jim Edgar, and the other activities. Without pushing me, I could always tell that his hope for me was having an impact on other people. He was sure that if I was tenacious I could find a way to make a difference in Illinois—but the road was fraught with zigs and zags, some of them self-inflicted.

In the summer of 1991 I was approached by a number of Republicans, including some close to the governor, about running for the U.S. Senate seat then held by Alan Dixon. "Al the Pal," as he was called, was widely viewed as unbeatable, getting 60 percent or more of the vote in statewide races. The established Republican pols were reluctant to take him on. I had shown in the earlier Senate race that I could raise money, and it was widely believed that George Bush had made a mistake in encouraging me to get out of the earlier Senate race in 1989. Again, I thought, an Illinois U.S. Senate seat offered a chance to be a voice for change on the issues for disadvantaged families, though much more indirectly and perhaps less effectively than hands-on work at the state level. I evaluated the idea for a couple of months with the help of some fine staffers I had worked with in the earlier effort. In the meantime the other leading potential candidate pulled out. I did some political soundings, and some polls done in Washington showed some unexpected Dixon vulnerability. Governor Edgar said he would support me, and he had a speech ready to endorse me at a rally at Miegs Field, where a chartered plane was going to take me on a "fly-around" of the four or five largest Illinois cities to announce that I was going to be the Republican to take on Dixon. The media assumed I was the one.

About a week before the Miegs rally, I decided to check in with some of the big Chicago names that were on my letterhead as my finance committee in the earlier effort against Paul Simon. I had every expectation that these leading Republicans would once again be on-board as I made my calls. The response of my friend of twenty years, billionaire Bob Pritzker, whose family owns Hyatt Hotels and many other less visible companies, was representative of many of the rest. "Gary, you'd be the best senator—I'll send you a one-thousand-dollar check, but I'd better not be on your letterhead this time. Dixon's on the banking committee and we own . . ." Good government, when put up against personal financial interests, too often comes out second best. A meaningful number of my friends didn't care as much about the larger issues as I thought they should, but perhaps they were also somewhat pragmatic. It would be a tough race for me to win, and what can one junior senator out of one hundred accomplish anyway?

Former Governor Thompson told me, "It would be great for the party if you did it, but you have already been successful, why would you want to put yourself through all of that?" I had become engaged that summer. Charlene, then my fiancée, after making a hit at a Chicago Polish political picnic meeting people and eating brats, sat at the breakfast table one day and gamely said she would support whatever decision I made—but then, uncharacteristically, a tear just popped out of her eye against her will. I was sure she would be a tremendous asset in the campaign, but the strain would be tremendous.

Knowing of the huge personal price I would be paying for the next fifteen months, and knowing that it would take about $9 million to have a fair shake against an incumbent, I figured I'd be left at the $3 to $4 million level. This was counting a $1 million commitment from Senator Phil Gramm, head of the National Republican Senatorial Committee in Washington and half a million of my own money that I decided I would be willing to spend. To spend more of my own money didn't seem right to me. If I was to credibly represent the Republican Party, and if I was to sacrifice fifteen months of my life campaigning, I shouldn't have to pay for most of it too. I pictured running all over the state in a van and running out of money to respond to the attacks at the same time. The first candidate to launch an unanswered advertising blitz painting the other candidate as an out-of-touch extremist, either left or right, tends to win.

I made several trips to Washington during this time to meet with party leaders and gauge the level of support I might get for fundraisers and direct financial support. On one of these trips the energetic, rising Congressman Newt Gingrich gave me a ride to the National Republican Senatorial Committee building in his car. I said hello to his driver as we got in the backseat. Gingrich gave me a friendly tip: "Gary, if you're going to be a successful politician, you're going to have to introduce yourself to everyone and really make a connection." I found him very stimulating. Little did I realize, of course, that he would become Speaker of the House and lead the way on the most profound welfare reform legislation in decades, giving my Illinois reform effort a big boost. To me he is aptly characterized by a newspaper cartoon showing an office filled with filing cabinets stuffed with paper, all but one labeled "Newt's Ideas." The final one is labeled "Newt's Good Ideas."

Two days before the scheduled announcement flyaround, I paced back and forth most of the night before calling Jim Edgar and telling him I had decided not to run. Jim was sorry to hear that, saying, "You just have to have faith that the money will come from somewhere." I then called Phil Gramm, who earlier had made a personal visit to my apartment to persuade me to run, and told him of my decision. "Gary," he said in his Texas drawl, "when yore seventy years old, you'll look back on this decision as the biggest fucking mistake of yore life." I'm not seventy yet, but I have no regrets.

Later, a bestselling book titled *Strange Justice*[1] was published on the Clarence Thomas nomination and contained a discussion of my potential run, quoting Bush White House political operatives as making a deal to get me out of the race in return for Dixon's vote. The book stated that I was "thought to be a serious contender who could raise large amounts of money," but when Dixon was persuaded to vote for Thomas, a "high ranking GOP (White House) political aide" was quoted as saying, "Dixon was led to believe he'd get a weak opponent," "it was done with a wink and a nod," "MacDougal withdrew." Dixon went on to cast one of the few Democratic votes for the Clarence Thomas nomination, which barely passed. Two "on the fence" senators, voting for Judge Thomas, one of whom was Dixon, made the difference.

The White House politicos took credit, rightly or wrongly, for drying up my financial support. I subsequently queried one of them on the statements in the book and he said, "Someone may have hinted to Dixon that we'd do something like that, but nothing was done." My guess, though I'll probably never know for sure, is that the reticence of my Chicago CEO friends stemmed mostly from fear of offending Dixon, a feeling that he was more a friend of business than most Democrats and therefore not a real target for elimination, and a feeling that the odds were against beating him. Ironically, Dixon was beaten in the primary, and the general election race was against the then–relatively unknown liberal Carol Mosely Braun, the Cook

County recorder of deeds. She was charged with bending Medicaid rules and manipulating income tax regulations in handling her mother's finances, and a big issue was jobs and the economy. I had been given public credit for helping to bring a new 4,500-job UPS facility to the Chicago area, and with jobs the issue, as a businessman my credibility was high. It may be egocentric, but despite her symbolic advantage as an African-American woman, I believe I would have won. Edgar was right, the Republican wallets would have opened wide.

This distraction had run its course by the end of 1991, and as the New Year dawned, I decided to step up my campaign to get Governor Edgar to face up to the welfare/human services challenge. If he wasn't going to take the initiative, I was going to push as hard as I could. I started giving him aggressive pitches when I ran into him at political events in Chicago. He would listen politely and suggest someone on his staff whom I should talk to. It took me awhile to appreciate it, but he is a very closed person in many ways, with a rigid approach to decision making and management. He needed the comfort of one of his staffers championing an idea that he could then evaluate. In addition, from his perspective as governor, I'm sure he was getting aggressive pitches all the time. Most of them end up revealing some sort of self-serving angle having more to do with private interest than public interest, so I'm sure there is a natural reflex to use your staff as a shield. I finally figured out that my solo pitches weren't going to be enough, and though he cared about disadvantaged people, taking a political risk to do something about it was not high enough on his list of things to do.

I had developed a friendship with smart, curmudgeonly Mike Lawrence, his longtime colleague, advisor, and communications chief. Mike was a longtime downstate newspaper reporter with a passion for keeping politicians honest by digging deeply into suspected scandals and writing the exposé. He had a nose for how something would look on the front pages, and even turned over to the state police an anonymous letter he received that unearthed a scandal in the Edgar administration resulting in the indictments of Edgar administration officials. Mike wears a permanent scowl, but underneath is a warm, caring human being with an unwavering moral compass. Mike seemed very interested in and supportive of my reform ideas, but after a few months I realized that, although he would be an ally, he wasn't the one to get the ball rolling. Perhaps he figured that if it was a really good idea, others in the administration would step forward and he would then help.

I was very busy that year with my corporate boards, foundation trusteeships, trips out of the country, chairing the UPS finance committee in Atlanta, an appointment by President Bush to the U.S. Commission to Improve the Effectiveness of the United Nations, and working with Charlene to prepare for our June wedding. Charlene had just retired from a highly successful career as a ballerina, most of it as a principal dancer with the Joffrey ballet. She had been the legendary Rudolph Nureyev's partner for a year and performed in *West Side Story* on Broadway as Clarice, a member of the Jets street gang. Charlene choreographed our wedding dance, and it was clear that I was way out of my league in the dancing department. I needed Fred Astaire's help, which I obtained, plus many Sunday afternoon practices to be a respectable partner on the big day. In addition, George Bush's reelection campaign was in trouble, and the campaign manager, Fred Malek, a friend from our McKinsey days together, asked if I could spend from mid-August to mid-October working in the campaign in Washington. He asked me to lead an effort to go after a few hundred thousand swing votes in five key states by better organizing key coalitions of high Republican potential: Evangelicals, hunters (whom we referred to as gun nuts), veterans, and Catholics. It was hard to say no, since the race looked close at that time, and I wouldn't have been able to live with myself if Clinton just squeaked in. However, we failed to convince the President to come up with an aggressive response to the Los Angeles riots that year—and this became one of several pieces of political "evidence" that he seemed out of touch. In addition, Ross Perot siphoned off crucial support, and without the benefit of a Greenspan interest-rate cut, the economy was weakening. It began to feel like a lost cause, which of course it was.

This work, though in Washington, kept me in touch with leading Illinois politicians, and every chance I got I'd bend their ears about the need for major welfare and human services reform. I felt that the way to begin was with a first-rate, blue ribbon governor's task force on human services reform that would include the directors of all the major state departments involved, top people from the governor's office, leading businessmen, an academic or two, and other key civic leaders.

During one of a number of pitches I made to Governor Edgar at various political events where I would see him, he had referred me to Felicia Norwood, a very bright Yale Law School graduate, experienced in Illinois state government, who had become his human services point person. Felicia was enthusiastic about the task force idea and reforming the system, carefully reading the material I prepared. However, she made it clear that she would support the ideas, but was not going to be the initiator of a major, visible effort. Her boss, Kirk Dillard, Edgar's chief of staff, a lawyer with no visible affinity for welfare and human services issues, was emerging as the key. Kirk had the reputation of being a very nice fellow with lots of friends accumulated over many years in government, but not well organized. Returning phone calls, or even having someone else return them, was not his strength.

I started calling Kirk every week, and I could picture the little pink phone message slips piling up on his desk. I also knew he was dealing with such problems as a fight between Governor Edgar and Mayor Daley, a pitch by the Chicago Bears owner for a new stadium, riverboat casino licenses, Illinois Tollway Authority corruption, major speeches, and whatever other high-media-visibility issues were on his plate the day one of my many calls came. I had launched perhaps a dozen unanswered calls over a several-month period. Finally I saw Kirk at a political event and asked him to step over to the side of the room for a couple of minutes. With unseemly intensity, I insisted on an hour of his time to talk about a topic I said "would become one of Governor Edgar's greatest accomplishments, both substantively and politically." He apologized for a long period of nonresponsiveness and set up the meeting. A week later we had a fine meeting in his office—I gave him an outline of the main points of my proposal for the task force, passionately selling each one. He asked good questions, and at the end said, "This is terrific. You, Felicia, and I should meet with the governor."

The meeting with the governor went well—with Kirk, Felicia, and Mike Lawrence onboard he felt safe. Apparently he had reached the point where he trusted me enough to feel comfortable that if he launched this very public, very sensitive reform effort I could be counted on not to hurt him politically. We were, I hoped, starting a snowball down a big hill. There were several keys to selling the governor to make this commitment:

First, I assured him that our approach would be to focus on how to use the *existing* billions now being spent on the myriad services for poor people more effectively. I promised him I would not lead an effort that would join the long line of people asking for more money for this or that worthwhile cause. Child care, mental health treatment, drug treatment, and job training were only a few of the many worthwhile areas which had armies of lobbyists and advocates working hard for more spending. I asserted that no one knew what the right amount of money to spend would be until we figured out how to spend the existing dollars effectively. Only then would we know whether we were spending too much or too little. I also made it clear that this was not going to be an effort to cut spending, but rather that when we found places where money was not well spent, we would attempt to redeploy those dollars to more productive uses. This "spending neutral" approach was crucial in positioning our effort as bipartisan. Liberals were happy that this Republican administration was not out to take money away from poor people, and the conservatives were pleased that our effort was not going to make a case for pouring more money into a system that they knew wasn't working.

A second very helpful selling point was the political desirability of doing something in the area of welfare reform. Jim Edgar is a straightforward person who is strongly motivated to do what is right and to help disadvantaged people, but like any politician, it has to make sense to him politically. For years, governors around the nation were reelected without any expectation that they would, or could, do anything about the welfare morass. Occasionally the issue had popped up on the political radar screen in the form of Ronald Reagan's "welfare queens" or other scandals. However, in the early nineties the issue was emerging, stimulated by the Los Angeles riots, increasing violence in cities, and an intensive media focus on inner city problems. For Jim Edgar, formation of the Governor's Task Force for Human Services Reform showed the public a sensitivity to these issues, and inoculated him (as they say in politics) against attacks that he wasn't doing anything on this traditionally Democratic turf. At the national level, Newt Gingrich was still several years away from his very helpful national reform effort.

As an example, the "inoculation" ended up working very well in Governor Edgar's 1994 reelection campaign when his Democratic opponent, State Senator Dawn Clark Netsch, wife of famed architect and Air Force Academy designer Walter Netsch, attacked him for having "fragmented, underperforming, unfocused, multibillion-dollar" human services systems. Governor Edgar shot back immediately that she either hadn't done her homework, or was plagiarizing his ideas, because his task force was already hard at work with plans to rationalize the human services systems.[2] I followed up with an opinion piece carried by the *Chicago Tribune* outlining those plans.[3] Surprisingly, despite all the attention now given to welfare reform at the national level, and the efforts of states to reduce their welfare rolls and meet their welfare-to-work targets, it is still the case that only a few states have made major changes in their highly fragmented systems.

A third selling point that made a difference to Governor Edgar was the willingness of the Annie E. Casey Foundation to help support the reform effort. One would think that in relation to the $36 billion state budget, the prospect of a few hundred thousand dollars from a foundation to help staff a task force effort wouldn't mean much. It was a real eye-opener to me to learn how limited the governor's staff resources were. It is, of course, politically risky for governors to spend too much taxpayer money on staff salaries. In addition, the head count of the governor's staff is limited by legislative budget agreements and there are salary level limits as well. All of these constraints make it hard to staff a new effort, and they also result in a governor's staff made up of a large proportion of low-paid young people. Being able to say "This effort will not cost the state anything except for office space" was more powerful than I anticipated. Finally, the imprimatur of a large, well-known national foundation as a partner in the enterprise added to the credibility of the effort and provided some degree of protection against the critics who were certain to emerge.

I really had no idea what the end product of our work would look like, but I knew things were a mess, and I was sure we could come up with ideas to make things better. In my heart, I knew we had to do something about the fragmentation of the many programs and funding streams, the dead hand of the bureaucracy, and the dearth of measurable results. But something told me to be very quiet about speculating on possible changes that might come out of the task force. We didn't need to energize any opposition to ideas that weren't solidly grounded, and I also didn't want to scare the governor with visits to him by powerful lobbyists. This was a process that had to unfold.

The governor committed Felicia Norwood and Joan Walters, his director of the budget as task force members, along with the heads of the principal human services departments involved. The participation of the state budget director is important in an effort like this for two reasons: there is some inherent clout with respect to the agencies involved, because she has a big impact on their budgets, and there are important financial implications and needs for data that are essential to the process. In this case, Joan, a very bright, extremely hard-working divorcee and former nun in her late forties, also brought an uncommon passion for helping disadvantaged people to the table. She also was one of a small number of the governor's most trusted confidants.

The other state people were the directors of the departments of Public Aid, Public Health, Children and Family Services, Alcohol and Substance Abuse, Mental Health and Developmental Disabilities, and Rehabilitation Services—initially six departments in all. The superintendent of the Illinois State Board of Education also joined later. To provide balance I recruited a Goldman Sachs partner, the CEO of a big Chicago bank, a Northwestern University professor, and the president of Governor's State University (who had been a top policy director for Jim Thompson, the previous governor). I also recruited the head of the giant and beleaguered Chicago Housing Authority—custodian of the notorious "projects," as well as an executive from the Casey Foundation. I was the chairman, but it was clear that my ability to lead rested on my ability to develop a partnership with Joan and Felicia and the continued support of the governor.

As important as who was on the task force is who was not included. The most active people in the human services and poverty arena are advocates for the poor and the private sector people who contract with government to provide services for the poor. Advocates get paid for pressing in every way they can for more money for their cause, be it substance abuse treatment, children, job training, or whatever. Advocates normally wouldn't be expected to advance ecumenical solutions that might involve diminishing in any way the focus on their cause—they are paid to do the opposite. For similar reasons, top leaders of organizations like Catholic Charities or Lutheran Social Services are involved daily in the scramble for state money to keep their organizations viable. They know where their government funding streams originate, and they understandably see protecting and enlarging their organizations as their primary duty. It took me awhile to realize that the state funds the majority of the budgets for most of the "private" provider organizations. Not including providers and advocates as members of the task force was something Felicia felt strongly about, and I later came to realize how right she was. It would have been divisive to include some and not others, and most of them could be counted on to be fiercely partisan.

Because a broad, statewide consensus was going to be needed, and to enhance our credibility, I put together the Leadership Advisory Council, which would meet occasionally to serve as a sounding board for Governor's Task Force ideas and serve as an additional source of ideas. This gave us an opportunity to include people who were unlikely to become involved as deeply as task force members, and to include some knowledgeable people for whom GTF membership would be a conflict. I had a lot of recruiting lunches, and ended up with such notables on the advisory council as William Julius Wilson, then of the University of Chicago and perhaps the nation's leading poverty sociologist; Adele Simmons, president of the important Chicago-based MacArthur Foundation; the heads of the Chicago Urban League, Chicago Community Trust, the Latino Institute, Salvation Army, United Way, social services leaders from Carbondale and East St. Louis, and others. The governor approved all of these appointments, since their formal addition to the group associated them with him, and therefore represented some political risk.

The big day I had been working toward since Nepal arrived on February 26, 1993, when Mike Lawrence and Jim Edgar scheduled a press conference to announce the formation of the Governor's Task Force on Human Services Reform. The stage was set in the bizarre, Helmut Jahn–designed, coldly institutional and not very functional, State of Illinois Building in Chicago. A huge atrium dominates the glass building, with the offices sandwiched around as a sort of afterthought. I heard Jim Edgar mutter in his office one day, "I hate this building." He later had an elaborate ceremony and named the building the James R. Thompson Center after his predecessor, who had hired Jahn. This building is Big Jim's "whiff of immortality" and I'm told he has an almost full view of it looking down from his nearby offices where he now heads the law firm of Winston and Strawn.

I was very excited as the TV cameras, tape recorders, and fifteen to twenty scruffily dressed scribes with small spiral notepads found their way up in the painfully erratic glass elevators and through the rabbit warren of partitions to the sixteenth-floor press room. Governor Edgar stepped to the microphone and muttered magical words: "the most comprehensive review of welfare and human services in memory," and "the purpose is to improve the lives of disadvantaged families and children in the state of Illinois." He read off the names of the task force members, I made a few remarks, and then the questions came.

"How can such a small group possibly know what to do about such a big and complicated problem?" I gave a vigorous response committing the task force to forming a broadly inclusive leadership advisory group made up of advocates, providers, and other experts to help us with ideas. I also emphasized our commitment to an ongoing outreach effort to all interested individuals and groups statewide. That seemed to do the trick.

Then came the best question, one I remember vividly. It came from Hugh Hill, the grizzled veteran Channel 5 political reporter. Hugh had positioned himself in the front row, right in front of the governor's lectern. "Governor, the state has had lots of task forces, commissions, and the like. Most of the reports end up gathering dust on a shelf somewhere. Why should this be any different?"

To my great pleasure Jim Edgar really rose to the occasion. "Hugh, you've got to look at my record going all the way back to my time as secretary of state. This is how I change things—I get a team of good people to come up with good ideas, then take action." He went on to describe drunk driving reform and some other accomplishments that came out of task forces that he appointed. The cameras were whirring, and there was the governor on record in the most public way possible, not only charging the task force to come up with sweeping reform, but committing publicly to take action on our findings. It's a great day when at least part of your dream comes true. Now the monkey was on my back to make something truly worthwhile emerge from the Governor's Task Force on Human Services Reform. Someone once said, "Be careful what you wish for, you may get it!"

We had the first task force meeting right away, and it was both awkward and interesting. The outsider nonemployee members were excited and eager to get on with the job of making things better. The insider agency directors, with some exceptions, were watching carefully. It was clear to me they hadn't decided how to play it. To be a top-level government administrator is to be engulfed in a daily swirl of meetings, many of them called by others, where attendance by a director of an agency is symbolic. They are treated internally as minipotentates, each with their own public relations department, government relations department, state car, and obsequious deference: "Director X will see you now." They had seen governors, reform efforts, and new program ideas come and go. They were the B team: "B here when you come, and B here when you go." Unlike me, they were deeply familiar with the legislative, provider, union, and other barriers to change. With the capitol in Springfield, many agency heads are drawn from a constantly recycled pool of Springfield residents, no matter who is governor.

Given the governor's press conference, they had to show up, but they hadn't figured out how seriously they had to take the GTF. I subsequently found out that one of the things some of them were trying to do was figure me out: why is he doing this? What does he want, a state contract? One assumption was that I was there to add to my resume for a future run for public office. The idea of someone investing lots of personal time for free to make government better just wasn't in the equation. One of my most satisfying moments was to come six months later, when one of the strongest directors, Jess MacDonald, head of DCFS (Children and Family Services) came to me and said, "I have to admit that at first I was suspicious of your motives, but I've come to realize that you really care about helping people, and that is why you are here."

During the early meetings, the eyes were often on the two members closest to the governor—Felicia and Joan. Were they supporting this guy MacDougal? Did Felicia and Joan really want to change things? One of the chief proponents of the status quo was "Director Bradley," as he liked to be called, head of the massive $6 billion Department of Public Aid—the place that passed out welfare checks, food stamps, and Medicaid cards. Phil skipped the second meeting, and I saw this as a danger sign and a test. I talked to Felicia about it, made a special visit to Phil, and got him back at the table. He ended up moving over to the receiving end of the government contract pipeline, and his replacement was more modest and more interested. Both Felicia and Joan made it clear that the task force was a serious effort that they cared about, and the right tone was set.

In these early days I began to get a feeling for some of the limits the directors felt as we embarked on the process of rationalizing the system. They had many responsibilities that would not normally be expected to affect the ladies in the backyard. For example, the Department of Mental Health and Developmental Disabilities had responsibility for the state institutions for people with developmental disabilities and mental illness. Public Health, among other duties, had a responsibility for inspecting nursing homes and funding AIDS education. The Department of Rehabilitation Services (DORS) didn't have any particular mandate to help welfare recipients. In addition, much of the money administered by the directors must be spent the way Washington dictates. It's just not possible to spend food stamp money on drug treatment, no matter what the states determine is the top priority. Further strings are added by the state legislature. There is some flexibility in some of their budgets, but lobbyists fight hard for those scraps. Finally, the task force was formed at a time when the directors had just come through several years of tight budgets and budget cuts where no new initiative seemed affordable. These facts combined with union limits and the knowledge that some lobbyists had more power than directors did must have sometimes made the task force mission seem like naive idealism.

However they also knew that they had a large overlap among their department caseloads. The majority of DCFS cases were also Public Aid cases. In turn, most tough neighborhoods where poor people lived had disproportionate need for Public Health's prenatal care, DMHDD's mental health services, and DASA's alcohol and drug services. They also knew that each of their agencies had an array of special programs mostly directed to these same people and neighborhoods.

Concurrent with these early meetings, I was busy building a small staff to support the task force activities. One of the state agency directors and GTF members gave me an office in his area in the state building. He also offered with a high recommendation a top staffer, Vivienne Charles, a savvy, experienced, well-connected bureaucrat, to help support the task force. I needed someone who knew how the various bureaucracies worked. The interview went well and I needed to get going quickly, so I took her—a big mistake as it turned out. Vivienne was a great talker and a master of the bureaucratic skill of ensuring that meetings fill the time allotted, generate paper, and assiduously avoid any firm conclusions or action steps. I would listen to her talk or read her memos, marvel at the use of words, but then have no idea what was really said. I began to sense that she absorbed phrases into her vocabulary without knowing what they meant. In an unguarded moment she said, "You know, working in government is like swimming around in oatmeal." She was an expert oatmeal swimmer, but I began to suspect she was offered to me in an effort to ensure the task force got nothing done. She often talked about how much money proposals she prepared brought to the state. She had the skill of filling almost any size binder with words and exhibits on almost any subject, feeding back to the recipient the words in the proposal request. I was working with a classic bureaucrat close up, and it was scary. I thought of the thousands of administrators who were going to have to change their ways and start achieving measurable results, and wondered how many Viviennes were in the ranks. At an appropriate transition point, I gave her back to my donor.

I also needed an energetic staffer from outside the system. Terry Mulvihill, the Goldman Sachs partner, was very active with the Catholic Church, and enthusiastically recommended Michelle Arnold, a member of the management team at the giant Catholic Charities organization. Michelle was eager to help change things and struck me as being very good with people. References were terrific. She was interested in taking a twelve-month leave of absence, but said that to help make that happen I needed to meet with the legendary Father Conway, the longtime head of Catholic Charities and close confidant of Cardinal Bernardin, the much revered archbishop of the archdiocese of Chicago. Terry was close to both the Cardinal and Father Conway, so I felt reasonably confident as Michelle picked me up for the short drive to the Catholic Charities executive offices just outside the Loop. We waited awhile in Michelle's office and then were ushered into a small conference room, where we waited some more.

Finally an overtly unfriendly bishop appeared, dressed, of course, in black except for a white collar that held back some loose reddish skin. He was tall, gray-haired, and paunchy, with a face that seemed to have a built-in scowl. I looked at him and following my normal kill-them-with-kindness approach, smiled my most sincere smile. I told him that I was extremely pleased to meet him because I had heard so many good things about his accomplishments over the years. I thought I would win him over with the excitement of finally fixing things in that giant state bureaucracy that supplied him most of his budget and which I suspected had been frustrating him for much of his career. After all, we were on a mission for the governor, and the cause was helping disadvantaged people become self-sufficient.

After what I thought was my most persuasive and eloquent pitch, he looked at me and said, "What you are doing is a waste of time. There is no way you are going to change the state, so I don't know why Michelle would want to waste her time either." Wow! I did my best to counter his extreme skepticism, but the meeting ended on a very depressing note as he left without the normal courtesies. Michelle had been sitting quietly, embarrassed by her bishop, I thought. She said she was sorry about the meeting, and I said that I needed her badly, and it was up to her. I told her I was sure Catholic Charities would take her back, even though Bishop Conway didn't want her to leave. Fortunately she joined us, did a great job, and they took her back. Bishop Conway was an early one-of-many key players in the reform process strongly skeptical and/or resistant to change. It was depressing, but I had to get used to it. I was very fortunate also in hiring Kathy Ward, a very bright longtime top management secretary and executive assistant at Mark Controls who had gone on to get her law degree and was working for a Chicago judge in a job that didn't challenge her. Kathy became my reliable eyes and ears on the task force, especially valuable when I was away from the office. I filled the staff out with part-time help from Hanns Kuttner, a very smart and knowledgeable former Bush White House policy staffer and now University of Chicago Ph.D. student, and Stan Hallett from the Northwestern University faculty and also a Governor's Task Force member.

Chairing a government task force where, for all the members, the work is an extra, part-time duty, there is a realistic limit to the number and length of meetings. It seems there is a natural pace at which progress unfolds, with needed time for digestion and staff work between meetings. I was committed to being a hands-on chairman who made things happen. However, it was still a part-time commitment, I thought, so when I was approached about a unique job by a top executive search firm, I listened.

The job was general director of the New York City Ballet, the ballet company that most critics agree is the best in the world. With the largest budget, longest season, its own theater, and its own school in Lincoln Center, NYCB is a national culture treasure. To some extent, the fragile future of classical ballet depended upon the leadership and success of NYCB, but attendance was falling, George Balanchine the genius founder was gone, and the company lacked a strategy and plan for the future. I was suggested to the search firm and the NYCB board by a number of friends who knew of my longtime love of ballet, apartment in New York, interest in challenges, and recent marriage to a ballerina. I had long ago determined that I had absolutely no artistic talent, despite my love of the arts, but I am an avid consumer.

I didn't want to slow down my welfare reform work in any way and rationalized that building a good team in both places would allow me to run back and forth successfully, keeping both balls in the air. I had followed a similar approach with the many businesses that were part of Mark Controls. I talked with Felicia and Joan, and then disclosed my Illinois requirements to the ballet board chairman and the president. I offered to buy my Mondays from them (20 percent of the workweek) for a $50,000 contribution to the ballet (20 percent of my new salary). The ballet was dark on Mondays, and that was a good day for task force meetings in Chicago. Planes went back and forth hourly, so the commute was relatively painless. The ballet thought this was fine, and I took the job.

I was excited about a new experience, but Harvey was definitely not excited. As usual, he was not overtly critical, but I could tell from the vibes I got over the phone wires that he thought I was getting off the track. He loved the arts, raising money for the Phoenix Symphony, collecting Taos School and other beautiful early Western art, haunting museums and performances around the world, and taking watercolor lessons in his seventies. But there was no doubt that my volunteer work on the problems of the disadvantaged in Illinois, despite the long odds of change, was where he thought I could and should make a difference. I knew I had to make sure my Illinois work did not suffer, and I had to work seven days a week to make sure it didn't.

Drawing on my McKinsey background, the agenda for the first two Governor's Task Force meetings largely focused on how to define the mission the overall human services complex should pursue, and on developing a list of principles to guide us in that mission. This made for an interesting discussion, but one that was hard to complete in a normal three-hour meeting. One of the GTF members, Dr. Paula Wolf, the president of Governor's State University and an experienced, smart, and well-respected former government hand, suggested an all-day retreat to really nail down the guiding principles. It was set for April 3 at the private, ornate, wood-paneled Union League Club downtown. I was nervous. Would this be a day of talk, or would we have some tangible results?

Based on the discussion in the first two meetings, my personal tour of the various human services systems, and a few ideas I came to embrace in business, I prepared a "Discussion Draft" list of possible principles. I had to be wary about being too assertive. Even though I was the chairman, I had to be very careful not to manage proactively as I did in my longtime CEO role at Mark Controls. I had to keep reminding myself that my standing depended in large measure on the support of Joan and Felicia, so I watched them for clues. If they became alienated, it would be harder for the governor to support me, given his consensus style. They in turn were sensing the vibes of the group—after all, the directors were all gubernatorial appointees confirmed by the state senate. The directors had the potential to stir things up with the legislature. The whole process was like herding cats—I could facilitate, but I couldn't really lead. Fortunately, the outsiders weren't constrained, and they were a critical ingredient needed to drive the process forward. I was not above planting a key question or idea with them from time to time.

We already had a general mission outlined in the governor's remarks, "To improve the lives of disadvantaged children and families in Illinois," and to do this he said we must "Improve the delivery system in our state." This was later sharpened, with the help of federal welfare reform, to emphasizing self-sufficiency as an overarching goal.

The meeting went surprisingly well. We spent the day working on the draft list that I brought along. Ideas were added, such as a focus on prevention and on community economic development, some were dropped, and wording was modified on almost every principle. The list, though not profound, truly guided the welfare reform effort in the succeeding years. At the end of the day we all agreed that we would work toward a system guided by the following principles:

We are helping *families* and children *help themselves* by seeking to increase the capacities of families to meet *their responsibilities* to their children. This one is more profound than it sounds. Myriad programs are now directed toward a specific category of individuals—single mothers with children, pregnant teenagers, individual drug abusers, and the like. This principle defines a system that works with the whole family. If, for example, one family member gets a job, it affects the entire group. The definition of a family is the subject of endless debate, which we decided wasn't necessary at this stage, since this statement pointed our work in the right overall direction. The other key terms "help themselves" and "their responsibilities" clearly state that we intended to move government toward a "hand up" and away from a "handout," a transaction where the recipient has the ultimate responsibility to climb the ladder.

Only with a *partnership* effort involving parents, businesses, the community, schools, churches and synagogues, and local, state, and federal government will restructuring, redirection, and renewal be successful. This one also sounds obvious, yet there are almost no examples where this really happens. Veronica, the caseworker, was typical in her narrow focus on the specifics of what she felt was her job. There are examples of a level of government working with individual organizations, and lots of examples of private organizations getting a government contract to do a specific task. The GTF decided that the truly rare but crucially important objective would be to have broadly based local community representatives sitting at the same table with key people from state and local government to develop mutually agreed upon approaches to community problems. I remember vividly when, later in the process, Joan Walters, in her role as state budget director, spoke to a broad-based group that came together in an inner-city Chicago community and said, "You know so much better than we do, sitting in Springfield, how state money can be best spent to meet the priorities of your community." Joan was telling the inner-city folks that *they* knew better—a very important idea.

Involving businesses is quite rare, yet it is the jobs that are the key to self-sufficiency, and most job creation is with the smaller employers at the local level. Churches, synagogues, and mosques are islands of stability and values in distressed communities, and yet rarely work in partnership with government. All of these players, the GTF agreed, represent a key piece of the puzzle, yet they rarely all come together at the community level. Government is usually viewed by local communities—especially state and federal government—as inaccessible, inflexible, and uninterested. Skeptical looks and even laughter greeted me in some of the early meetings with community leaders when I said, in effect: "We're from the government and we're here to help you."

We need to make fullest use of, work with, and learn from highly effective private sector and community-based organizations, rather than presume solutions through additional effort by the state. This one clearly leans toward the increased flexibility, lower costs, and better outcomes often found in the private sector. I was mindful of the envy my caseworker friends in Springfield had for the flexibility and accomplishments of the private agency across town as we discussed this one. This principle did not declare war on AFSCME (The Association of Federal, State, County, and Municipal Employees), the huge government employees union, but they did get very nervous. Interestingly, the state directors, well aware of the difficulties of working in the government environment, supported this one fully. This meant that in the future new and redeployed funds would probably flow to the private sector, which they did. It avoided the war involved in eliminating jobs by privatizing activities now performed by state union employees.

We will emphasize cost-effective *prevention* over inefficient, after-the-fact treatment, amelioration, and crisis management. This one was added by one of the state directors and is, like many of the others, very hard to argue with, and very hard to implement. Clearly, money spent on family preservation has a huge payoff compared to the costs of institutional and foster care after a family breakup. The suggestion that the mother in Springfield lock out her teenage daughter is a good example. Switching funds from crisis work to prevention is hard, but this principle clearly points the systems in the right direction, and that's the whole idea of the principles.

Local/community efforts are likely to be more flexible, relevant, and effective than centralized, uniform statewide efforts. If there is one lesson government needs to learn, it's that one size does not fit all—what works in Wyoming may not work in Manhattan. The state of Illinois is almost as diverse, from unemployed coal miners south of the Mason-Dixon line to gang bangers patrolling Robert Taylor Homes, as tough as the inner city gets anywhere. This principle nails down Joan's point in her speech to the community group, "You know better."

We will be working to *integrate* services and to work with the whole family—bringing together programs historically separated by bureaucratic boundaries and categorical funding. This includes an emphasis on case management and fund decategorization. Once there is an agreement to *integrate* services, the separate unconnected pipelines to clients are history. In effect, the directors were agreeing that most of their jobs weren't going to exist if we were successful in implementing our principles. Some of the directors clearly realized this was the implication, and to their credit were willing to sacrifice for a better system. Others may not have thought it through, or believed it was unlikely to happen. Of course how we made it happen is the biggest part of the story. Categorical is bureaucratese for rigidly defined, single-purpose funds that flow through the system and can't, under any circumstances, be used for any other purpose. Our friend Fred Collins at Project Chance should be able to pursue his van idea.

We will eliminate the disincentives to preventative and integrated responses that have inevitably appeared with the hodgepodge of laws and programs that have been patched together over the years. Perhaps the biggest disincentive that existed in Illinois, and still exists in many states, is the incredibly unfortunate situation of a family being punished financially when someone gets a job. The loss of the welfare check and Medicaid card plus the addition of transportation, clothing, child care, and other job-associated expenses can make this happen. This principle comes at the ideas of integration and prevention from a somewhat different angle, explicitly recognizing the need to clean out the barriers by eliminating regulations, changing laws, getting waivers from Washington, or whatever it takes.

We will find ways to *end permanency of participation* in and dependence upon the welfare system. After a thoughtful discussion involving both outside and inside (state employee) task force members, *no one* thought welfare should be permanent. There are, of course, people with mental and physical disabilities for whom it may not be possible to be fully self-sufficient, though some type of work may be possible. For this group, properly defined, there seems to be bipartisan agreement that some kind of ongoing government role may be required. For all others, the GTF easily agreed on the principle that welfare is temporary. The ladies in the backyard will have to do something different. Three years after our GTF retreat, of course, welfare time limits became national law.

We will explore opportunities to increase the effective use of volunteers (companies, community groups, individuals, etc.) providing social services. I'm convinced that there are literally millions of people (most without the benefit of Nepal!) who would like to make a difference helping on the problems of the disadvantaged, but find it hard to connect properly in a way that they feel is a worthwhile use of their time. The GTF felt that the human services systems could get great leverage from tapping this resource, and they were right.

We will increase the proportion of caregivers (those in direct con-

tact with disadvantaged people) in relation to record keepers, administrators, etc. I borrowed this one from the corporate world from a friend who used this principle to help turn around sick companies. The stories of caseworkers like Veronica in Chicago give meaning to this one, plus the redundant cost of maintaining separate systems. GTF members easily supported this one, even though many of them were administrators themselves.

We will find ways to strengthen community economic development, utilizing resources coming into the community to provide training and jobs for residents of the community. This principle, proposed by Dr. John Lumpkin, the director of Public Health for the state, aimed to capture some of the billions of human services spent on behalf of a community in the form of jobs for people who live there. Early in the work of the GTF I remember well a session we had with all of the state workers from all six relevant departments who were scheduled to be involved with the pilot project in the Grand Boulevard test site. The session was held on the South Side of Chicago in a big meeting room at the Illinois Institute of Technology, and about two hundred people attended. These were just the state employees who worked with and in Grand Boulevard. As I was explaining the GTF and what was going to happen in the test site, I paused and asked, "How many of you live in the Grand Boulevard community?" Only five people raised their hands. All of the rest of that middle class economic power escaped elsewhere at the end of the workday. The attraction of better schools and a safer environment is understandable, but Dr. Lumpkin's principle stimulates creative thinking on ways the state might use the $10 billion human services budget to strengthen economic development in poor communities. The problem of the often inappropriate geographic placement of state facilities in relation to the location of those in need falls under this principle.

After we completed our work at the retreat, I walked out of the club with government veteran Paula Wolf and she said, "This is amazing, Gary. We got this diverse group to come together and agree on a strong group of principles, and the task force in only ninety days old. We're off to a great start!" We both knew that we would regularly be returning to these principles to resolve turf wars and the other complex decisions that inevitably lay ahead. We also both knew that there was no way that the present top-down, highly fragmented, and unfocused array of organizations could survive if we moved forward zealously with our newly adopted principles.

We published our principles in June 1993, and many of us used them in speeches, with the media, with legislators, and in every other way that could help solidify a bipartisan consensus. This wasn't hard, since in the abstract the principles sound like motherhood: "integrate services," "work with the whole family," "partnership . . . involving the community," "measure the real outcomes and real costs." However, the existing state and private welfare/human services systems did *almost none* of those things. In fact, from my work as a Casey Foundation trustee it was clear that the other forty-nine states for the most part didn't do these things either—in fact, most still don't. The dichotomy, puzzling to many, is that many of these principles have been common in literature on social services for years, but implementation just doesn't happen. Once a broad-based agreement on the principles is reached, it should lead inexorably to a new, integrated, community-based vision for the human services systems, and major change becomes mandatory. When the governor and the GTF implemented the principles, virtually everything done by the 26,000-person, $10 billion human services systems would be overhauled—reinvented from the ground up. That was where we had to go.

From a personal perspective, the journey through this process of establishing principles taught me that welfare and human services reform didn't need to be about harsh or easy, or even more money or less money. Rather we, as a country, can achieve a broad nonpartisan agreement that major philosophical and systems changes are essential; changes that are more revolutionary and more important than any called for by even the most extreme liberal or conservative attention-getting rhetoric. Almost no one in our initial process defended the present system, but a thoughtful vision of what the giant complex of human services/welfare systems ought to look like was going to be quite a challenge.

Shortly after adopting the principles, Felicia, speaking with the authority of the governor's office, said, "We talk about how we're fragmented with multiple caseworkers overlapping with clients and the like. Why don't we put together a chart showing how things are now?" This turned out to be a great idea, and shows the mess Illinois was in. Most states still preside over systems comparably illogical and dysfunctional. How could this be? I wondered when I first ran across this mess on my tour with Jeanette and in discussions with the ladies in the backyard. The answer is a complex archeology involving Springfield and Washington political forces and management inattention on the part of preceding governors. Pieces were added and modified, and almost no one looked at the whole thing.

The "Felicia Norwood chart" turned out to be a fabulous communications device, used in speeches, legislative presentations, and with the press. Felicia's chart was wonderfully and accurately captured by a Rube Goldberg cartoon done by Mike Thompson of the Springfield *State Journal-Register* (Figure 3). Literally no one—conservative, liberal, or anything else—stepped up to defend the present organization. The stage was set for change, but change to what?

The task force discussed ideas for a new "integrated" system that would embody what Jim Edgar came to call "one stop shopping," a front line, bottom-up approach that would enable clients to get most or all of the help they needed to become self-sufficient in one place guided by one caseworker. Ira Barbell, a member of our task force and a professional staffer from the Casey Foundation with considerable experience in other states, led a number of blackboard discussions on possible systems design concepts. Ira (subsequently Dr. as he completed his Ph.D.) was perfect for the role. With his scraggly beard and thick glasses, always just off the plane from working with the welfare system in some other state, he was the right discussion leader. Ira and I would prepare for these sessions together, trying to capitalize on his value as an outside expert. However, we both knew no state had ever done this before, so we knew this was going to be an immaculate conception.

After a few sessions where considerable progress was made, I

Figure 3. Felicia Norwood Chart–Cartoon Version

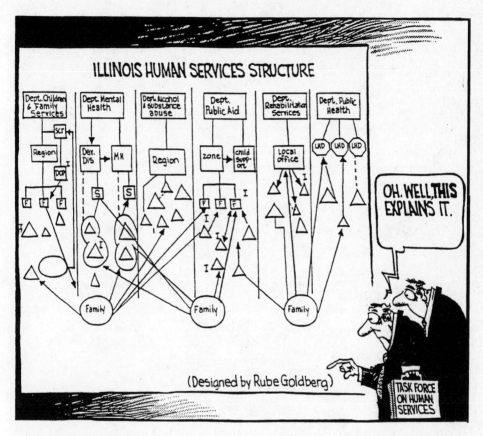

Figure 4. Linking Communities and Government–An Ambitious Vision
(June 1993)

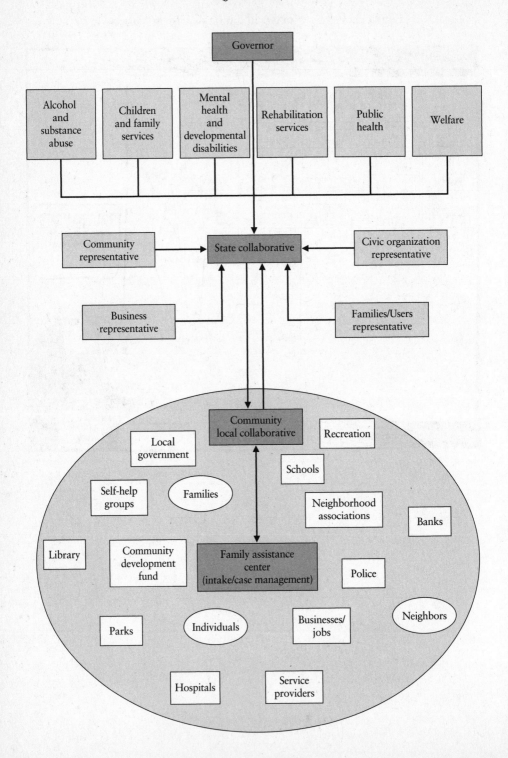

sensed we had pushed the "Casey expert" approach far enough. We had general agreement on front line integration and community involvement, and we were in danger of the directors avoiding ownership of what they might perceive as the "Casey design." I persuaded several of the directors to lead future discussions, and within a few months we had variations on a theme that had a single caseworker, aided as necessary by specialists, empowered to represent the entire range of state services necessary to achieve self-sufficiency. We also agreed upon the importance of listening to communities identify their priorities, and then redeploying state resources to respond to those priorities. Throughout these discussions I carefully steered the discussion to avoid talking about what would happen to the organization chart boxes at the top of the six bureaucracies which, of course, included the directors' jobs. The operative words were, "Once we know what we want to do on the front lines, we can then organize the boxes in Springfield in the best way to support the new system." Based on the established principles, we had a good conceptual idea of how a reformed system should work (Figure 4).

The governor's office, clearly a crucial element in leading change, is constrained by many limitations: intense, day-to-day pressures and crises; severe salary and staff size limitations; lack of media interest in fundamental structural reform (as opposed to their intense interest in embarrassing incidents); pressures of state human services contractors and their influential, high-paid lobbyists; unions; legislators; etc. Keeping Governor Edgar comfortable in the face of impending change and the growing publicity our effort was receiving required lots of thought, regular communication with his trusted advisors and measured doses of public opinion pressure stimulated by advocates, the media, and others.

Though we had a pretty good idea of what needed to be done on the front lines and in the communities, we needed the experience and credibility of trying the principles and organization ideas in some test sites if we were really going to reinvent the system. Especially important were the principles of integration and community involvement. Test sites would take us beyond thoughtful principles and theory to a

Figure 5. Illinois Test Sites: A Cross-Section of the State (and the Nation)

1. Jo Daviess County
2. Stephenson County
3. Winnebago County
4. Boone County
5. McHenry County
6. Lake County
7. Carroll County
8. Ogle County
9. DeKalb County
10. Kane County
11. Cook County
12. DuPage County
13. Rock Island County
14. Whiteside County
15. Lee County
16. Mercer County
17. Henry County
18. Bureau County
19. Putnam County
20. LaSalle County
21. Kendall County
22. Grundy County
23. Will County
24. Kankakee County
25. Henderson County
26. Warren County
27. Knox County
28. Stark County
29. Peoria County
30. Marshall County
31. Woodford County
32. Livingston County
33. Ford County
34. Iroquois County
35. Hancock County
36. McDonough County
37. Fulton County
38. Mason County
39. Tazewell County
40. McLean County
41. Champaign County
42. Vermilion County
43. Adams County
44. Schuyler County
45. Brown County
46. Cass County

47. Menard County
48. Logan County
49. DeWitt County
50. Piatt County
51. Pike County
52. Scott County
53. Morgan County
54. Sangamon County
55. Christian County
56. Macon County
57. Moultrie County
58. Douglas County
59. Edgar County
60. Calhoun County
61. Greene County
62. Jersey County
63. Macoupin County
64. Montgomery County
65. Shelby County
66. Coles County
67. Cumberland County
68. Clark County
69. Madison County
70. Bond County
71. Fayette County
72. Effingham County

73. Jasper County
74. Crawford County
75. Saint Clair County
76. Clinton County
77. Marion County
78. Clay County
79. Richland County
80. Lawrence County
81. Monroe County
82. Washington County
83. Jefferson County
84. Wayne County
85. Edwards County
86. Wabash County
87. Randolph County

88. Perry County
89. Jackson County
90. Franklin County
91. Williamson County
92. Hamilton County
93. White County
94. Saline County
95. Gallatin County
96. Union County
97. Johnson County
98. Pope County
99. Hardin County
100. Alexander County
101. Pulaski County
102. Massac County

tangible reality. The challenge was to pick places that when taken to-gether reflected a cross section of the entire state. We decided that most of the communities selected should have a higher-than-average poverty rate, that they should be widely dispersed geographically, and that one should be a tough inner-city community, one a challenged suburb, and one a rural site with high unemployment (Figure 5).

The staff put together candidates of each type with all the demo-graphic data, and an energetic discussion ended with the selection of Grand Boulevard, a 35,000-person, almost entirely African-American community with some of the highest poverty, unemployment, and crime statistics of any community in the nation. The suburb selected was Waukegan, a gritty semi-industrial, semiresidential city of 68,000 on the lake north of Chicago. Waukegan had a disproportionately large Hispanic population and higher-than-average poverty and social problems. For rural poverty the Southern Seven Counties (Pulaski, Union, Johnson, Massac, Pope, Hardin, and Alexander), with 70,000 people and two thousand square miles at the tip of Illinois, were se-lected as a group. In the Southern Seven distances are great, and un-employment is high because of closed mines, marginal farms, and little industry. I was happy with these three test sites, but saw a great deal of work and travel ahead. Then, to my surprise, the state agency directors pushed to add two more—the city of Springfield and Du-Page County. I protested that five test sites might overload the staff, and besides, those two places have *below* average poverty. Finally the light bulb went on in my head that Springfield had the huge advan-tage of being in the front yard of the state's political leaders, lobbyists, administrators, and everyone else who counted when it came to systems change. For its part, DuPage was, perhaps, the most potent political county in the state, home of the senate president Pate Philip and then–house speaker Lee Daniels. I soon saw the advantage of including a "medium-sized downstate city" and an affluent county with "pockets of poverty" to our list. These additional sites were not only suggested by some of the state directors, they volunteered to help manage them and to pay for them. This was a turning point—the in-siders had decided that the Governor's Task Force was for real, and they were going to get on board.

We ended up with a terrific statewide cross section with so much diversity that it could arguably be representative of the nation as well as the state. In 1993, 42.8 percent of poor people in the U.S. lived in a central city, 32.6 percent lived in a suburb, and 24.6 percent lived in small towns or rural areas.[4]

To move the task force ahead, I had worked with the Casey Foundation to earmark a modest level of start-up funding for each community and funds to support the small task force staff for the coming three years. I figured if we couldn't demonstrate success in three years, we wouldn't have a practical model.

I also decided we needed a high-level full-time advocate on the governor's staff to keep the momentum accelerating. Though I was eventually spending more than half my time on task force activities, we needed stronger connections to key players in government, to our task force communities, and to the outside stakeholders. To make this happen, I proposed to create the position of assistant to the governor for human services reform paid for by the Casey Foundation at a level of $90,000 per year (low in relation to the task, but at the level of the directors and one of the highest levels of pay on the governor's staff). It was important to have someone on the governor's staff working solely on changing the systems. At this point some of the directors became nervous and competitive. One of them said, "The position is okay, but the title will cause resentment—this person can't be perceived to be more important than we are." I decided that the title was needed both as a visible commitment to change and also to attract the right person, but I was the only one other than the outside task force members wanting the visible, high-level title. I then decided that this title and position would be a litmus test of the governor's commitment to change. Consensus is great most of the time, but sometimes it is important to act alone.

I set up a meeting with Governor Edgar and Doug Nelson, the Casey Foundation president, in Springfield as a sort of progress review and to set the stage for the possible Casey grant, which would total $2.5 million.

The state capitol building in Springfield, up on a hill with its huge dome visible for miles, is impressive and quite beautiful. It seems no expense was spared back in 1888 when this much larger building replaced the original capitol, now a nearby museum. As cathedrals define many towns and cities in Europe, the capitol building, constructed in the form of a Latin cross, really *is* Springfield. Most of the rest of Springfield's commercial center is home to various state agencies housed in boxy, nondescript buildings with lowest bidder/political pal architecture. Halfway up the hill to the capitol's main entrance is a larger-than-life-size bronze of Springfield resident Abraham Lincoln, standing tall and looking very strong, wise, and caring—the way we used to think of our presidents. Closer to the capitol entrance is a statue of U.S. Senator Stephen Douglas of Lincoln-Douglas debate fame, who also rates another statue inside. The inside is beautiful, with impressive scale, broad marble stairways, oversized doorways, and lavish use of rich wood paneling. Large oil paintings and portraits abound. A statue of Chicago's former mayor Richard J. Daley is prominent, recognizing his role as a former state senator and longtime boss of large delegations of state representatives and senators from Chicago and Cook County, home to more than half of Illinois's citizens.

The governor's office is the featured center of the capitol building—the coveted mountaintop for the hundreds of state politicians who swarm through the building when the legislature is in session. After passing through two huge glass doors to the outer office, a visitor is confronted by a palace guard of state police, secretaries, and assistants. As we were ushered into the governor's main office, with its impressive combination of vast scale, rich wood paneling, historic paintings, and beautiful furniture, it struck me as ironic that we were here to talk about poor people. I found myself wondering if the governor had ever been in an apartment in one of Chicago's housing projects. This lavish cocoon, together with the governor's mansion, chauffeured cars, plane, and helicopter must make it very hard to feel the pain of the ladies in the backyard.

Governor Edgar greeted us cordially, and we sat at a large mahogany table. We were joined by his two top staffers who sat on the task force, Felicia Norwood and Joan Walters. We started by bringing him up to date on task force activities and talked about the desire of the Casey Foundation to help. Then, in a nice way, at a propitious moment, I told him that I thought it didn't make sense to bring in the $2.5 million without having a high level person with regular access to him working on his staff. We needed that to make sure that we got a return on the investment and to demonstrate to his top people his determination to effect real change. I went on to suggest the title assistant to the governor for human services reform. Politicians know horse-trading when they see it—he looked at me and at Doug, thought for a minute, and said fine. The snowball was rolling down the hill with greater size and speed—harder and harder to stop. It was an experience I would normally have shared with Harvey on our weekly phone call.

Harvey was and is still with me, even though he died on October 26, the previous fall. I lost him two weeks after his eightieth birthday, and when I got the news from his son-in-law in Arizona I cried for the first time that I could remember since I was a child. He had gone into the hospital for the first time in his life the preceding June, and had shocked me by telling me on the phone, "Don't worry about me, I'm fine. If the Lord think's it's time for me, I'm ready." He really sounded strong, calm, and ready, but I wasn't. Life without Harvey was hard to imagine.

I was thrilled when he got out of the hospital that first time and I asked if Charlene and I could come out and have dinner with him and his wife, Sally, the next Saturday night, July 3, my birthday. As we got on the plane in New York at 7:45 that Saturday morning, I thought about what a long way it was to go for dinner, but that I was receiving an incredible birthday gift. When we drove up to his modest but beautiful home, he was standing on the front steps in his usual erect, alert way, waiting for us. We were not great huggers historically, but we hugged warmly and gratefully and went inside for a long talk around the kitchen table. After a couple of hours he then gathered strength for what was to be his last outing to his favorite art gallery in Scottsdale, where he and Charlene were drawn to a Burt Phillips Taos School painting of an Indian hunter and an Alaskan landscape by Albert Bierstadt. I had admired Harvey's collection of Western art ever since I had known him. On a totally uncharacteristic impulse I bought both paintings, feeling that I would be bringing home and holding on to part of Harvey. We had a wonderful, warm dinner, and then stopped by Sunday morning for a good-bye brunch before heading back to New York. Sadly, it really was good-bye, but I'll be forever thankful for that birthday weekend.

Harvey's hopes and dreams for me weighed heavily as I continued my work on the Governor's Task Force and at the New York City Ballet. At the ballet I was busy developing a strategic plan, restructuring the management, planning tours, negotiating contracts for a movie and a CD, sorting out alleged sexual harassment in the orchestra, and attending lots of terrific ballet performances for the special one hundredth season (fifty years) of the New York City Ballet. After a year, when the long-range plan was completed, it was clear that because of lack of resolve by the board and old-timers, further changes would come very slowly. I decided that I didn't have the patience to wait around. I came to believe that I could have more impact on the Illinois human services systems, and also knew that if Harvey was looking down, he'd tell me to spend my time in Illinois. I left the ballet with a good return on their investment in me, and I still help them from time to time. The progress we made in Governor Edgar's office gave me the feeling I could make much more difference investing that additional time in Illinois.

Meanwhile all was not rosy—there were those who did not share our vision. Unions and providers, deeply vested in the status quo, turned out to be primarily interested in preserving their own jobs and their own organizations. I was shocked to learn some of them even feared success in reducing dependence—a cut in their customer base. These groups have clout—buildings full of lobbyists in Springfield and important campaign contributions to legislators. Like Washington, revolving door relationships are common—pass out contracts in one administration, lobby to receive contracts in the next. The interests of the poor are not ignored, but I learned it pays to keep a close eye on the money trail and personal job security.

PRINCIPAL POINTS

1. Commitment of the governor and his or her top staff persons is essential.
2. Establishment of a broad-based collaborative at the state level is essential, with membership from the governor's office (human services and budget), agency heads, business, academia, and community leaders.
3. A successful reform effort must start with broad agreement on the mission and principles that should undergird both the reform effort and the ultimate system. These principles should be nonpartisan.
4. A simplified version of the Illinois principles calls for an overall mission focused on *client self-sufficiency,* supported by a one stop, *family-centered* system at the local level, *strong community* (churches, schools, business, United Way, etc.) *involvement,* and clearly *measured performance outcomes* (e.g., number of people in jobs).
5. Community test sites (probably three to five) should be selected carefully and should reflect a cross section of major state demographics.
6. Once agreement is reached on the principles, it becomes clear (in almost any state) that dramatic systems reform is essential if those principles are to be realized. The bureaucracies must be turned upside down.

5

Is Anyone Really in Charge Here? The Clout of Unions and Providers

Every body continues in its state of rest, or of uniform motion in a straight line, unless it is compelled to change that state by forces impressed upon it.
—SIR ISAAC NEWTON

I was having a bratwurst and sauerkraut lunch with Jimmy Lago at one of his favorite restaurants right near his office in downtown Chicago. My enthusiasm for bratwurst is limited, but my interest in building an effective relationship with Jimmy was intense. Jimmy is the shrewd, handsome, fiftyish head of the Catholic Conference of Illinois, the lobbying arm of one of the biggest Illinois human services contractors, Catholic Charities. I had targeted Jimmy as a desirable ally early in the reform process since he is one of the most influential Springfield players and knows and is well thought of by the governor and most legislators. Jimmy is close friend and associate of the cardinal and could, if he wished, speak for many of the more than 3.7 million Catholics in Illinois.

I had first tried to get Jimmy inside the Governor's Task Force tent by getting the governor to agree that we should ask Jimmy to work with the task force as the liaison to the other big contractor/providers. I suspect he would have preferred to be a member of the task force, but Felicia Norwood and I decided that major government contractors would have conflicts, and should be involved, but not as members. I told him of the governor's and my desire for his help, and we agreed to start with his arranging a breakfast with other providers and provider lobbyists in Springfield, with the idea of obtaining input and sharing ideas. I came to believe that Jimmy is looked to by the other providers as their informal leader.

Jimmy dutifully arranged the breakfast, giving the appearance of being helpful to the governor. He knew that the governor was aware he was being asked to help. However, I had the feeling he was only going through the motions, and he did nothing further despite my regular encouragement, or perhaps more accurately, my cajoling. I would periodically track him down, always attempting to sell the virtues of integrating services, involving communities, and measuring outcomes, but I could never strike a spark. Jimmy was a very shrewd fellow, so I knew he understood what I was talking about. Early in the game I tended to rationalize the lack of enthusiasm shown by some as a pragmatic reaction to my naive idealism. I was determined to see things change, but the Father Conway–type veterans of the poverty world had been around a long time, seeing things only getting worse. Did Jimmy see all this as a waste of time? Or was something else going on?

Finally, halfway through the bratwurst lunch, Jimmy came clean. He said he was *not* enthusiastic about our reform effort—in fact, he felt threatened by it. "Gary, my interest is Catholic Charities, and my job is to keep my organization healthy. If you are successful in empowering communities, how do I know some community group won't want to take a state contract away from Catholic Charities and give it to some undercapitalized, undertrained local group."

In his mind, the value of my idealized vision wasn't the issue—the government funding stream into Catholic Charities was the issue. I made the point that quality standards combined with checks and balances would minimize the risk of funding unqualified local providers, but he was still very uncomfortable. I had missed the point. Whether smaller, community-based providers did a good job or not was only part of his concern. If they were funded with dollars that would otherwise have gone to Catholic Charities he didn't like it. I knew also, and I'm sure he knew, that there was a geographic mismatch between the location of a number of their major facilities and the communities in direst need of services, particularly in the city of Chicago. I tried to reassure Jimmy we could work together over time to correct these imbalances. The mismatch issue is a big one.

The meetings with Jimmy fit with a lunch I was invited to one day by the Reverend Hallberg, my friend from Lutheran Social Services. Attending the lunch was a group of the major Chicago area providers that Don led, and I was asked to explain where I thought the task force and the state were headed. Apparently this group met frequently to compare notes about state funding and other activities. The meeting was in a private room of the Metropolitan Club, high up in the Sears Tower, and I remember coming away from it feeling like I had been part of a high-level meeting of businessmen. The discussion focused more on dollars and cents than on helping people. Of course these big providers *are* big businesses—I was getting educated about the poverty industry.

Somehow my assumption that we were all working together to maximize the number of people who become self-sufficient and get out of the system was *not* the leitmotif of my various conversations with providers and unions. I finally understood why I couldn't get the state's big contractors to help us make the needed changes. Further, I wasn't surprised as various provider groups did what they could to slow down or stop the reform by lobbying the governor's office and legislators for the status quo. In Jimmy's case, his judgment seemed to be that it would be easier to protect the sources of Catholic Charities income by dealing with the same legislators and administrators who were now supporting his organization. Getting communities to the table would be too risky—clearly some of them would advocate, as I would want them to, for human services to be physically located in their community. I've long been convinced that the economic development of distressed inner-city communities has to be an important part of the reform agenda and, in fact, it was one of the principles adopted by the task force. Over time it's very hard to argue against keeping community economic development in mind when contracts are awarded, assuming the contractors meet quality standards. In distressed communities, government spending is known to be a large proportion of the economic activity. Just as states compete for a new auto factory or military base, it makes sense that communities push for community-based human services activities, especially when their community residents are the customers. Employees of the facilities are more likely to live in or near the communities served, improving community-buying power. This, of course, would help encourage retail activity and other services to return to these communities. It would be a problem for the big providers to decentralize and reconfigure—probably requiring capital they're not sure they could raise. Jimmy had another problem: some inner-city community leaders see Catholic Charities as a big, remote bureaucracy run largely by white folks.

As the discussion with Jimmy Lago illustrates, the Governor's Task Force work was surrounded by a constellation of very interested people whom we might call the stakeholders, if not shareholders, of "poverty industry" organizations. From my very first Governor's Task Force meeting and in private discussions with governor's office staff and department directors the word *provider,* a new word to me, kept coming up. I began hearing things like "We don't want to get in trouble with the providers"; "Providers will fight us on that"; "The providers will never let that happen." It was also clear that the directors spent lots of time meeting with providers, whether they wanted to or not. This was really puzzling to me, since in the world I came from contractors were always extremely eager to do their customer's bidding. Why should people to whom we give billions each year intimidate us? It turns out there are lots of reasons. For starters, I subsequently learned that moving to a job with a provider was a common career path when administrations changed.

A closer look at the Catholic Charities organization was fascinating to me. As an Episcopalian, I have always been awed by the much larger size and scope of the Catholic Church, from St. Peter's and the Vatican treasures right on down to Cardinal Bernardin's Holy Name

Cathedral on State Street in Chicago and his mansion near Lincoln Park. We Episcopalians have gotten used to thinking of ourselves as the junior varsity to the multifaceted Catholic juggernaut. In hearing about the many good works of Catholic Charities and seeing their many facilities around Chicago and around the state, I had the impression that I suspect many have of overwhelming generosity to the poor on the part of Catholic parishioners. However, a close examination of the annual report of Catholic Charities of Illinois reveals that more than 80 percent of the operating budget ($75 million per year)[1] comes from the government, primarily the state of Illinois. We taxpayers are the generous ones. Catholic Charities of Illinois can be thought of, like most other "private" provider organizations, as a "majority-owned" arm or subsidiary of the state. Having said all this, I have no evidence that they are not a generally competent dispenser of state services, primarily in the areas of monitoring child welfare, including foster care and adoption.

On the national level the story is pretty much the same. Catholic Charities USA is one of the largest social services nonprofit organizations in America, with a $2.1 billion budget, 1,400 local agencies, and 46,000 staff members.[2] In a typical recent year, government sources were the dominant source of income at 64 percent, with the Church contributing 5 percent. United Way and other sources provided the rest. I also learned that Catholic Charities is a highly political organization on the national level as well, vigorously opposing welfare reform, for example. The 1995 annual report states that "the Scriptures command us to speak out" against such "dangerous propositions" as block grants, devolution, and family caps.

National president Father Fred Kammer, a Jesuit priest, said, "There has been a lot of romantic nonsense lately in Washington to the effect that state and local governments are always more effective and efficient than the national government. The (erroneous) claim is that local people know best." Kammer's views are the opposite of those expressed in the catechism: responsibility for the needy first rests with the individual in need, his or her family, friends, and neighbors. Then come churches, charities, and local governments, and finally with state and federal governments. His views also oppose the principles of human services reform in Illinois. Catholic Charities does much good work, but the point of all this is that they are primarily an integral arm of government, and a highly political arm at that. The big surprise for me was that this army of private providers, who I assumed would be natural allies in reforming government, turned out to be actual or potential *barriers* to reform.

Without the support, or at least acquiescence, of Jimmy Lago and a critical mass of his counterparts in the hundreds of provider organizations in Illinois, any reform effort could be stopped in its tracks. How could this be? The state is by far the biggest source of income of almost every provider, typically representing two-thirds or more of their revenue. For example, Chicago's famous Jane Addams Hull House receives 85 percent of its $37 million annual budget[3] from government, and the ninety-year-old Abraham Lincoln Center on Chicago's South Side, an operator of a wide variety of mental health, child care, Head Start, and other counseling programs receives 90 percent of its $10 million[4] in revenues from the state. To keep the billions of dollars flowing, providers have built a tremendous network of highly paid, very effective lobbyists, and have become important contributors to legislative and gubernatorial campaigns. As is the case with Hull House and the Abraham Lincoln Center, it is not uncommon for these providers to be run by well-connected former legislators or government officials.

Unlike Washington, in Illinois a decisive difference in the outcome of a legislative race can result from a contribution as small as $10,000, making lobbyists very potent. Also unlike Washington there is *no limit* on contributions. The sky's the limit in Springfield, and there is not a lot of oversight. An iron triangle of clout has been created—legislators and the governor need money from the lobbyists and providers, and the providers need money appropriated by the legislators and contracts awarded by the governor's executive branch. How do you introduce major change in such a situation? Reform can't happen without them. Their pervasive influence, their problems, and their point of view count.

I remember being asked to speak to the Illinois Alcohol and Substance Abuse Association (IASAA) one cold February day. I was happy to be invited to talk with this group, since they were an association of the heads of a very important provider coalition, and most of the state's alcohol and substance abuse budget was spent on the treatment their organizations provided. The alcohol substance abuse industry in Illinois is big business, with a budget for the Department of Alcohol and Substance Abuse of about $240 million per year, most of it subcontracted. Optimistically and perhaps naively, I speculated that my invitation meant they were taking the work of our task force seriously, and they thought something might actually come from it. After I went through my presentation which, as usual, included the Rube Goldberg organization chart and our mission and principles for a reformed and reorganized system, it came time for questions and discussion. A barrage of sharp-edged questions and statements followed with the thrust that any interference with the present separate Department of Alcohol and Substance Abuse was unnecessary, and would diminish service. I was a threat to the orderly flow of funds from "their" department to their organizations and livelihoods.

The alcohol and substance abuse executives said they were already out in the communities and had local advisory groups and boards. I was holding my own but not making any converts to the idea of integrating services, when one member sitting at the end of the table stood up and said, "Look, he's right. When we get finished with a drug treatment program, if there's no connection to a job at the end, the odds are we'll see recidivism. We've got to connect these services together to get the best results." This fellow later told me that what he said was unpopular and possibly even risky to his organization, but he thought it was right. I was learning a lot about how government operates. In the end, this group was not happy with the reorganization, but did not mount the kind of opposition it might have.

IASAA employs as one of its lobbyists Bob Kjellander who, together with his associate Bill Cellini, is one of the very top money raisers for Republican candidates statewide, especially governors and house and senate leaders. Their way of operating is illustrative of the tangle of Springfield interests—interests that usually aren't apparent to the average voter. Bill's sister Janice was on the governor's staff as the personnel patronage czar. Kjellander is also the IBM rep in Springfield, and he just happens to be the Illinois Republican National Committeeman. Cellini gets considerable leverage on politicians in many ways. For example, for many years he headed the Illinois Asphalt Paving Association, a group that was so intensely interested in good government that Governor Edgar received at least $375,000 from its members over thirty months. Not surprisingly, Cellini, a former director of the Illinois Department of Transportation, does lots of real estate and other business with the state, developing and leasing back to the state six major office buildings since 1979 and receiving millions in annual payments.[5] With considerable financial help from the state he developed the main hotel in downtown Springfield, and personally made millions on a sweetheart deal for the state's first riverboat casino license, among other activities. In my opinion, much of this activity should be illegal, but it is not.

A cynical but often accurate view of this process is put forth by Washington pundit Jim Pinkerton, who calls this situation "Vealocracy," harkening back to the traditional political pork barrel.[6] He says, "The first step in Vealification is that [special interest] groups wrestle the government to the ground so they can feed off it; the second step is the institutionalization of this process by corralling government programs, just as farmers lock up calves and turn them into veal." He continues, "The critters are the government agencies themselves, penned and helpless, continuously fattened up for fiscal slaughter to feed ravenous interest groups."

The "private" provider organizations, so ably represented by their Springfield lobbyists, are also so huge that human services reform can't stop with the reforming and restructuring of government, but must extend into their world if services really are to be integrated, communities involved, and real results of their activities measured. For example, Catholic Charities provides almost no data on the overall effectiveness of its programs,[7] i.e., how many people gain self-sufficiency as a result of its services. There's always the argument that money spent on evaluation and outcome measurement is better spent providing more services, but there is little point in offering more services if their long-term effectiveness is unclear. Incentive-based contracts with payments based on results is a good place to start, but providers can be expected to resist on the grounds that each case is different, complex, and hard to measure. Very few, even in the corporate world, like to be measured and paid on the basis of results, but stockholders demand it, so that's the way it is. Stakeholders in human services include taxpayers, clients, and legislators, most of whom will support incentive contracts based on results, assuming the contracts are thoughtfully structured and fairly negotiated.

There is an oft-enunciated war cry that has become part of the stump speech of some politicians that shifting money away from government programs toward "faith-based private charities" is a big piece of the answer to solving the problems of our welfare/human services systems. As a conservative Republican, I am a strong believer in the efficiency and resourcefulness of the private sector, and I also yearn for the values that church-based organizations are able to contribute. However, shifting resources from one unmeasured inefficient bureaucracy (government agencies) to another unmeasured, inefficient "majority-government-controlled subsidiary" (many providers) is not helpful unless the private provider is proven to be efficient and effective. Care must be taken to pay for results, not activity. A notorious example of this point is the Oprah Winfrey saga.

As much of the world knows, Oprah Winfrey has moved well beyond her role as a legendary talk show hostess and has built a highly profitable business empire which makes her one of the wealthiest Americans, and perhaps the wealthiest African American in history. Understandably, and to her great credit, she wants to help others less fortunate, and so she announced a $3 million personal commitment[8] to move one hundred families out of public housing, off public aid, and into better lives—$30,000 per family that could be spent free of government red tape. She picked one of Chicago's best-known social services agencies, Jane Addams Hull House, to run the program, called Families for a Better Life. Two years and $1.3 million later, only five families had completed the program, and the program was stopped. The president of Hull House is Gordon Johnson, a large, gregarious, articulate, fiftyish, bespectacled man with thinning tufts of gray hair. Gordon is a former head of the Illinois Department of Children and Family Services (DCFS) and was regarded by some as part of the problem at DCFS, which was unusually troubled under his rein. I asked Gordon one day what happened on the Oprah project, and he answered, "Getting people out of poverty turned out to be more complicated than she thought it would be."

"How are you two getting along?"

"Just fine, we're good friends," he said with a smile.

A *Chicago Tribune* expose of the project described how the $260,000 per family was spent. Essentially the middle class poverty industry operatives gobbled it up. One such operative, a Dr. Richard Cox, the president of the Forest Institute of Professional Psychology, a Missouri graduate school that helped with the program for an undisclosed fee, was quoted as saying, "There is such a huge amount of front-end investment, and one has to be willing to put it in up front with a great deal of faith and trust." To make matters worse, the seven families initially selected for the program were creamed from 1,600 families who submitted applications, four thousand of which were mailed after screening thirty thousand phone calls that came in about "Oprah's program." Drug tests and psychological tests (to determine motivation among other things) were given to nineteen people, and all participants but one had a high school diploma or GED. The seven families were then given ten months of seminars covering a gamut of subjects including: "Identifying daily actions," "Preparing for change," "Housing" (which included meeting real estate agents and visiting communities where they may want to live), instruction about meal planning and nutrition, and so on. Oprah made an introductory video for each session, and the Utah-based Covey Leadership Center, founded by self-improvement guru Stephen Covey, helped train the Hull House staff (not the seven families) and reviewed the curriculum. All this for seven families, five of whom completed the course. There is no convincing evidence that, on balance, the families are better off for having completed the program.

Presumably Mr. Cox is better off, perhaps sending his kids to better colleges than they otherwise might have attended, and Mr. Covey's huge bank account is even larger. Oprah should ask Gordon Johnson, who still serves as president of Hull House, for her money back. The best way to test motivation is to connect someone with a job and then help keep him or her there. This doesn't cost very much money. An irony in the abortive Oprah effort is that the majority of those on welfare don't have high school diplomas and GEDs, and large numbers have other major problems, such as drugs, and all these challenges were screened out. This example serves to illustrate a not-uncommon private sector social services mentality—lots of preparation, extensive use of consultants, cream skimming, and vague unmeasured outcomes. There are important exceptions to this, but in my view, "nonprofit" providers often suffer from the same lack of bottom line accountability often found in government, perhaps because they *are* part of government. With incentive-based (pay for results) contracts based on measurable outcomes, providers can experience some of the discipline stockholders provide in the business world. Performance has to count.

One day in my pursuit of data on the economics of the UPS welfare-to-work effort, I needed information on the pay and benefits given to Delrice Adams, the self-sufficiency coach assigned full-time to facilitate twenty-five recently employed long-term welfare recipients. UPS had agreed to hire fifty welfare recipients, people who didn't meet their normal hiring standards. Delrice told me she was paid in the low twenties, but she didn't know the cost of her fringe benefits. I then called the agency from which she had been reassigned, introduced myself as senior advisor to the governor (the administrator who answered the phone knew who I was), and asked for the costs associated with Delrice.

In retrospect, this was a naive approach, probably stemming from my many years in the business world. For years I fielded calls from Wall Street analysts and others asking for details on costs, labor contracts, product pricing, etc., which we always provided. In addition, the Securities and Exchange Commission required that management compensation, stock ownership, and conflicts of interest be made public in the annual report and proxy. However, my innocent question met a stone wall at the nonprofit agency. "I can't release that information," she said. I couldn't believe it. Unlike Mark Controls Corporation, these weren't private dollars, but mostly taxpayer dollars. Private charities should be more open, not less, I thought. Several phone calls later, and after convincing the president of the organization that I was going to get the information one way or the other, I was told that they charged the state $120,000 for Delrice's services. Wow, no wonder dragging that number out was such a sticky process.

I'm not implying that large amounts of money are stolen, and I'm sure that an overhead allocation is necessary to pay management salaries, but I began to worry about the economics and efficiency of nonprofit agencies. There is a proliferation of hundreds of small nonprofit agencies, each with its own president and staff. It makes sense that without some consolidation or mergers within given communities, disproportionate taxpayer dollars go to the middle class administrators of the poverty industry rather than directly facilitating the self-sufficiency of those in poverty. Mergers are forced in business by competitive conditions and stockholders. Unfortunately there is no equivalent force for nonprofits, though enlightened board members, combined with a push from government could stimulate rationalization and greater community focus. However, poverty industry leaders and their lobbyists will fight forces for change long and hard. In addition to the omnipresent and potent providers, the huge state employee unions also represent a major force to be reckoned with.

Henry Bayer, the Illinois head of AFSCME, the government employee union with 44,000 state employee members, paid a visit to my task force office early in the reform effort. I knew Henry had plenty of clout, with AFSCME making contributions to legislators totaling six figures in a typical election. I also became aware of the substantial AFSCME building a stone's throw from the capitol in Springfield, presumably well stocked with lobbyists. After brief pleasantries, Henry looked at me and said, "Gary, I want you to understand my objective in all of this is not to lose a single union member or a dollar of pay or fringe benefits." I was startled at his bluntness, and the fact that his objective omitted any mention of the people all those thousands of union members were supposed to help. But then, I had dealt with many union leaders in the business world, and it was not unusual to see a single-minded focus. They usually don't get paid for statesmanship, but I would have thought he'd want to be a little more subtle in a situation where poor people are supposed to be the focus.

"You should be clear that my objective is to find a better way to help the hundreds of thousands of Illinoisans who need to become self-sufficient. Hopefully, there will be some overlap in our objectives," I responded. I remember at the time that I felt his objective was very selfish. Didn't he care about Illinois's disadvantaged people? Unions were formed in the first place to help those who were less well off. Shouldn't he want to help us reform the system? Instead, it was clear that the purpose of his visit was to put me on notice that he was ready to fight us.

However, further discussion shed more light on Henry's point of view. The state did not have a very good labor relations history, and it's arguable that the state had earned Henry's distrust. Compared to Mark Controls, where we worked hard over many years to build constructive relationships with our ten or so unions, Henry faced a rotating cast of negotiators as administrators changed. Central Management Services, usually headed by a loyal political appointee, has never been known for outstanding management capabilities—they're the same folks who maintain a grip on the archaic computer systems and other office practices, and they handle union negotiations. Further, I had to remember that his members hired Henry for the sole purpose of protecting their incomes and working conditions. He shared with me his fear that flexibility and choice at the local level might be a Trojan horse for a *real* agenda of privatizing state services with lower-paid, lower-fringe-benefit, nonunion community providers. This was a variation of Jimmy Lago's fear. The state and the community would get together, set up local, private, nonunion service provider organizations—say for foster care services—shift state dollars to these lower-paying organizations, and effectively privatize many of the present, higher-paid government union jobs. Their fears are understandable. However, there was *not* a hidden privatization agenda. But there is no question that our reform leads to a much better ability to evaluate the costs and effectiveness of human services spending—evaluations that in some cases could lead to privatization.

Henry Bayer went on to agree that change was needed, that his members were often expected to do things without being given the proper tools, training, and support necessary to be successful. He was too smart to defend the present system, and we agreed that the frontline workers appreciated the need for change—they just wanted to be involved to ensure the change was sensitive to their needs. I felt we could work together, and AFSCME's substantial political contributions served as a reminder to be alert to the union issues. Involvement was the key, and setting up the Employee Involvement Committee that included the three largest state employee unions was a crucial move. This kept them plugged in and, in my view, may have helped convince them that the motives of the reform were sincere and not directed at them. As the reform proceeded, the union agreed to contract modifications that allowed the state to broaden the duties of caseworkers, giving office managers more flexibility.

Working with the scores of state contractors and the government unions was a totally new experience for the me, and it took longer than it should have for me to realize how much power they had. We subsequently found some things about the reform for Jimmy Lago and the others to like. Providers dealing with multiple state agencies were subject to myriad audits and reviews, and state reimbursements were slow. A commitment was made to simplify and make more efficient the dealing between the state and its contractors, and a committee was set up to develop an action plan. Steps like these staved off intense resistance and moved the providers to a sort of passive acquiescence, probably the best we could do. Their access on an as-needed basis to everyone in state government from the governor, senate president, and house speaker on down is a fact of life and part of the messiness inherent in a system so dependent on campaign contributions.

Through all of this, in the back of my mind I started to think about a fundamental dichotomy. If I were to reach my dream where almost everyone currently on welfare or otherwise disadvantaged became self-sufficient, most of Henry's human services union members would not, in fact, be needed, and Catholic Charities and the other providers would have to shrink dramatically. They'd never had to think much about this before, but *real* success worked toward putting them out of business, though some would remain to deal with new problems and to engage in prevention activities designed to maintain the success. Initially, a reduction of the caseload would merely free up resources to do a more intensive job with the tougher cases that remain, but true success means largely going out of business. Studies in factories have shown that when workers sense demand going down, they slow down production enough to ensure that they look busy. This is human nature. Was I sensing some of this fear? It must be tough to think that the harder you work and the greater success you have, the more your organization shrinks. Perhaps perversely, I was looking forward to that problem, but we had a long way to go.

As a CEO, I had learned long ago a sort of universal law: in large organizations people are usually certain that impending change will have the worst of all possible consequences for them personally. They will often think of negative consequences of the change that you've never dreamed of. Constant communication and alertness to rumors is essential. As I fought my way through this morass and ways to deal with the many important stakeholders were developed, I was strengthened by thoughts of why I got into this in the first place: the ladies in the backyard, what's good for our country, and Harvey.

Now the challenge was to go to those five communities identified by the task force and see if we could get them to join in our adventure. The communities were the place to really learn what was needed, and they could emerge as an important political counterpoint to some of the self-interest I was coping with. I started to worry. Who was "the community" anyway? The idea of community is great conceptually. How do we transform it to reality? Can I earn their trust? How am I going to get the time to build these relationships all over the state? How do we handle the public relations? Where do we start on Monday morning?

PRINCIPAL POINTS

1. Surprisingly, most "private" aid organizations, such as Catholic Charities, get most of their funding from the government and have tremendous political clout.
2. Over the years these organizations, which form a sort of poverty industry, become an end in themselves to their top managers, and perceived threats to their government funding can transcend the focus on changes which can help clients.
3. The traditional union focus on jobs and wages makes organizational change threatening.
4. The worries of providers and unions are very legitimate if we are successful. Suppose the changes were successful and most of the caseload became self-sufficient (a goal I believe to be realistic)? What happens to the level of union dues and the staff at union headquarters? What happens to the private providers?
5. These threats must be understood and overcome through some combination of forward momentum, win-win solutions, involvement, and placation.

B. Herbert Martin
leading a service at
Progressive Community
Church, 1999:
inspiration and therapy

In search of a future:
trekking in Nepal and
looking at Mount
Everest, 1988

Harvey Branigar *(right)*, my inspiration, with author

The author *(right)* with George W. and Laura Bush: "You'd be a great HHS Secretary, but . . ."

Author with former President Bush in the Oval Office: discussing the Illinois Senate race

Ladies-on-welfare focus group with Dolores Martin *(left)*, Springfield Federation director: a study in barriers and opportunity (PHOTO BY GINNY LEE)

A welfare family in Robert Taylor Homes: strong feelings about a better life for the children. Pictured are a grandmother (age 35), daughter (age 18), and grandchild (age 2)

(below left) The stairway to the front yard at Robert Taylor Homes

(below right) Robert Taylor Homes: the view from the family's front door

Stateville Prison *(above)*: welfare fathers away from home (PHOTO BY ILLINOIS DEPARTMENT OF CORRECTIONS)

Lives on hold: a welfare office waiting room in Chicago, 1998

Welfare office form storage racks, 1998: headwaters of the paperwork river

Illinois governor Jim Edgar *(left)* with the author, 1999: cautious governor who made a bold move

State Budget Director Joan Walters, a strong key to change

The foundation as catalyst: Doug Nelson, president of the Casey Foundation

Terry Mulvihill: Warren Buffet's stockbroker and Governor's Task Force member

Felicia Norwood: a leader who charted
the mess

A shrine to bureaucracy: Chicago's Thompson Center

Jerry Stermer *(above)*, Voices for Illinois Children: an intense advocate

Jimmy Lago: protecting Catholic charities

AFSCME Union Springfield Headquarters: a power in a mansion

Grand Boulevard Federation: a distressed inner-city community coming together and working with government

The monthly Springfield Federation meeting: a new power center (PHOTO BY GINNY LEE)

Opening the Lee Center One Stop, Springfield: community and government in tandem. Pictured from left: Governor Edgar, Mayor Karen Hasara, and Mrs. Lee (THE STATE JOURNAL REGISTER)

The Lee Center: self-sufficiency services under one roof

Grand Boulevard community leaders Greg Washington *(left)* and Sokoni Karanja *(right)*

Joyce Aldridge, just promoted to Air Operations at UPS

The lifeline: Delrice Adams, self-sufficiency coach

State's troubled families may get 1-stop welfare

Edgar panel seeks grant for pilot plan

By Rob Karwath
TRIBUNE STAFF WRITER

Illinois officials have a radical plan to make it easier for the state to help troubled families.

Instead of sending them to six different state offices, send them to one. Or even bring services into their homes.

That's the idea behind a simple but unprecedented attempt to streamline and improve Illinois' services to troubled parents and their children. Families now often get more frustration than help when they deal with any of the six state agencies established to address social problems such as poverty and child abuse.

The state hopes to make the system more user-friendly and efficient through a two-year test project that could start as early as this year. The plan is currently riding on whether the state receives a $2.5 million grant next month from a Connecticut charity.

In February, a task force established by Gov. Jim Edgar submitted a plan for testing a streamlined social-services system to the Annie E. Casey Foundation of Greenwich, Conn.

Officials of the Casey Foundation, the country's largest charity devoted to disadvantaged children and their families, met recently with Edgar and Gary MacDougal, a Chicago businessman who is heading the Illinois task force. MacDougal also happens to be on the Casey Foundation's board of trustees, and Casey financed his task force with a $200,000 grant.

After the meeting with Edgar, Casey Foundation officials expressed optimism that Illinois would receive the $2.5 million grant, according to MacDougal and Felicia Norwood, Edgar's top aide overseeing human services.

But the Casey Foundation board of directors will make the final decision next month.

"It sounds favorable," Norwood said. "We're kind of excited. It really could be a dramatic change here. We have our fingers crossed."

Under the plan, the state would

Illinois' centralized welfare proposal

Illinois welfare officials are seeking a $2.5 million grant to establish consolidated centers for Illinois' child-welfare program. This would be a test pilot program for national welfare systems.

▶ Agencies in current system

A person must contact or visit caseworkers at separate agencies for different problems. Each agency keeps separate files; often, the agencies don't know what help the person is getting from other departments.

Department of Children and Family Services
• Child abuse and neglect.

Department of Public Aid
• Welfare checks, Medicaid health insurance coverage, food stamps.

Department of Alcoholism and Substance Abuse
• Drug and alcoholism treatment.

Department of Mental Health and Developmental Disabilities
• Help for people with mental illnesses or mental retardation.

Department of Rehabilitation Services
• Help for people with disabilities (such as transportation assistance, in-home services).

Department of Public Health
• Health issues, birth certificates, teenage pregnancy prevention and disease-transmission programs.

Source: News reports

▶ A case study

For example, a single mother has children taken by DCFS for allegations that there's not enough food or supervision. The family must deal with DCFS and the Cook County Juvenile Court system.

Agency referrals
In an effort to reunite the mother with her children, DCFS may refer the family to numerous agencies.

Welfare check problems: The mother contends her welfare check isn't sufficient. To get it increased, she would have to go to the Department of Public Aid.

Disability issues: The mother of children would go to the Department of Rehabilitation Services.

Mental health problems: The family would go to the Department of Mental Health.

▶ How the new system would work

A person would walk into a central office. A caseworker, who works either directly for the state or for a private agency under state contract, would help the person get access to all of the services he or she needs from the state's human-service departments. The program also would allow the state to keep one computer file on all of the person's needs.

Chicago Tribune

set up test programs in at least three and as many as five locations statewide.

The state has settled on the Grand Boulevard community on Chicago's South Side, Waukegan, and seven southern Illinois counties. DuPage County and Spring

See WELFARE, PAGE 14

Welfare

CONTINUED FROM PAGE 1

field also may be included.

Illinois families now must deal with as many as six separate state agencies to address problems of child abuse and neglect, poverty, drug and alcohol abuse, mental illness and retardation, physical disabilities and general health problems.

The agencies usually have separate offices. And, by the state's own admission, they often don't work well together.

A person with multiple problems who goes to several agencies for help usually is assigned a caseworker at each agency. These caseworkers keep separate files on their clients. Frequently, they don't talk to each other. And sometimes they propose treatment that conflicts with help the client is getting from another agency.

The result is confusion for the client and inefficiency for the state.

Under the plan submitted to the Casey Foundation, the state would establish offices in the test areas where individual caseworkers would try to get clients help from the state agencies instead of merely referring them to another state office across town.

"Very few families come into our system that don't have contact with multiple agencies," Norwood said. "Unfortunately, many families have difficulty navigating through the system."

For example, in Cook County, about 80 percent of the abusive or neglectful parents who run afoul of the state Department of Children and Family Services have drug-abuse or alcoholism problems. Resolving parents' addictions is crucial if their children are ever to be returned home from the expensive and over-crowded state system of foster homes.

But even when DCFS caseworkers refer parents to treatment programs, many don't seek help, either because they perceive the process as too difficult or because they refuse to acknowledge that they have problems.

Under the test project, a caseworker still would have to refer parents to outside treatment. All of the state's drug and alcoholism treatment is performed by private companies under state contracts.

But the caseworker would follow up to make sure the client was receiving treatment and would be available to help if the client hit any bureaucratic roadblocks.

"Will we try to bring together

services in the form of one-stop shopping? Yes," MacDougal said. "Will it be in just one office? We don't know."

MacDougal and Norwood said another part of the plan is to establish networks of neighborhood groups, churches and local social-service agencies that could assess and treat clients, possibly in their own homes.

These groups also would search out families in need of help before they reach a crisis that brings them to the state's attention, MacDougal said.

"The idea is accessibility and integration, so you don't have to go eight different places," MacDougal said. "We have a wonderful chart showing what this system looks like now. It's an unbelievable can of worms. You'd have to have your own lawyer and be smart as hell to know how to work through the system."

Kathleen Feely, Casey Foundation associate director, said foundation staff members are trying to clarify details about the Illinois plan before the board of trustees votes.

"We believe the governor is serious about this," Feely said. "We want to understand how exactly it will play out with the agencies and the communities."

If Illinois gets the grant and starts the project, it would be "one of the more comprehensive major approaches to human services reform in the country," MacDougal said.

"Other states are doing pieces of it. You have a county pulling together services. You have somebody else working with neighborhood organizations. You have two or three state departments working together. But this time we'd be forming a collaborative at the state level that would be totally involved in this problem."

If the project shows promise, it could serve as a national model for reforming how states provide social services, MacDougal said.

But two years probably would not be enough time to do a thorough test, and Illinois would most likely ask an outside source for more money or use state funds to complete the project, Norwood said.

State officials have long discussed consolidating or simplifying the operation of human-service agencies to make it easier for families to get help and to save the state money. But agency turf wars and concerns about any changes initially causing problems have frustrated such attempts in the past.

"Change is not something that comes particularly easy around here," Norwood said.

LaRue Martin: on-the-job mentor for fifty workers from the welfare rolls

Howard Peters *(right)* and B.J. Walker *(below right)*, with author: strong change leaders

Rosetta Dunbar: a life dramatically changed, and a guest of the governor

The legendary State Senate President Pate Philip: shrewd, tough pol

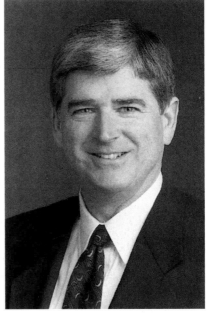

Senate Appropriations Chairman Steve Rauschenberger: helped bring warring factions together

House Speaker Lee Daniels: strong advocate for accountability

Historic milestone: Governor Jim Edgar signing reorganization bill, July 3, 1996

House Democratic Leader Barbara Currie: working in a bipartisan way to help distressed families

McKinsey & Co. Partner Mike George: crucial donation of organization design team (ONE HOUR MOTOPHOTO & PORTRAIT STUDIO)

Kenny, 28-year-old unmarried father of twin boys (age 2) and a daughter (age 1): a typical noncustodial father/convicted felon. A key to the future

Michele Hare, Human Services administrator: after 23 years, a new, exciting self-sufficiency mission

6

Linking Community
Groups with Government
—A Historic First

The sense of community is indispensible . . . to full self-realization.
—HERBERT J. MULLER

*Above all we need, particularly as children, the reassuring presence
of a visible community, an intimate group that enfolds us with
understanding and love, and that becomes an object of our spontaneous
loyalty, as a criterion and point of reference for the rest of the human race.*
—LEWIS MUMFORD

I t's the third Wednesday of the month and, as usual, the large
meeting room in the Grand Boulevard Urban League building is
jammed for the monthly meeting of the Grand Boulevard Federation. It is September 1997, and the Federation has been in exis-
tance and growing for almost three years. There is a palpable air of
energy in the room as people get coffee and arrange themselves on
both sides of about a dozen tables arranged into a big E shape. There
are also seats along the walls, and the overflow is standing. It looks
like about seventy or more people are here, and the fact that they
are almost all African American accurately reflects the 99.5 percent
African-American presence in this community where they live and
work. There is a remarkable diversity of occupations and interests in
the room—more diverse and reflective of the people they represent
than most legislative or other governing bodies. Lt. Ken Brown and

Lt. Don Woods from the Chicago Police Department, looking sharp in their uniforms, take their accustomed chairs on the corner. Lucy Watson and Jennifer Shaw, welfare recipients and public housing residents, are seated along the center prong of the E.

Judge Sophia Hall of the Cook County juvenile court system with her stylish gray hair and Lavert King from the staff of the Chicago Housing Authority with his signature kinta cap are present, and nattily dressed Jesse Madison, former Chicago parks commissioner, former Illinois state senator, and now head of the legendary nonprofit Abraham Lincoln Center, is also here. Larue Martin, the six-foot-eleven pro basketball player–turned–UPS human resources executive, is easy to spot as he takes his seat at the end of one of the tables. Pat Dowell, one of the driving forces behind the ambitious Bronzeville (Grand Boulevard) Redevelopment Plan, along with one of the founders of the Grand Boulevard Federation, Marrice Coverson, head of the local Elliott Donnelly Youth Center, and Dr. Charles Mingo, principal of the truly challenged DuSable High School and a fixture in the African-American community, were there. Dr. Mingo, a giant, gregarious man with a big gold chain around his neck, once told me that his dropout rate at DuSable was 50 percent, and although, because of a lawsuit, he wasn't allowed to collect the data, he estimated the pregnancy rate at 50 percent. He also told me of a previous year's valedictorian who was a model student in all respects but became pregnant halfway through her senior year. He told me that he thought the pregnancy was likely to have been on purpose. I asked him why she would do that, and he said, "She might have been nervous about facing the outside world upon graduation. Though not really logical, that welfare check represents a kind of security, even though it is not enough to support a baby—someone knows you are there. It's hard for you to imagine how isolated they feel." Dr. Mingo hosted the federation meetings at DuSable until they outgrew his space.

The meetings are open, though there are membership dues. Particularly interesting and important attendees are Mary James, the head of the Department of Human Services (DHS) office on the edge of Grand Boulevard, along with Delores Shoemate and Gail Terrell, two state employees redeployed, at the request of the community, to the

Grand Boulevard Federation. Looking around the big room it becomes clear that all of the elements of this inner city community are represented—from top leaders to welfare recipients; community, city, and state government administrators; police officers; school officials; church leaders; and business people. Within the community the federation is referred to as the go-to place, where all the pieces of the poverty puzzle are at the table and where things get done.

The buzz in the room just doesn't seem to fit with the grim Grand Boulevard statistics[1]: median household income of $8,143, approximately one quarter of the state average; unemployment many times the state average at 34 percent; infant mortality rate at 28.5 per 1000, almost three times the state average and in line with Third World countries; and 83 percent of the children in poverty compared to 16.8 percent statewide. Grand Boulevard, sometimes called Bronzeville, is a tough place, having descended from its historic position as the economic and cultural center of Chicago's lively and thriving African-American community in the first half of the twentieth century. In its heyday Grand Boulevard was the home to such greats as the legendary gospel singer Mahalia Jackson, world heavyweight boxing champ Joe Louis, and singers Nat King Cole and Dinah Washington. However, in recent decades middle-class families and jobs moved out, and massive housing projects and crime moved in. The Grand Boulevard Federation is engaged in nothing less than the process of reversing that history and bringing its community back—and it is making meaningful progress.

Seated at the top of the table are Greg Washington and Dr. Sokoni Karanja. Greg is described variously by those in the community as "a wonderful human being," "brilliant," and someone who really "organizes things" and "makes things happen." Greg is the executive director of the Grand Boulevard Federation. He is also blind, a handicap that came upon him when he was a student and athlete at Beloit College in Wisconsin, where he was student body president and editor of the school paper. With a Braille typewriter and other devices, he operates in a way so efficient that those of us who work with him tend to forget that he is blind.

Dr. Karanja, clad in his usual African kinta cloth garb, with curly gray hair surrounding the edge of his omnipresent cap, is the leader of Centers for New Horizons, a multifaceted provider of services to the poor. He is often referred to, sometimes with a smirk, as "our village chief." Today he doesn't look much like the student revolutionary who led a takeover of the administration building at Brandeis University, where he earned his Ph.D. Sokoni Karanja has dedicated his life to helping the less fortunate, and he works effectively with the downtown foundations and with state bureaucracies to get money for Centers, winning a $250,000 MacArthur Genius Award along the way. He is a frequent public speaker, often articulating his dream of restoring Grand Boulevard to its historic greatness as the Black Metropolis when the area had jazz clubs, the first black-owned insurance company in the nation, a thriving retail district, and a solid black middle class. He has on his desk a Bronzeville plan, illustrating a future vision for each block of the currently largely devastated area. Sokoni changed his name after a transforming residency in an African village, and he is a well-informed student of African history, naming a housing program Akhenaten after the black king of Egypt of Ethiopian descent.

Sokoni calls the meeting to order, and Greg starts through a fascinating agenda: a report on the job successes of longtime welfare recipients with little previous work history, a meaningful number of whom have been working for over two years; a request for candidates for a trial employment program for convicted felons who had served their time; a report on the new responsibilities assumed by the federation as the community network for the child welfare/foster care system; the redeployment of some additional state caseworkers and about 350 Department of Human Services welfare cases to the federation; announcement of a healing service involving families and victims of a highly publicized incident of racial violence in a neighboring white community; discussion of the formation of a consortium which would bring together the large number of organizations involved in job training and placement in Grand Boulevard; announcements of upcoming events; and much more. What brings all of these people together? What is going on here? How did this happen?

We go back to the fall of 1993 and the strong conviction of the Governor's Task Force that involving communities with government in the solution of the problems of those communities is crucial— bottom-up, grass roots thinking rather than top down. To establish a sound basis for systems change, we needed to learn from the pilot sites in Grand Boulevard, Waukegan, the Southern Seven Counties, DuPage County, and Springfield. Illinois would be the first state to reform the system working at both the community and state levels at the same time. The GTF had hired a young white University of Chicago Ph.D. student to do some fact gathering in the white communities, and a bright young African American who was a foundation grant recipient did the reconnaissance work on Chicago's Grand Boulevard and other predominantly black communities. Their initial evaluations were used to provide background for picking the sites. Then, after the sites were selected, they did some networking to identify community leaders and others who might be interested in working on a whole new approach to welfare and human services reform.

The Governor's Task Force had identified the five pilot sites as a good cross section of the state, but figuring out how to generate the right kind of community interest and involvement was another matter. This kind of government–private sector relationship hadn't been done in Illinois before, and from the Casey Foundation perspective there were no precedents anywhere in the country. Not having any better ideas, Felicia Norwood and I decided to start in Grand Boulevard by inviting about fifteen people to a luncheon meeting at Dawson Community College, named for the legendary Congressman Bill Dawson. "Big Bill" was the longtime leader of the black community during the days of the late Mayor Richard J. Daley, the present mayor's father. Legend has it that the senior Daley assured himself of black votes and a minimum of racial trouble by keeping Bill Dawson personally happy. Obviously this was a lot easier and less expensive than doing things for the black community at large. Attending the lunch were Drs. Mingo and Karanja, Greg Washington, Lavert King, Marrice Coverson, and others.

A nice lunch was prepared and served by the culinary arts students, but I sensed a feeling of strained hospitality in the air. Felicia's position as assistant to the governor and mine as chairman of the GTF made their attendance more or less obligatory, but you could feel pent-up resentment. In the first meeting, one of the community leaders came right out and said, "We've had important people from the government come in before and talk about change, but we don't see them again, and nothing changes. Why should we think you are any different?" To them, government was an unreliable, bureaucratic, often negative presence in their lives, and past experience taught them that people from government, though often well intended, did not keep their word.

"We're from the state government and we're here to help you and your community. This time it's going to be different—we're going to stay with it, and things *will* change if we work together," was a message we brought without much initial credibility.

We passed out the Felicia Norwood chart, outlined the new principles, and got their comments. "Interesting" was the polite reaction, but you could see no one believed real change could happen—especially in Grand Boulevard. Then we offered up what turned out to be one of our most effective attention getters—a table (Figure 6) showing all of the state human services funds flowing into their community. They had never seen anything like it, of course, because *nobody* had ever put the numbers together like that before. Government requires very accurate accounting by funding stream, which usually means by program or expenditure type (food stamps, doctors, welfare checks, etc.) on a statewide basis or by contractor, not by community. Further, checking with my friends at the Casey Foundation who have insight into most states, I found that no other state had this local-level information either. There is always some political talk about the importance of communities, but little of this talk is reflected in the way government does business.

Task force staffer Michelle Arnold had worked hard developing personal contacts in the budget departments of the six human services agencies so that she could come up with the first ever identification of funds flowing into or spent on behalf of a given community. Significantly, just identifying the funds geographically (by zip code) for the

FIGURE 6. A RIVER OF GOVERNMENT MONEY FLOWING INTO THE GRAND BOULEVARD COMMUNITY

Community Size: 35,574
56 percent in Poverty, or 20,000 people

Illinois State Department	Primary Services	Annual Expenditures ($millions)*
Alcohol and substance abuse	Drug treatment	2
Children and Family Service	Child Abuse Protection and Foster Care	26
Mental Health and Development Disabilities	Treatment and Support	2
Rehabilitation Services	Therapy, Training, and Support	2
Public Aid	Welfare and Medical	112
Public Health	Women, Infants, and Children Food Supplement	2
	STATE GOVERNMENT	146
	FEDERAL (PRIMARILY HOUSING)	73**
	CITY OF CHICAGO	30**
	TOTAL	$249,000,000 per year

* Fiscal '93 Expenditure Source: Governor's Task Force (estimated $)
**McKinsey & Company research[2]

five pilot sites took a tremendous special effort—no one had done this before. The numbers were later updated by a study team from McKinsey & Company to include direct federal programs, such as housing, and city of Chicago human services spending, bringing the Grand Boulevard total to an amazing $249 million per year. While a very large proportion of the human services funds flowing from the state originate in Washington and have lots of strings attached, the state administers the largest portion of the programs and writes the checks, and can request waivers from Washington. The city of Chicago administers some programs, like the Workforce Investment Act (WIA), but the states are, in most of the country, the nine-hundred-pound gorillas. The total annual *state* human services spending for Grand Boulevard was over $146 million![3] This river of money flows into a community (Figure 7) whose borders can be walked around, though not safely, in a few hours, starting south down Cottage Grove Avenue near and parallel to the Lake Michigan shore from Thirty-ninth Street (Pershing Road) on the north for twelve blocks to Fifty-first Street; west on Fifty-first Street the equivalent of about ten blocks to Federal Street next to the Dan Ryan Expressway; then north on Federal to Fifty-first and back east to Cottage Grove.

When you finish your afternoon walk, you will have circumnavigated the more than $249 million per year of your federal, state, and local tax dollars and the 35,574 Grand Boulevard residents, of whom 56 percent, or 19,921, are in poverty and 35 percent, or 12,457, are on welfare.[4] This works out to annual spending of over $12,000 per poor person, again a real attention-getting number when juxtaposed with that $18,850 poverty line for a family of *four*.[5] These numbers further reinforced the position I had taken with the governor, the press, and others that more money is *not* the answer.

Since state fiscal pressures made discretionary increases in social services budgets unlikely, and since there already seemed to be huge amounts of money flowing into the various human services systems, I argued that ways must be found to redeploy existing funds to get better results. I reached back to my days as a corporate chief executive officer when I always looked at the lowest performing 10 percent of any budget item, knowing that it could be spent better, often moving the money to a more productive activity. I told them that I was sure that, with community help, we could do a better job, since they were really the customers in an important sense, and they had critical additional community resources (e.g., churches, volunteers, schools, businesses, and jobs) that are crucial for self-sufficiency, and can provide great leverage to the taxpayer dollar investment.

Well, the group at the Dawson lunch decided that we were worth

Figure 7. Grand Boulevard/Bronzeville: A Dangerous Two-Hour Stroll

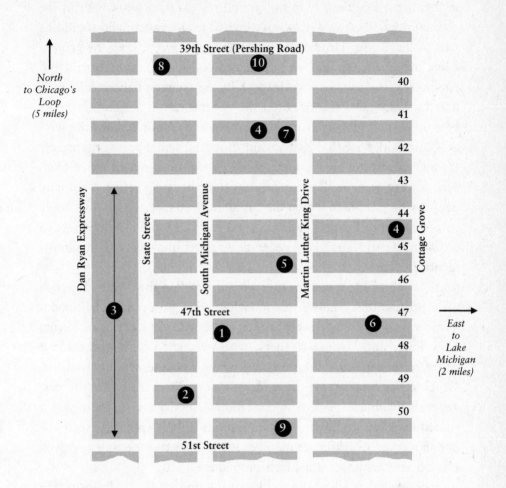

1. Progressive Community Church

2. DuSable High School

3. Robert Taylor Homes

4. Other public housing projects

5. Chicago Urban League headquarters

6. Grand Boulevard Federation Office
   (space in state unemployment office)

7. Centers for New Horizons

8. Dawson Technical Institute/
   Community College

9. Provident Hospital

10. Donnelly Youth Center

Community area 38
Census tracts 3801–3820
City of Chicago Department of Planning

trying. We asked their help in figuring out who to work with in the community and how. Who wasn't invited to our lunch who should be part of the group? How could we avoid duplication, keep the process open, achieve legitimacy as representatives of the community, avoid conflicts of interest, select a leader? In the course of the meeting we heard a number of stories about the fragmentation and intractability of state human services. At one point Dr. Mingo pointed out the window and said, "See that half-vacant shopping center across the street? If you really want to do something you could move an office from each human services department into that shopping center. That way people who need help would have it all in one place, and many people could walk to it." Not a bad idea for a start, I thought. As we were to see later, an early Springfield Federation project implemented an almost-identical idea.

Felicia and I left the meeting with the feeling that we had kicked off a process that could lead somewhere. The group had identified a number of additional people, among them church leaders, recipients of welfare, and business leaders, who needed to be at the table if we were to maximize the potential of real community involvement. Nothing like this had ever been done before. We agreed that the majority ought *not* to be providers of human services, since there was a risk of members competing for state funds (a "pie-splitting exercise," one Governor's Task Force member warned) as they became involved more deeply with key state decision makers.

I decided that I had my work cut out for me. In addition to the deeply ingrained skepticism of grass roots community people about state government, I had a personal challenge. The meeting at the Dawson Center was the first of many in Grand Boulevard where I was the only white person in the room. People in the community were cautiously glad to see me, but I had the feeling that I was being watched very carefully. It was clear I had to get to know them well— something I was really looking forward to doing.

As Felicia and I discussed our next moves it was also clear that we had to get the state to quickly change some things for the better. Some changes needed to happen early to establish credibility with Greg,

Sokoni, and the other Grand Boulevard residents we were getting to know in the process of establishing the Grand Boulevard Federation. To me, Grand Boulevard was the flagship. I had been warned that some communities were in such bad shape that the concept of the state working with grass roots community residents and their leaders was naive. In addition, I was told by some that the problems in these most acutely distressed inner-city communities were so severe that we'd be whistling in the wind to think we could make any kind of meaningful dent. In my mind, the success of our reform effort hinged on our ability to help mobilize this community.

As part of my effort to build relationships in Grand Boulevard, Charlene and I had Sokoni and his talented wife, Ayana, to our home for dinner. After a pleasant dinner Sokoni leaned back on the couch, put his hands behind his head, looked out at the lights of the city and Lake Michigan, and said, "I am so glad that I am black." I know he really meant it, and I'm glad he felt relaxed enough to express that thought to us. I wondered what he was thinking that made him say that, but it seemed awkward to ask, since my question might imply that I was in some way questioning the statement. A couple of years later, sitting together at a civic leaders' retreat, the topic of racism was being discussed. As an aside, I asked him: "What percentage of whites do you believe are racist?"

Sokoni answered, "One hundred percent." I swallowed hard, and tried not to take it personally. I decided not to pursue it further, though my curiosity will probably cause me to ask him some time in the future what he meant. Needless to say, race issues are complicated, and I still have a lot to learn.

To truly broaden the process we agreed to hold a wide-open, broadly advertised, town hall–type meeting where the reform effort would be described and interested people solicited. This had to be the whole community at work, not some kind of small group with a special connection to state dollars. In addition, this group would limit itself to being a convenor and facilitator for solving the highest-priority community problems and avoid becoming yet another group competing for funds to provide direct services. There was one other group in the community, Mid-South Development, that was active as a broad community convenor, but their emphasis was more on physical redevelopment, so the two groups agreed to work together in a complementary way. We were determined not to duplicate, but rather integrate and fill gaps. If we were to identify an existing group in a community that was even close to the kind of broadly based collaborative Grand Boulevard became, the state could start working with it right away, saving lots of time, and avoiding the reinvention of the wheel. Unfortunately such a group is rarely found, since existing groups tend to have narrower purposes and ties to a specific organization and its goals. However, groups have emerged in Decatur, Freeport, and a number of other Illinois communities that show real promise.

The Grand Boulevard community involvement process, with some occasional bumps in the road, grew broader and deeper each month, leading to the very tangible reform activities discussed in the monthly Grand Boulevard Federation meetings in the Urban League conference room. An important milestone was reached in June 1998 when seed money from the Casey Foundation for the two-person staff ended and the federation became self-financing. The Casey philosophy is that if value has been demonstrated, the market test will allow the work to continue. It worked. The Grand Boulevard Federation has already changed many lives for the better, and the list of real accomplishments is growing. A special lesson I learned over the years in observing the growth and contribution of this collaboration in Grand Boulevard is that even in the most distressed inner-city communities, there *is* a leadership group that can emerge to fill the vacuum and knit together the community. In addition, the opportunity to link the community to the enormous state resources is a very effective, probably essential, catalyst to make that happen. I believe this can and should happen anywhere in any state.

Another lesson for government policy makers is the sharp differences between what is happening in Illinois today and Lyndon Johnson's infamous Great Society movement in the 1960s. The Great Society/War on Poverty effort rained money down on communities and much of it was wasted. Political competition for dollars transcended need and management was poor, with some taxpayer money even ending up financing weapons for gangs. New money from Washington is *not* needed to get communities to the table working together with government. All that is needed is the legitimate chance to play a role working with government to determine community priorities and recognizing the need for negotiation and checks and balances to work toward utilizing *existing* government resources more effectively. If you are a concerned player at the table making sure that government dollars produce real self-sufficiency results for the community, you don't need to touch the dollars with your own hands. That's been my motivation, and it is the motivation of the vast majority of community volunteers involved in the Illinois transformation.

Grand Boulevard, with all its progress, still has many major challenges, of course. The federation has set up a working group on housing and one on violence. Some gang members have made a convincing case to me that much of the violence would cease if jobs were available for gang members—even jobs that are not high paying. Elliott Taylor, a former gang member now in his fifties, runs a small construction company where he hires only gang members. "Elliott, why would a gang leader give up all of that drug money to go work in an ordinary job?" I asked.

"They're easy to convince," he responded. "I tell them, 'Just do the numbers, one hundred thousand dollars in a year followed by nine years in prison works out to ten thousand dollars a year—even McDonald's pays better than that, with much less chance of getting killed.'" Elliott and his younger partner Marvel Thompson are convinced that if we could get jobs for just two hundred leading gang members in Grand Boulevard, that violence would diminish dramatically. A different youth role model would be established, and choices could be made. Gang members need a ladder of opportunity, too. He suggested that I meet with a large group of gang members under the auspices of the Reverend Martin at the church. The prospect made me nervous and Charlene apoplectic. My anxiety escalated when he said that some of them have never talked to a white man before. There would obviously be no security beyond whatever atmosphere the church and Reverend Martin provided, but Elliott and Marvel told Reverend Martin that even he still had a way to go to earn the trust of some of them. This process is still unfolding, and shows promise of being a very important element in the next phase of the Illinois reform effort.

Elliott and Marvel have been working for a number of years with gang members trying to create alternatives to violence. I asked what usually causes the gunfire, and Marvel answered, "Usually something silly—I've seen gang fights over a pair of sneakers, and once they get started most of them are scared and looking for a face-saving way to stop."

When he said this, I was embarrassed at a thought that flashed through my mind. A few years ago Charlene and I were out in the wilds of Papua New Guinea when our Jeep was accosted at a bridge by a group of very fierce-looking warriors with painted faces and bows and arrows. We were really frightened, even though we had an escort armed with a shotgun. It seemed we had wandered into a fight between two tribes. "Would kidnapping a couple of tourists help one side or the other?" I worried. I was also keenly aware of New Guinea's head-hunting history and the famous disappearance of Michael Rockefeller in New Guinea, where his head was cut off and displayed on a pole because he was a guest of an enemy tribe.[6] It seems one of the most common causes of tribal warfare in that part of the world is a stolen pig—and the fact that the men don't have much else to do. There is also a warrior tradition. Was that a racist thought—was Sokoni right that 100 percent of white people are racist? Or was my mind jogged by the parallel of men who don't have much else to do fighting with deadly weapons over something small—independent of color. I believe the latter. After an animated discussion with our armed escort and the driver, the warriors let us proceed across the bridge and on to the small airstrip.

Violence in our inner cities is so commonplace that it needs to be understood if we are really to make a dent in persistent poverty. Violence is a huge barrier to self-sufficiency not only for those on welfare but also, perhaps more important, for the young men like Julius in a community mired in poverty. The police are viewed quite differently in a place like Grand Boulevard—almost like yet another gang. There is no respect for the police, and much of the lack of respect has been earned by arbitrary actions on the part of police. Poll after poll shows that African Americans believe that they are unfairly singled out and picked on by police. In the years that I have been active in Grand Boulevard I have come to believe that both the perception and the reality are true, but all police brutality and misbehavior is not racist.

Gary, Jr., my older son, was a victim of police brutality in New York when he came to the aid of Greg, his college roommate whom he thought was being mugged. The fat, swarthy, unshaven mugger in grungy clothes turned out to be Benny Goleta, a plainclothes cop. Benny grabbed Greg, who happens to be philanthropist Walter Annenberg's grandson, when Greg's token jammed in a subway turnstile and Greg slid past the barrier. An enraged Benny and his partner took the 155-pound Gary, who prior to his experience had never even been in a playground fight, into a small room off the subway platform and beat him badly. They then arrested both Greg and Gary for resisting arrest, and took them back to the police station where there were further beatings. Gary called me in Chicago from the station at 3:00 A.M., afraid to talk. Although Greg's family and I facilitated a lawsuit to get Officer Goleta disciplined, neither Gary nor I necessarily see the police as a refuge or a source of justice anymore. All it takes is one incident of brutality to change your view, and the African-American community experiences many such incidents. The traditional big city police officer often comes from an intensely ethnic community like Irish Bridgeport in Chicago, where tolerance is sometimes low and things haven't changed as much as we might hope over the years.

The Reverend Martin, in his community leadership role, became involved in quieting racial tensions in 1988 after an African-American teenager rode his bicycle into the Bridgeport neighborhood, an all-white bastion—the home of both Mayors Daley and much of the city's political leadership. The boy was badly beaten by a group of white teenagers, presumably for breaching territorial borders, and tensions, fanned by newspaper stories, flared. Unlike Al Sharpton, the Reverend Martin, among other relationship-building activities, invited all the families involved to his church and conducted a healing service. Governor Edgar attended and offered a prayer, preempting Jesse Jackson, who sought to gain press attention by inviting Governor Edgar to a news conference at Operation Push headquarters. When the dust cleared, the Reverend Martin said that the divisiveness between the Irish and Italian residents of Bridgeport, each group blaming the other for the attack, seemed worse than the black-white divide. Big cities are complicated places.

This work again drives home to me the fact that local communities are very different from cities. Viewed from Washington, it may feel like real devolution of decision-making to pass things down to local government. However, from the Grand Boulevard perspective, Chicago's city hall is a huge, complicated bureaucracy not much different from Springfield and Washington, and certainly not able to do local problem solving the way that Grand Boulevard has. The distinction between communities and local governments is crucial in Chicago and in the other big cities. The city of Chicago is often described as being made up of seventy or more community areas (Hyde Park and Woodlawn being two of the most famous), as originally laid out by the Chicago Planning Commission (refer to Figure 2). City government needs to be connected and involved, but grass roots people must take the lead. This fits also with the management philosophy that whenever possible, big problems need to be broken up into bite-sized pieces.

Even though, statistically, the city of Chicago and Cook County represent about 60 percent of Illinois poverty and welfare, a credible statewide effort was necessary for reform, so parallel efforts were underway in the other four pilot sites.

Meanwhile, it took several months, but I was fortunate to recruit a dynamic outsider, B.J. Walker, to fill the Assistant to the Governor for Human Services Reform position that Governor Edgar had agreed to. B.J. is a very bright, articulate, hard-working Mt. Holyoke graduate with an M.A. from Northwestern. She had a background with an education think tank and was a top Casey Fellow as part of the one-year program offered by the Casey Foundation to help train high potential human services practitioners for top management positions.

Serendipitously, she had grown up poor in Grand Boulevard. She joined in the effort to connect all of the test sites to our reform effort.

. . .

The Southern Seven experience was a very different ball game from Grand Boulevard. Vivienne Charles had been doing the scouting in the Southern Seven, so she and I got on a TWA Express twin-prop puddle jumper for Marion, Illinois (population 15,000), just outside the northern edge of the Southern Seven Counties, where we would be met for the ninety-minute drive to our meeting. The other commercial air point of access is Paducah, Kentucky, just south of the Ohio River from the Southern Seven. It turns out there are no commercial airports in the Southern Seven Counties despite the fact that they stretch over two thousand square miles and contain 71,000 people. However, no town is over eight thousand in population. These counties are often linked together since individually they lack a critical mass, and they also share government services, such as Shawnee Community College, in the tiny town of Ulin, the sole institution of higher education in the Southern Seven and the location of most of our meetings. The government in one form or another is the largest employer through the Choate Mental Hospital, human services offices, and schools, with the economy also linked to agriculture, river traffic, a few small scattered manufacturers, and what's left of coal mining.

As we drove, I enjoyed the beautiful rolling and green countryside, but the small towns had a hollowed-out feeling about them, reflecting the underlying reality. Unemployment in the Southern Seven was roughly double the state average. Twenty-eight percent were in poverty, and 20 percent on welfare.[7] This was a tough one. Somehow it was hard to digest the fact that more than one out of every four people we would see was in poverty. As we drove through the small town of Dongola at about 10:30 in the morning on our way to Ulin, I suggested we stop and join the beaten-up pickup trucks at the lone cafe in town. I walked in and saw a heavyset woman who appeared to be in her fifties wearing an apron that had seen better days and pouring coffee for about a dozen jeans-clad patrons—young to middle-aged white men. It reminded me of a recent visit to Albania, where unemployment and chauvinism were very high. The kiosk cafes were full of men all day long, and women were working hard at home cleaning, cooking, and taking care of the children.

When the waitress paused, I introduced myself and inquired if I could ask her a few questions, with the idea of learning enough to be helpful. She cheerfully said, "Sure, but you ain't goin' learn nuttin' from me." The discussion quickly spread to include the whole cafe group, and soon focused on the lack of jobs. I was standing in the middle of the cafe listening to a sort of seminar on life in the Southern Seven.

An informal leader, an unshaven craggy-faced fortyish fellow named Charlie started the ball rolling. "Since the Bunny Bread factory moved out there ain't no jobs."

I was curious: "How do you make it now?"

Charlie answered, "We get food stamps, do a few odd jobs, and grow some vegetables—barely get by."

I offered what seemed to be considered a naive suggestion: "Have you thought about moving someplace where there are some jobs?"

"How'm I gonna do that? I ain't got no high school graduation, got a wife and two young 'uns. Now I have a small place on a plot of land and don't pay no rent. I don't know of no jobs no way."

They thought the government ought to help them, but they weren't sure how. They seemed willing to work, but not particularly eager. I'd have liked to continue the discussion, but the others in our car had finished their visit to the grocery store and were waiting—we needed to push on to Shawnee Community College for the "town hall" meeting. I thanked them for their thoughts and returned to the car.

During my time working in the Southern Seven I came to believe that we were looking at a different kind of poverty. With all the land around, people weren't going to go hungry and there would be wood for a stove, so the low levels of income might not have the same impact as in a rubble-strewn neighborhood in the inner city of Chicago. The visceral impressions were supported by the data—the infant mortality rate in the Southern Seven was eleven per one thousand births[8] compared with a state average of 10.69, despite the poverty numbers and the typically great distance to a hospital. By contrast, the Grand Boulevard infant mortality rate was more than twice as high, at twenty-nine per one thousand, despite the close proximity of a big hospital. In fact, in the Southern Seven it is necessary to go to Cape Girardeau, Missouri, Paducah, Kentucky, or up to Carbondale, Illinois, to have a baby in a medical facility. The Southern Seven was below the state average for children removed from their homes by the state child welfare agency for neglect and abuse with 105 cases in one year, while Grand Boulevard, with half the population, had 735 kids removed from their homes, or almost seven times the state average.

Unlike Grand Boulevard, violence didn't come up as a barrier to self-sufficiency. The conditions in the Southern Seven seemed similar to those surrounding the ranch I bought 20 years ago as a kind of retreat for my family in Sequoya County, Oklahoma. The families in that area typically get by on a few acres and occasional jobs in agriculture or construction. Just as in Sequoya County, here in the Southern Seven nobody had much cash, much savings, or anything fancy—they were poor but not distressed. They had needs, but the dimensions were quite different than those of the ladies in the backyard. We passed numerous shacks with junk in the yard, a small garden, and chickens running around, and a visit inside one of them is a much more comfortable experience than my scary visit to the Robert Taylor Homes apartment. The home ownership rate in the Southern Seven is an impressive 76 percent, compared with 8 percent in Grand Boulevard and a statewide average of 64 percent.[9] Though I'm sure most of them have rifles inside for protection and for the hunting season, there is no feeling that random violence is a risk. Beaten-up pickup trucks abound. However, as with their poor counterparts in Grand Boulevard, it's hard to identify a realistic ladder of opportunity for our friend, Charlie, from the cafe in Dongola. What about the kids? Perhaps some of them can get through high school, find transportation to Shawnee Community College, acquire a skill, and move out. Those not so fortunate will probably repeat the cycle.

We went on another forty-five minutes to the "town hall" meeting at Shawnee Community College, hosted by the college president Dr. Jack Hill. Dr. Hill was, I was told, perhaps the most respected leader in the Southern Seven community, and in a previous meeting indicated a real interest in helping us in our effort to form a community collaborative to work with the state to reform the human services systems. Michelle's data showed spending of $54 million a year, or $2,700 per person in poverty, not counting the $21 million per year to operate the Choate Mental Hospital. I was told by a director of the Department of Mental Health and Developmental Disabilities that the state had too many residential mental health facilities, but like excess Pentagon military bases, each was protected by a powerful legislator. The prospect of freeing up those wasted resources and making them count is exciting, but that's another story. A shortage of resources is not the problem at the moment, and it's important not to get bogged down in peripheral fights. I remember thinking that as a dutiful taxpayer for years, I really had had little understanding of what happened to my money.

Choate reminded me of a medium-sized college campus where there was little activity because of summer vacation. Choate provided jobs in an area that had few—but was this the way to do it? I continued to find further support for our thesis that there is plenty of money flowing, we're just not using it very well.

The town hall meeting was jammed, with all the seats filled and standees in every available space. Almost everyone was white, despite the presence of over seventeen thousand African Americans in the Southern Seven, making up 24 percent of the population.[10] The African Americans were mostly in the river towns like Cairo, a long drive from Ulin. We would address this mismatch in the future, but it wasn't easy.

The meeting went well, and the principles were enthusiastically endorsed. The Felicia Norwood chart drew its usual groans and laughs. An open discussion ensued with some give and take. Up at a blackboard I encouraged the group to take a first pass at identifying community needs, and transportation problems easily topped the list. There was no public transportation other than school buses, so access to jobs and assistance was a major problem for those on welfare. Further, regulations denied welfare to anyone who had a car worth $1,500 or more, a real catch-22 in an area where you might have to drive forty-five minutes each way for groceries, not to mention training, human services, or work.

We came away with a good list of names of people who were interested in forming a collaborative, ending up with strong representation across the Seven Counties and the various community occupations. The local publisher, Jerry Reppert (*Metropolis Sentinel, Anna Gazette,* and others), signed on and ran some good stories about our effort. Grover Webb, an energetic, caring farmer became an active participant, often getting a meeting back on track for action by using a farming analogy. "I can only put so much work and fertilizer in on a field before I have to see some crops growing—when are we going to see the crops?" he interjects at the appropriate moment. The head of a multicounty planning commission joined the group and helped create transportation ideas—leading the effort to get a federal grant to help on transportation, among other contributions.

Betty Wilson, the very articulate, soft-spoken high school principal of Metropolis High School, also joined the group. She represented both Massac County and the public schools, and as the group's only African American, she brought additional insight. However, I soon became aware of a racial divide in Metropolis that resulted in Betty being denied the opportunity to attend the meetings. In spite of a letter I wrote to the school superintendent and efforts by others to maintain her participation, it became clear that racial politics would win. The stories I heard about what was going on in Metropolis reminded me of the South in the fifties. Of course Cairo, not far from Metropolis, was the scene of one of the worst race riots and burnings in the sixties.

The group soon took shape, named itself Focus of Southern Illinois, set up a small office in empty space at Choate, took on a pilot group of twenty-five families that successfully tested the integrated case management model, and paved the way for jobs and self-sufficiency.

On a later visit I was invited to talk at a lunch in the Choate conference room with a group of about twenty employers about how, working with state help, hiring people from the welfare rolls is a "reasonable business risk," and "enlightened self-interest." At the end of the lunch, every employer made a commitment to hire a specific number of welfare recipients, with the largest being a commitment to hire twenty-five clients by the human resources director of the riverboat casino tied up at Metropolis. It turns out he needed restaurant and bar workers for the evening shift. In addition to transportation, night child care was an important issue. Night child care is an example of the kind of barrier to work that shows up in a community problem-solving process, but is highly unlikely to be thought about in Springfield or Washington.

An important initiative created and implemented by the Focus collaborative and the state in the Southern Seven was the initiation of a new bus route that allowed three hundred unemployed people access to jobs, connecting unemployed people in several towns with several previously inaccessible factories. The jobs typically paid $8 to $9 per hour plus benefits. The buses brought meaningful numbers of African Americans into previously all-white areas, and there were some demonstrations, including rock-throwing, that have since ended. When Focus first identified transportation as the number one barrier, the plan was to obtain a subsidy for the bus route. It turned out that the first bus was so popular that a modest charge to the users made the subsidy unnecessary, and the demand so great that additional buses were added. Without the local government/community collaborative seeking local solutions to the self-sufficiency challenge, taxpayers would be sending those now employed people welfare checks indefinitely.

I made a number of trips to the Southern Seven, and it often felt somewhat like a visit to the old South. A great treat was a barbecue with Great Boars of Fire, the nationally recognized Anna, Illinois, barbecue team. Winner of the grand prize at the previous summer's two-hundred-team national championship cookoff in Louisiana, this group sported a huge custom-designed welded steel cooker, specially selected and processed pork, and an exotic, top-secret barbecue sauce. Sitting under a tree eating spectacularly good food with the very thoughtful barbecue team members, a local farmer, and some small businessmen, I was pleased that we were connecting people to our self-sufficiency effort who represented a real community resource, and who otherwise would be unlikely to get involved. Again, the prospect of the state with its major resources being willing to listen to community people had drawn them in. They were the first to elevate the importance of transportation, among other issues, and they made something happen. Continued improvements in transportation are being implemented by several arms of government—the momentum has been established. The overall Southern Seven/Focus collaborative worked well on many levels, reinforcing the statewide reform effort principles and helping make the statewide case for system change. However, the great distances combined with weaker staff support have left this federation short of its potential compared to others, and more work is required.

. . .

The DuPage County Federation, chaired by the dynamic, well-connected Margo Schreiber, had a somewhat different configuration but provided additional support for systems change. DuPage is an affluent county overall, but among its very large population are almost as many people in poverty as Grand Boulevard. We thought of it as pockets of poverty amid affluence, another type of situation to learn about. With its stronger tax base, DuPage had a small human services budget of its own and a county board chairman, Gayle Franzen, who became very interested in systems reform and measuring the real outcomes from human services investment. He stimulated a good outcomes measurement effort and enthusiastically supported the idea of community involvement and integrating services.

Margo, an executive in the DuPage County human services department, ensured that state senator Pate Philip and house speaker Lee Daniels knew what was going on as she put together a broad coalition of members from churches, businesses, and schools. This collaborative includes the United Way and DuPage Easter Seal, and volunteer organizations such as the Junior League. Human services provider organizations such as Metropolitan Family Services are also included, but care was taken to make sure they did not become a majority. The federation became a historic coming together with government of organizations that shared considerable commonality of purpose.

The DuPage Federation and the state again utilized the integrated-services, one-stop idea, together with other innovations and, in the initial project, jobs were found for sixty welfare recipients. The federation is now housed in the local Department of Human Services office and, with redeployed state workers, is taking responsibility for some of the more difficult welfare cases. In one federation innovation, used vehicles are donated to the nonprofit People's Resource Center and then given to qualified low income workers, most of them homeless or on welfare. To support this effort, in-kind donations are obtained from auto-related businesses who donate auto safety inspections, repairs, tires, batteries, insurance, used vehicles, etc. Thirty cars were donated in the first six months.

The DuPage Federation also identified child support (deadbeat dads) as a big issue, convening a Child Support Summit of local leaders. They came up with a number of good ideas, and the Department of Public Aid, impressed with this local effort, and, of course, headed by a Governor's Task Force member, has agreed to change a number of procedures to make the system more effective and is transferring part of the responsibility and authority for operation of the system to the county.

As is the case in Grand Boulevard and in the other initial sites, the DuPage group is still working years later. All of the communities saw a need for a facilitator who integrates the efforts of those in the community and who can draw upon the state as well. In the process of each individual community deciding how to organize itself, there were lots of differences, but one awkward, somewhat political question always emerged: what is the right way to involve the people and organizations that get money from the state? State contractors always show up. They know a lot and definitely can contribute, but there is a built-in conflict of interest, and they are not the broader community. Each community figured out a way to involve the providers while not being run by them—a crucial point for credibility. The two main approaches were either the formation of separate but connected provider advisory groups, or their inclusion on the federation leadership group, but in the minority.

• • •

In Waukegan, a high-energy entrepreneur, Lucy Rios, emerged as the builder and head of the local federation. A heavyset woman in her forties, Lucy saw no limits to what hard work could bring in this country compared with her native Mexico. Though not affluent by any means, she had built a small secretarial and travel business and now was giving back, both as the elected leader of the federation and as a member of the Waukegan City Council. She said, "I just got myself on the ballot and then rang doorbells." She was an excellent link to the Hispanic community (24 percent of Waukegan, and disproportionately poor and on welfare) and to local government. She was also particularly good at involving churches and businesses in the federation.

Waukegan's largest employer, other than the almost bankrupt Outboard Marine Corporation, is Cherry Electric Corporation, a maker of electrical components. With over three thousand employees, we needed Cherry to be involved in any self-sufficiency effort. I worked hard in several visits to his office to get Peter Cherry, the CEO of Cherry Electric, to join the Waukegan Federation personally. He came to a meeting, but trips to Japan and other commitments led to his asking his human resources director to participate. She became an active federation member and pledged jobs at Cherry for welfare recipients. A lot was learned at Cherry about drug problems in the welfare population, since they did drug testing as part of every employment decision. Language problems also required special attention, and this realization was also helpful to the reform effort.

All of the federations did considerable work linking the churches, temples, and synagogues into the self-sufficiency effort, but Waukegan more than most. The federation initiated and developed the Waukegan Clergy Planning Council, whose mission is to help coordinate human services in Waukegan and to help address the issues of diversity constructively. In addition to the 24 percent Hispanic population, Waukegan is 19 percent African American and 3 percent Asian American for a total 46 percent minority population.[11] As another important challenge, Waukegan has its own problem-filled public housing projects. The Clergy Planning Council conducted a two-day Better Together citywide seminar, which addressed how the faith community can help in the welfare-to-work challenge. Out of this came volunteer family mentors who are assisting the caseworkers in moving families to independence—once again helping to fill that omnipresent need for a thoughtful, caring, sensible adult in an otherwise traumatic life. The Clergy Planning Council is now working on expanding quality, affordable child care in the city.

The Waukegan Federation has also launched a successful effort to connect human services more closely to schools, especially the most distressed schools, and it has added considerable evidence, based on a fifty-family pilot project, of the value of integrating human services in a single primary caseworker. All this because government, of all things, reached out and asked for help from those closest to the problems in the community. The modest Casey seed money has run out in Waukegan, but the federation has proven its value, and the community has seen to it that the two-person staff is maintained. As with the other federations, the real impact for Waukegan is redeployed resources and the connecting of the key community elements, especially employers and volunteers.

• • •

The Springfield Federation, in a very short time, came up with the most visible early project to show what can be done when a truly broadly based group is formed for the first time to begin knocking down the walls among bureaucracies. Like many small cities, Springfield has a poor side of town, largely African American, where the Springfield Housing Authority projects are located. This part of Springfield has earned a reputation for being dangerous—a smaller, low-rise version of Grand Boulevard. After an early town hall–type meeting held in city hall, the Springfield Federation started to come together in a way similar to the other four community collaboratives, and they began to hold their meetings in the Springfield Housing Authority conference room, on the tough side of town. Initially I was worried that the group might become all African American, and not sufficiently bridge all the community interests.

After weak early leadership, Frank McNeil, an African-American Springfield city councilman, became the chair, and Mike Boer, executive director of the Springfield Chamber of Commerce, emerged to head the jobs committee, connecting the federation with the predominantly white Springfield business community. Delores Martin, a former state government lawyer, was recruited as executive director, and supplied crucial support. Like the other four federations, the issue of finding jobs for those on welfare was picked by the community as one of the top issues—again before the federal welfare reform of 1996. Like the other federations, they were encouraged by the Governor's Task Force to pick a tangible project to see what the community could accomplish, now that they had a pledge from the state that they would work together.

After considerable thought, the Springfield Federation decided it wanted to make all of the state human services available *in one building, within walking distance* of the majority of the welfare population. They were going to bring to life the offhand comment of Grand Boulevard's Dr. Mingo. There was a time in my life when I would have yawned at the obviousness of this idea; however in the context of the world of welfare systems, this is profound—almost a revolution! Remembering the Felicia Norwood chart, to connect these pilot sites to the human services systems, each federation had six liaisons in attendance at each community meeting—one for each department. This crowd grew to seven when the Department on Aging joined the Governor's Task Force. These liaisons came to the evening federation meetings in their own communities on their own time and became quite interested and quite helpful, going back to their department heads sometimes to fight for a change—such as redeploying a state worker—that the community felt was needed to carry out a community welfare-to-work project. The fact that, in order to cover all the services, the state had to be represented by six or seven liaisons in each community graphically illustrated what was wrong with the present structure.

The Springfield Federation identified a building that was within walking distance of 60 percent of the city's welfare population. It was the former medical clinic of the beloved, recently deceased Dr. Edwin A. Lee, an African-American doctor and community leader who provided care to this poor community. The building was perfect functionally, and since Dr. Lee was a local legend, there was a terrific symbolic value. The city of Springfield donated $300,000 for rehabilitation, and unions and community residents donated labor. The cooperation from all walks of life evoked, for me, the image of community barn-raising in an earlier, healthier America in years gone by or in today's Amish communities. Working together, the state liaisons and the Springfield Federation relocated caseworkers to the building, thus providing access to all state human services in one place. The visible example of the state's willingness to redeploy resources and people at the behest of the community sent a powerful message. For security, the Springfield police set up an office in the building with a duty officer. All this was done in less than a year. Importantly, the Lee Center also became a test site for the new state management information system that integrated entire families, all human services systems, and relevant private community resources in a single caseworker's personal computer. In spite of the fact that this systems support is essential for a caseworker's effort, a nationwide search by the Casey Foundation failed to turn up any software systems in any state that could provide this basic tool. We would develop the model and make it available to other states.

The opening of the Lee Center on November 22, 1996, was a great day. I was to participate with the governor in the ribbon cutting, and since the weather was still nice, I decided to take the twenty-minute walk from my downtown Springfield hotel to the ceremony. Springfield is a town steeped in history, primarily because Lincoln lived there, and it's fascinating to see his law offices, his church pew, the railway station where he left to be president, and his tomb, among other sites. Since it was on the way to the Lee Center, I walked by Lincoln's home, complete with much original furniture, where the Republican Party delegation came to ask him to run for President. It wasn't far from the Lee Center. I wondered what he would think if he saw Springfield now, with its large area of black poverty, crime, and a trouble-plagued public housing project. I imagined he'd wonder where we went wrong after the good start he gave us by abolishing slavery in the Civil War. I decided he would come to the conclusion that we had screwed up somewhere along the way, but I'm sure his words would be more eloquent! As I crossed over the tracks toward the Lee Center, I saw lots of Springfield and Illinois state police closing off the area to protect the governor. I'd been to many events with the governor, but this was the tightest security I'd seen—right in his and Lincoln's hometown. When the event was over, my cab couldn't get in to take me to the airport. It felt like we were in the small-town version of Grand Boulevard.

After the speeches, Governor Edgar was standing at the front door of the Lee Center, posing for the cameras, and I noticed a very old, stooped-over, white-haired black woman with a happy look on her face at the edge of the crowd. I went over and found out she was Geraldine Lee, the doctor's widow. I introduced her to the governor, and the picture of the two of them ended up in the newspapers. The event got excellent coverage by both the print and electronic media, and the governor was pleased to get his picture associated with the "one stop" human services image all over the state. From the task force perspective, it was another chance to get him to reiterate publicly his commitment to the reform and its principles. A bonus was the chance to sit him down at the caseworker's personal computer so he could see firsthand what an integrated system looked like. In addition, all the attention reenergized the volunteers who were doing such good work leading the Springfield Federation.

It took a couple of years for the Springfield Federation to go through the town hall meeting stage and other collaborative steps leading up to the Lee Center effort. Along the way there were some bumps in the road. The first chairperson was replaced, and some of the early meetings were filled with more words than action. In retrospect, this early groping seems like part of the process, and the discussions have value. I attended most of the Springfield Federation meetings in the early days, and I remember a presentation by the then–deputy director of Public Aid, Joe Antolin, to the federation meeting one Wednesday evening. Joe, a very smart, hard-working, and articulate bureaucrat, explained to the group the then–Public Aid system as background for the federation suggestions for change. When Joe finished his presentation, Pat Boston, a heavyset, fortyish African-American woman who was one of the welfare recipients on the federation board, said with a winning smile, "Mr. Antolin, you've just told us how the system is *supposed* to work. Now let me tell you what *really* happens." She went on to describe fragmentation, inefficiency, and barriers to self-sufficiency. For me this was a rare and priceless moment.

As one would imagine, Springfield is an unusually political city, even at the local level. The majority of jobs in Springfield are connected with state government, directly or indirectly, though there are two good-sized insurance companies, a couple of hospitals, and well-developed retailing, banking, and hotel businesses. Finding entry level jobs for welfare recipients is more of a challenge than in Grand Boulevard, Waukegan, or DuPage, and it had to be done on a more widespread basis, with only one or two jobs per employer. Mike Boer, from the chamber of commerce, became a truly inspirational federation member and contributor in the employment challenge. Mike and the federation formed Jobs First, a partnership to develop employment opportunities for low income families. The partners connected together for this effort were the Springfield Urban League, the Sangamon County Department of Community Resources, and United Cerebral Palsy of Land of Lincoln. In addition to assisting in the mainstream welfare-to-work challenge, this group has a special emphasis on finding employment for people with special challenges. From day one, the Springfield Federation experienced strong advocacy on behalf of the handicapped, and this interest and involvement continues to be important. These kinds of connections among community organizations with a common purpose and their connection, in turn, with government are at the heart of the value of community collaboratives and the Illinois reform effort. Mike Boer also came up with the idea of "contracts" with a large number of employers in the area. The contracts explained what the federation would do in terms of mentoring and supporting welfare recipients who otherwise would not be hired, and the employers agreed to try. With the state services and the federation, these hires became a "reasonable business risk" and "enlightened self-interest." Mike Boer, of course, also provided the federation with access to the top managers of most of the employers in the area.

To illustrate the energy that can come out of community collaborations that were ignited by and are connected to government, it is worthwhile to highlight some of the other Springfield Federation efforts. The federation formed Teen Reach, connecting three well-established youth programs (Boys and Girls Club, Springfield Housing Authority, and Springfield Urban League) with the purpose of coordinating, upgrading, and expanding those programs. To increase the flow of volunteers for youth programs, the federation brought together the Junior League of Springfield, Imani Incorporated (a faith-based provider), and the Boys and Girls Club. Connecting the many providers of services together, eighty private service agencies meet monthly under the umbrella of the federation to work on joint efforts such as housing, truancy, child care, and transportation. It may sound obvious that all of those with overlapping interests in serving the disadvantaged should work together in a community to strengthen their efforts, but these kinds of collaborations are very rare.

To ensure that government is informed by the voices of the "customer" or client, the Springfield Federation formed a Consumer's Council with a membership comprised of people who are currently receiving or recently received state services. They identified problems in the child support system, child care, and other areas, the state listened, and changes were made. For example, as a result of the efforts of this council, the local child care office was restructured, including a new phone system and extending hours of operation into the evening. This Consumer's Council gives me special pleasure because it represents the institutionalizing of the ladies in the backyard—a real bottom-up way of getting a check on the front line reality and helping to counteract the naivete of top-down practitioners such as Lester Thurow and his ilk. In these matters, ladies in the backyard know more than Rhodes Scholars or their equivalents.

In Springfield once again transportation, that heretofore underappreciated barrier, emerged as crucial, and the federation responded by forming Access, which connects the Springfield Mass Transit, the Springfield Chamber of Commerce, and the federation's Jobs First organization. One of the first accomplishments of Access was the arrangement of transportation to and from work after 6:00 P.M., when public transit ends. Springfield became yet another local group calling attention to the fact that really poor people don't have cars and that public transportation wasn't designed to fit many entry level work requirements either geographically or in scheduling. This important step, like so many of the ideas and activities generated by the community collaboratives, seems obvious in retrospect, but grass roots people, not politicians or bureaucrats, identified the problems and found answers.

As with the other federations, the first cohort of recipients for which they implemented integrated case management was very successful, both in becoming self-sufficient and in demonstrating the value of integrating human services on the front lines. Through the Lee Center they provided case management for 116 families, found employment for 101 people, found mentors for many families, and performed numerous other activities. The Lee Center was highlighted on the PBS program *To the Contrary* and given a $5,000 innovation award from Mitsubishi Motors. I was told that the Springfield Federation represented for the first time *all* of the key segments of Springfield—Republicans and Democrats, black and white, city hall, business, providers, and welfare recipients—had come together under one roof and produced real change. In addition to the major elements of Springfield working together inclusively and effectively, they are also linked with the state agencies—the previously distant and nonresponsive government—in a way that is regularly producing change. These joint efforts have attracted money as well as attention, with the federation instrumental in attracting over $1 million in grants from private industry, nonprofits, and government.

All of the activities of the federations stemmed from a most unusual source—government reaching out to the communities and the private sector—and listening to their ideas! So simple to say, so rarely accomplished. Many lives have been changed for the better already, but even more important, the task force's ideas about how government and communities can work together to pursue the bipartisan principles are coming to life and providing momentum for statewide replication.

Though there were more commonalities than differences, each community worked on its own governance structure. As an example, the Grand Boulevard Federation is separately incorporated with an elaborate set of by-laws calling for a formal annual meeting, election of officers, payment of dues, etc. To minimize overhead, accounting and the small payroll is done by a member provider organization. They have also set up a parallel charitable foundation, a 501c3 corporation, so that tax-deductible contributions from foundations, corporations, and individuals can be received. A relatively small amount of money, $200,000 a year or so, is required for the glue to keep the modest community group support structure (an executive director and an assistant) in place. It is tempting for the state to fund this, but it is important that community people have as much independence from the state as possible, to foster a real sense of ownership. Besides, if there is real value added to the community, the community will find a way to keep it going. This has turned out to be the case as other funding sources, including contributions by providers, business, and other foundation grants, were found. Each community came up with some kind of wide-open democratic process to determine board membership and leadership. They set their own meeting schedules and agendas and have established their own priorities and projects. All have avoided becoming providers themselves, filling the valuable role of honest brokers among providers, the community at large, and the state. These community collaboratives have filled a crucial vacuum, becoming connectors of many elements of a previously much more fragmented set of systems and programs, both government and private.

I was taken aback recently when a high-level Central Illinois state human services manager described the Springfield Federation as *very powerful*. By that she meant that they had access to most all the resources, both state and private, so their influence was such that they were the place you had to go if you wanted to get something done in the human services arena in Springfield. The city of Springfield, the employers, the state, private citizens, and providers all look to the federation for priorities and direction.

There is healthy conflict built into this intensive community-state interaction. The process of the community identifying a better way for the state to do things and the state working with the community to make changes came to be called the *negotiation* process. Dr. Steven Preister, an outside expert hired by the Casey Foundation to evaluate the Casey investment in the Illinois reform effort, interviewed a large number of the participants statewide, and his report[12] contains a number of interesting quotes, including this one from one of the state agency directors: "One of the main reform elements of the Governor's Task Force is to change the delivery system from a provider-oriented one to a client-oriented one. The central process for accomplishing this is the negotiation process between the federations and the state agencies. What we've experienced so far is that the negotiation process is really a learning process. The state agencies are having to learn to work differently to create a client-oriented system. The federations are having to learn firsthand the constraints state agencies have to deal with daily—legal requirements, union rules, and so forth. I think all of us have been surprised at how much we are learning."

Another state agency head says, "The negotiation process has been a challenge all around. For the state agencies, we are being challenged through negotiation with the federations to change our system from one that measures our work by focusing on process to one that measures our work by focusing on client outcomes. We are challenged to do this because the negotiation process forces us to talk to citizens!"

All of the federation efforts were regularly reviewed, evaluated, and documented in thorough academic fashion. The report of another evaluator, Dr. Richard Sherman, emphasized some very satisfying quotes from welfare recipients:

"Focus is . . . helping people find jobs, also helping with transportation"; "My Focus worker made the poster board of all my strong points so that I could show them at an interview." (Southern Seven)

"They helped me get a job, and they are finding me a better place to live"; "I like being able to talk with a self-sufficiency coach to make plans for my future. . . . I am getting a professional point of view." (Grand Boulevárd)

"My case coordinator returns my calls—unlike other agencies I [used to] deal with." (Springfield)

"Information given about other (not just state) resources in my community has been appreciated"; "They are teaching me to be independent"; "The federation helps you with your family values and goals." (Waukegan)

"If it wasn't for this type of (help) I would've *not* got the initiative to change my life. I received my GED in December"; "I am able to express my feelings about the runaround system [government resources] and how frustration puts families in more problems than help. And how many resources need to change their policies." (DuPage)

Dr. Sherman concluded, "Each of the five projects has demonstrated success in expanding local resources through their community and agency networking activities. Some of these expanded resources resulted from the leveraging or maximizing of existing resources within the community, while others represented the securing of additional resources from external sources. Expansion of resources is considered to be one of the expected outcomes of community empowerment."[13]

· · ·

There is a long list of personal discoveries I made as I spent time in these vastly different communities. I once took a bus to a meeting in Grand Boulevard, and I was told by my community friends that being the only white person on the bus traveling down Martin Luther King Boulevard from the Loop past the housing projects with their snipers and armed bus riders was too dangerous, so I take a cab. However, to get back to Chicago's Loop another cab must be called, and the wait is usually a half-hour or so, if a cab will come at all. What does this mean to someone who lives in Robert Taylor Homes and has an emergency? Almost no one has a car, and public transportation is extremely limited. The sense of isolation is palpable.

While riding in a cab to Grand Boulevard one day, I thought about a conversation I had a while back with George C. Wolfe, a fellow board member of the Non-Traditional Casting Project, a New York–based organization dedicated to increasing minority employment in the theater. George, perhaps the hottest young director on Broadway (*Jelly's Last Jam, Bring in Da Noise . . .* , N.Y. Shakespeare/Public Theater), told me that when the shows let out, he had trouble getting cabs to stop for him, because he was black. I was shocked that this would be the case in this day and age and, naively, I wasn't sure it was true. A short while later, Charlene and I were riding with a black cab driver, and I asked him about his view of picking up African Americans in the evening. He said, "I won't do it—I don't want to get shot. Once they get in, by law you have to take them where they want to go. I ain't goin' to no Harlem housing project at night." The cab driver wasn't being bigoted, he was being Bayesian— playing the odds for what he believed to be his own safety. Yet another aspect of the omnipresent transportation challenge.

Another observation that would come back to me in the future as we worked on reform was the potential of churches. There were dozens of churches in Grand Boulevard, often the only institutional structure for blocks around. Here were community gathering places as well as sources of values. Separation of church and state is important to keep the pope or archbishop of Canterbury from running England, but it seems foolish to invoke that mantra at the neighborhood level where the churches are one of the few community anchors and sources of help for very needy people.

As I learned these kinds of facts firsthand, it became increasingly understandable why well-intentioned academics and high-level government leaders, sitting around tables in Washington, Cambridge, and Springfield, miss important pieces of the puzzle when it comes to finding the answers to problems of poverty. We know that government welfare/human services programs have only recently begun address transportation, while our community groups hit it right away.

Students of Chicago history know that transportation from the Black Metropolis into the white areas was limited *by design*. The first

Mayor Daley's plan to minimize racial problems back in the fifties and sixties then becomes a big factor in creating economic and unemployment problems now. As described persuasively by Nicholas Lemann in *The Promised Land*,[14] the mayor believed that he would best maintain his political strength by keeping the black community as separate as possible, concentrating thousands of blacks in the massive public housing projects. He then bought the black votes by bestowing favors on a handful of black leaders such as the legendary Bill Dawson.

Gaining trust and building effective working relationships in communities and with their leaders is a difficult and fascinating process, and the experience and challenges of each of these five test site communities was different. Connecting the *communities* to an integrated, vastly more responsive state system is at the heart of the reform effort. In each site the collaboratives developed their priorities, and then government policies were changed and workers redeployed to make things happen. Jobs as the key to self-sufficiency were at the top of each community's priorities, and each found a way to integrate the far-flung and uncoordinated state services. There is no other way to make the billions in state and federal dollars responsive to the problems faced by the ladies in the backyard, unemployed miners, and Waukegan Hispanic immigrants than by linking grass roots issues—which vary from community to community—to people in government who are at a high-enough level to make decisions and to change things.

Reactions of longtime state employees who became involved in finding out what communities needed to create a ladder of opportunity to self-sufficiency and jobs are an important part of the community story. The historic process in which state workers actually changed jobs to meet the priorities established by the community, and the comments such as "Don't ever make me go back to the old way of working" of the initial state employees whose assignments were dramatically changed as government responded to community needs are exciting and encouraging. We're freeing up the good people who have been trapped for years in a bad system.

From my personal point of view, the community work was both the most difficult and the most rewarding part of the challenge. Trust is hard to gain in these new and vastly different environments, but wonderfully satisfying when it is achieved. In the course of this multi-year effort, Sokoni, B. Herbert, Marrice, Farmer Grover, Margo, Lucy, Dolores, Frank, Greg, and many others in these varied communities showed me by their actions and words that I had earned their trust. They then became champions of community-based reform, and it became increasingly clear that the political cost to state leaders of turning back would be greater than the political risk of going ahead. Each of these champions had a real interest in helping to better their communities and, as it became clear that we could really deliver the connection to state decision makers, our common ground broadened and strengthened. Lots of well-placed favorable stories in community newspapers about the state reform effort added to the momentum. A powerful force for change had been unleashed.

I learned big things, developing, for example, the conviction that any community, even one with one of the worst demographics in the nation, has assets that can be built upon. Quality leadership is usually one of those assets. Each community also has other assets, such as the location of the Grand Boulevard community, only a half-hour bus ride from the downtown of one of our country's great cities. There are also skills—a disproportionately high proportion of the residents in poor communities are capable of such activities as fixing cars, carpentry, and other trades, since they've typically been unable to hire others to do this work. There is tremendous leverage connecting volunteers such as Mike Boer in Springfield to the community/state job-finding effort.

There is still much to be done to maximize the contribution and impact of the Illinois collaboratives as a force for grass roots change. There are more opportunities to make a difference in the additional areas of foster care (where all too many kids are shipped out of the communities where they live), juvenile justice, and community economic development, for example. In addition, there is a long way to go before every community in the state and in the nation has a collaborative, but we now know how to do it and how it works. We are on our way.

Perhaps most important, my belief that most of the people on welfare have many of the same hopes, dreams, and values as the rest of us, despite their presence in distressed neighborhoods, has been strengthened. Even though they may not have any successful role models, and badly need a caring adult mentor, most people on welfare and in poverty (an unscientific 90+ percent by my reckoning) place a very high value on doing a good job raising their kids, getting a job, and avoiding the gang bangers and drug dealers. My excitement that we're on the right track grows, along with my empathy. Nepal and Harvey put me on the right track—there is nothing I would rather do.

PRINCIPAL POINTS

1. Only in communities can *all* the ingredients (churches, schools, small businesses, etc.) come together in a way to create a ladder of opportunity that can enable people to turn their lives around.
2. Since government spending (an estimated $10,000 per person in poverty nationwide) is by far the largest resource, successful reform *requires* linking government to communities.
3. An effective, broadly representative community group, perceived by the community as truly representative, can be created in eighteen to twenty-four months from scratch, or built upon an existing organization. The opportunity to have an impact on the vast state resources is the primary incentive for voluntary participation.
4. A community should, early on, pick a specific, tangible project that addresses an important community problem, that draws on several state programs or departments, and that requires the state to redeploy workers, redeploy funds, or otherwise change the way of delivering services, and make it work.
5. To help a community become effective, government should designate liaisons to each community to help negotiate the changes in

the way the state does things that are necessary to facilitate self-sufficiency.

6. In even the most impoverished communities there are wonderful people who will come together around the self-sufficiency challenge.

7. Communities are usually different than local governments (especially in big cities), and vary dramatically within a given city and across a state and the nation.

7

Employers and Tough Welfare Cases—Enlightened Self-Interest and a Reasonable Business Risk

Work keeps at bay three great evils: boredom, vice, and need.
—Voltaire

The greatest charity is to enable the poor to earn a living.
—Talmud

Janice walked into the conference room at the big United Parcel Service package-sorting hub in Chicago, alternating between self-confidence and shyness. She looked directly at me, then averted her gaze. Janice was part of Grand Boulevard's initial effort to connect hard-core unemployed to jobs, an effort paralleled by initiatives undertaken in each of the Governor's Task Force community sites. We were in a building physically only a few miles from Grand Boulevard, but part of a world that was as far away in some ways as the mountains of Nepal. She had been working successfully for UPS for over two years now, sorting packages on the morning shift. This is hard work, both physically and mentally. For hours the conveyer belt brings an endless stream of packages, and each must be identified by destination and placed into one of a number of slots to send it on the next leg of the trip. Mistakes can be traced back to the sorter. Electronic tracking shows exactly at which point a package headed for

Tampa was placed erroneously on the conveyor belt with packages headed for the West Coast. Individual workers are rated and rewarded on the basis of keeping missorts to a minuscule percentage, because missorts lead to a late package. On-time delivery goals are a crucial focus for everyone from the UPS chairman to Janice, and poor performance leads to dismissal of anyone who doesn't meet standards, including her bosses. It occurred to me as I looked at her that she was much more accountable than her caseworkers used to be. Janice had been told by her mentor at UPS, Larue Martin, who arranged a series of one-on-one interviews for me, that "Gary is one of the governor's people who wants to get your thoughts on welfare and work, and he is a friend."

When each of the five community test sites, after much discussion at all levels, came up with their own priorities and plans for what they wanted to accomplish for their communities by working with the state, employers turned out to be really central players. In one form or another, successfully connecting people on welfare to jobs emerged at the top of each community's list. The image of most welfare recipients being lazy was disproved time after time, so the challenge really became one of getting the pieces together to make successful employment happen—building that ladder of opportunity. Understanding people like Janice and her relationship with her employer was crucial.

Janice was dressed neatly in work clothes, looking trim and quite a bit younger than her thirty-one years. She had a package sorter's bar code reader strapped to her wrist. I sensed a feistiness in her. After I had gotten her a Coke, we sat across from each other at the corner of the table. She stared at her Coke and the empty chair next to me as I explained to her that she could help me understand what was necessary to help other people like her get and hold a job—she could help me help her friends. I saw her as one of the ladies in the backyard, and was excited about what I might learn from her.

I asked Janice what she thought of her job, and she started to talk. "It's really hard work, but I like it. I enjoy coming to work and learning different things. It is important to me that my kids see me going off to work and know that I have a real job." She looked me squarely in the eye when she mentioned her kids and she conveyed a real feeling of determination. "I'm trying to get more overtime. Sometimes it seems like I have a thousand bosses, and I know some of them don't like women." It's clear she's had some problems adapting to the intense UPS work environment, but she says it in a way that tells me she's pretty much adjusted to it. As I sat with her and listened to her talk about her job, I felt proud of her and felt she had potential to do much more—perhaps become a supervisor, something she mentioned later. But I haven't really begun to hear the whole story.

"How did you get this job?" I asked.

She said she heard that "the Grand Boulevard Federation was helping people with problems who wouldn't normally get hired get jobs." The federation had announced the joint state/community/UPS jobs program at one of its meetings, and various federation members had put notices around the community in churches, schools, and private agencies. A community word-of-mouth network also stirred up interest. The small federation staff, made up of Greg Washington and an assistant, was now operating out of space in Grand Boulevard donated by the Illinois Department of Employment Security (the local unemployment office) and they coordinated the initial effort. I had persuaded UPS that it was reasonable to drop some of the normal employment requirements, given the willingness of the state and community to provide help. Janice applied, and her problem-filled background was actually a plus, since the community and the state wanted to be sure that the employee group hired was truly representative of the tougher, more-troubled segment of the welfare population, and UPS was willing to see what was possible. Janice dropped out of Tilden High School in the eleventh grade to have her first son, now fourteen years old. She subsequently had two more children—a daughter now twelve, and another son, now nine. She had suffered bouts of depression, occasionally resorting to "reefer," but, she says, not hard drugs. She has been on welfare for fourteen years, and prior to UPS never had a real job.

By now she seemed relaxed, and settled back in the conference room chair. She went on. "I've missed part of my work on ten days this past year, and this is more than UPS allows, based on the union contract. The packages must get there on time, and if someone who is scheduled isn't there, it's a problem. I live at State and Forty-ninth Street in the Robert Taylor Homes, and this is a gang border, and there is lots of shootin'. The gang bangers know that kids have to get off to school, so the mornings are usually okay, but sometimes I'll get a call that they are shooting in the early afternoon, and the kids can't get home from school." This rings a bell with me. I remember a woman at one of the Grand Boulevard meetings telling me that her kids miss lots of school because of violence, and that she has, in effect, chosen illiteracy over death for them.

Janice was starting to talk very freely, and she told me that her sister and brothers broke into her apartment while she was at work and "stole my stuff for drug money. They are jealous of my job and that I'm doin' good." I subsequently learned that this horrible phenomenon is relatively common, and is called the "crab effect" by psychologists—a desire by a group to pull back in and down one of its members who is making them feel jealous by breaking out. Janice has seven sisters and six brothers with serious problems of their own. For example, her twenty-five-year-old sister "is messed up with drugs," has seven kids, "can't read labels and doesn't care." Janice's mother is overwhelmed with family problems, and her father is "in and out," occasionally giving her mother some money. The father of Janice's oldest son is a drug dealer, and has given no child support.

She is the same age as my older son. I was struck by the sobering contrast—Gary Jr.'s life was guided lovingly every step of the way: Indian guides, extensive foreign travel, plenty of one-on-one time with his mother and father, mother home when he got home from school, his own computer at age twelve, Andover, a job at Radio Shack at age sixteen, Stanford engineering, partner in a venture capital firm at age twenty-four, president of a high-tech company at age twenty-six, and founder of a successful software company start-up at age twenty-eight. One child had a great ladder of opportunity presented at birth, the other child faced a ladder whose first rung would be beyond her reach, no matter how tall she grew to be.

Added to Janice's challenges was state bureaucracy that was not used to welfare recipients working. In an enlightened new approach, welfare payments in Illinois are now reduced gradually as earnings from employment increase—one dollar deducted for every three dollars earned. The old way was an almost immediate cutoff of all supports, which, given the costs (transportation, clothing, etc.) associated with work, often left the working person worse off than when on welfare. Most conservatives and liberals would agree that people who work, even at entry level wages or part time, should be better off than those who don't, and Illinois did something about it—restoring the incentive to work. Many states still have not. The state pays for child care and, having passed her trial period, Janice has medical insurance and other benefits for her family from UPS, eliminating government Medicaid costs.

But all was not smooth for Janice in making this big change. At one point a bureaucratic snafu resulted in a premature cutoff of her reduced state check, and she ran out of cash. Enter Delrice Adams, the redeployed state-funded caseworker from a private agency, now a dedicated self-sufficiency coach, who wears a beeper that connects her to Janice and twenty-four others like her. Delrice connects them to all needed state services including alcohol and substance abuse and mental health. For the Governor's Task Force pilot program, Delrice was the one stop for services. On one occasion, Delrice showed up with a bag of groceries to keep Janice from crisis. Delrice then straightened out the bureaucratic problem, using her connections with the state through the Grand Boulevard Federation. Another time, Janice was summoned for a 2:00 P.M. meeting with a caseworker from Project Chance, one of many unconnected government programs. Failure to show would also have risked the loss of that reduced check. Ironically, Project Chance is a program designed to help people get jobs. Delrice got Project Chance off Janice's back and made sure that Janice stayed out of further trouble with the bureaucracy.

Time and again the problem of fragmentation of the many bureaucracies rears its ugly head. Why can't all services come together in a single caseworker like Delrice? In addition to helping Janice with the bureaucracy, Delrice helped get her on her feet after the robbery and makes visits to her in her home, meeting with her at least once a month. Delrice will not make home visits during the summer because of increased gunfire, so Janice comes to Delrice's office during those months. Delrice, like other redeployed workers, loves her new job, because she has the flexibility to solve problems, whatever they might be, and can see real results—people breaking out of dependency and the poverty cycle.

The creation of the self-sufficiency coach position and the assignment of Delrice to it goes to the heart of the community involvement idea and the need to reform government systems from the bottom up. The community knew the people who needed jobs and the kind of transition help that was required. The state liaisons from each department who met regularly with the Grand Boulevard Federation entered into a negotiation process to figure out a way to try this new community idea. The state representatives struggled with various ways to come up with self-sufficiency coaches, and ended up deciding that they would pull people from some private agencies that were funded by the state. They took into consideration the fact that the nonunion private employees would be more likely to be available outside normal working hours and that some of the background and training was more suitable. Remaining work at the two agencies that loaned self-sufficiency coaches to the federation was redistributed. Undoubtedly these private agencies sought to get "credit" in their next state contract and were disappointed in the state's decision that Delrice's new job was more valuable than her old one, which was casework without the strong job and community connections. This type of "negotiation" went on in one form or another for all of the initiatives in each of the test site communities. Of course the state liaisons for each department in each community knew that their department heads sitting on the task force were supporting the redeployment recommendations. Imagine, government shifting resources around in response to communities!

In the course of our hour together, Janice said, "Without Delrice I wouldn't've made it." She also said, "Without Larue I wouldn't've made it." Larue, an assistant in the human resources department at UPS, has been assigned to mentor this group of employees, helping them be successful within the parameters of a very strong work ethic at UPS and very rigid union rules. This means counseling on lateness ("The packages on the conveyor belt won't wait—the load falls on your fellow employees") and other job-related problems. Larue, a six-foot-eleven former Portland Trailblazers basketball player from Chicago's inner city, already had a full-time job handling the many community relations activities and responsibilities that fall to a major community-minded employer in a big city. He somehow found the time to invest with this group of new employees who were hired without the normal qualifications. As a former inner-city resident, he cares about them, and they know it. They can count on him to respond to a call. Among other challenges, he finds himself squeezed between union pressures and the learning speed of his mentees. How can you show more flexibility on lateness, absenteeism, and back talk to supervisors for this group while disciplining others? When management ignores an infraction of the rules, union stewards are understandably quick to ask for relief for others who were disciplined for those same infractions. In addition, UPS has always been a highly disciplined organization focused on efficient, on-time delivery—flexibility on work rules is not common.

Larue evaluated Janice's early absences and decided to work with her supervisor and the union to keep her on the payroll. It was worth it. He meets regularly with his welfare-to-work cadre and helps educate other supervisors on what is needed to successfully assimilate these employees. Larue and Delrice talk frequently. It's probable that Delrice and Larue are the only reliable, caring adults in Janice's life. Delrice helps with the adjustment problems outside the workplace and Larue handles those inside. They're a great team, but Janice is the star player.

Before she went back to work, I asked her some policy questions, figuring she had better instincts for the behavior of people on welfare than most academics and policymakers. "What do you think of welfare reform?"

"It should've happened ten years ago. People get lazy if they're paid for not working," she answers.

"What about the limit on the number of children who qualify for welfare payments [the family cap]? "That will cut the number of kids," she says, mentioning as an aside that she has had her tubes tied. With that comment I *knew* I had succeeded in making her feel comfortable!

"If we're successful in finding opportunities like UPS for the others you know on welfare, what proportion would you guess will succeed?" I asked. "At least 50 percent," she answered, and I'm mindful that her group in public housing has negligible work experience, limited education, longtime welfare participation, and lots of problems.

Joyce Aldridge, a colleague of Janice's at UPS, estimated that 75 percent of the people she knew on welfare would work if they had the chance. Joyce has also been successful, completing her first year at UPS and getting good recommendations from her supervisors. Joyce became pregnant in the eleventh grade and dropped out. With three daughters, ages ten, eight, and six, and after ten years on welfare, her only job experiences were a brief stint with a suburban post office which required an unsustainable three-hour commute each way, and another five-month experience with an auto parts store where she "cursed out her supervisor who hit on her." She tells me that the father of her oldest child is in prison on a drug offense, and prior to coming to UPS she was also taking care of a sister's children because of a child abuse ruling against the sister. Joyce said, "Delrice is my big inspiration. I talk to her every month, and I have her pager number if I have trouble. Without her I wouldn't've made it. She even found a summer camp for my kids that I could afford." Joyce ended up telling me she was planning to drive a package car some day before long and become a UPS stockholder! Package car drivers, known to the world for their brown uniforms, brown trucks, and friendly smiles, make about $60,000 per year, including fringe benefits.

Delrice Adams is an angel. A very pretty twenty-eight-year-old African-American divorcée with an eight-year-old daughter, she has already made a huge difference in other people's lives. Her delicate appearance and soft-spoken demeanor belie an iron-willed determination to help people succeed. Her father was a teacher, and she was smart enough to get a scholarship to the University of California at Berkeley. Upon graduation she went to work for the Bank of America, and was doing well, but then decided to take the pay cut that comes with social work in return for the satisfaction of helping others. I asked her why she felt this need to help others, and like the many others I asked, she wasn't sure, but she added that the experience of dealing with alcoholism in her family might have been a factor.

Delrice knows intimately the people in the roughest housing projects in Chicago—the people many would put at the very bottom of our society. Her estimate of the situation fits reasonably well with what we learned from the ladies in the backyard, Joyce, Janice, and the others. "With help, at least 70 percent of this hard core group can work and become self-sufficient. The women at UPS no longer think of welfare as their alternative, but rather the possibility of other jobs. Their ability to hold a tough job at UPS has given them confidence that they belong in the world of work. Most of them are preparing for the next step. Both Janice and Joyce are studying for their GED, since it is required before they can be supervisors at UPS."

Delrice gave me her estimates on the overall situation of her public housing clients. "I'd guess about 50 percent of the women on welfare experience depression, probably brought on by the many traumas they have experienced, and the general hopelessness of life as they see it. About 70 percent abuse alcohol and drugs, with about 20 percent seriously dependent. Of the women on welfare, I would guess that about 10 percent of them have felony records, and of their men, 75 percent have felony records." Delrice also mentioned a preliminary effort with UPS in hiring ex-offenders—a crucial element of the welfare challenge. "One of our new UPS ex-offender hires, Ken Morris, hopes to use his new job to get custody of his three kids from their drug-addicted mother. The mother has seven other children, and they are all in the child welfare system due to abuse or neglect. This ex-offender project can make a huge difference." This is exciting to me, because it is a breakthrough on one of the most extreme cases. The average urban welfare mother has two kids and is a drug user, but not an addict. The felon father is typical, but normally he can't get a legitimate job. Once again Grand Boulevard and UPS are providing a ladder to climb. Ken and his kids have a shot at a real life.

In the first quarter of 1999 after over two years, thirty-four of forty-seven employees in the first Grand Boulevard Federation welfare-to-work group were on the job at UPS. The people selected for this very demanding work were among the toughest to place in the welfare pool. Normally they would not have been hired since, like the ladies in the backyard, they had almost no work experience, no high school diploma, and lots of additional problems. However, this group had a turnover rate *substantially lower* than the turnover of the average UPS hires. At the two-year point, the group on welfare had a turnover rate at least four times lower than the UPS average—a huge plus for UPS, given the substantial hiring and training costs. Four were terminated, one was incarcerated, and two resigned without explanation. The other six who left have not been tracked, but one woman took courses after work, qualified as a licensed practical nurse, and left for full-time work. The self-sufficiency coaches encourage all of them to take courses, and a significant number are following through. Three went on to other part-time employment, two returned to school full time. With successful UPS experience, they are more employable and able to go on to other jobs if they wish.

Though a rigorous academic evaluation was not run to isolate the important variables, and the evaluation would be difficult in any event, it's useful to identify the success factors. The self-sufficiency coach is probably the biggest reason for the remarkably low turnover rate. In addition, UPS has learned that for certain types of jobs the high school credential and work history requirements may have been keeping them from some good workers. These workers are more appreciative of their jobs and probably less likely to jump to other jobs than those with stronger histories. Some form of mentoring is also important, but it's also possible that there would be a payoff to UPS from more mentoring for *all* entry-level employees. Since most welfare recipients are single women with children, it's possible that the strong desire to help their families move toward a better life is a motivator that makes it harder to quit. On the cautionary side, since employees in the UPS Grand Boulevard Federation group had to volunteer, it's possible they may be more motivated than others deep in the welfare pool. However, I'm convinced that with encouragement, most welfare recipients would volunteer. The biggest and most exciting consideration is that the UPS women have been on welfare a long time, are high school dropouts, have little or no employment history, and lots of problems. Many said it couldn't be done.

The economics of this welfare-to-work investment are attractive to both the employer and the state. As shown in the accompanying chart (Figure 8), the cost of a self-sufficiency coach, additional child care in some cases, and other state expenses are more than offset by the reduced (and eventually eliminated) welfare payments, not to mention reduced use of other services (child welfare, mental health care, drug treatment, food stamps, etc.). We should also remember that Delrice is a caseworker redeployed from other state-funded work, and thus does not represent new spending. In my opinion, most government departments and systems have considerable slack and nonproductive activities, and meaningful gains can be made by redeploying resources. Delrice coaches twenty-five employees and can take on more as her group of employees gains experience on the job and as the most experienced employees no longer need her. This can vary from three months to two years, depending upon the difficulty of the problems. At the level of twenty-five employees, her cost per employee is only $120 per month, including fringe benefits, the discretionary support funds for emergency groceries, bus tokens, office costs, etc. Reduced government spending is at least twice that amount, even though the UPS job is a part-time, eighteen-hour-a-week, entry level position. Even part-time, Janice's family income increases $350 per month, not counting improved medical and other benefits, and the comparisons will improve as she gains experience and tenure on the job. In addition, despite the sibling break-in, the value of Janice and others as working role models in Robert Taylor Homes is almost incalculably important in my view, and the chances of her family members ending up in the expensive justice and prison systems are dramatically reduced.

One of the big problems in justifying investments in human ser-

FIGURE 8. THE SELF-SUFFICIENCY COACH
INVESTMENT PAYS OFF

WORKING FAMILY INCOME (3 CHILDREN)

UPS wages	$624/month*
Reduced welfare check	$230/month
Food stamps	$245/month
Total income	$1,099/month + medical after 90 days

COST TO GOVERNMENT

	Not Working	*Working*
Welfare check	$375	$230
Food stamps	$360	$245
Child care	—	$259**
Self-sufficiency coach	—	$120***
	$735	$854
Medical	$300	—
Total	$1,035/mo.	$854/mo. = $181/mo. savings to government

Working family income	$1,099
Nonworking income	$ 735
Family gain	$ 364/month

* UPS starting wages @ $8/hr., 18 hrs./wk., 4⅓ wks./mo. = $624/mo.
** $1/hr per child $8/day, $4/half-day
***Wages, fringe benefits, and expenses allocated over 25 clients

Note: All numbers as of 1997

vices has always been the argument that the investments could normally only be justified by longer term, tough-to-prove returns, e.g., failure to spend more money on a social service now will result in more people in prison at the cost to the taxpayers of over $38,000 per prisoner per year—the cost of most colleges. While the connection is surely correct, it is long-term, and tough to sell politically. By contrast, the welfare-to-work economics of the Illinois model give taxpayers an immediate, direct return on their investment.

UPS kept close track of any extra costs incurred (e.g., part of Larue's time), and the lower rate of turnover (compared to the average hire) produced, on balance, big savings. Reducing turnover is a very major savings for most companies, particularly those that are labor intensive. Learning how to broaden the labor pool is valuable to UPS in many parts of the country where labor is tight. In addition, UPS managers also know that being a good corporate citizen has an indirect payoff in customer goodwill. Finally, taxes, which are heavily influenced by human services spending, will hopefully be less onerous in the future. UPS truly believes this welfare-to-work effort is enlightened self-interest. Other employers are also joining in, and a broader acceptance is emerging.

The significance of this state/community/employer collaboration is profound, in my view, since unlike most welfare recipients put to work in the first phase of welfare reform, this successful, low turnover group was selected from deep in the welfare pool—no high school diploma or GED, no substantive work experience, and a problem-filled home life in the public housing projects. In other words, the cycle has been broken, and *we now know how to do it*. In addition, the economics make sense for the worker and the taxpayer.

Perhaps these employees value the jobs more than other employees because they had given up hope. If UPS had been unwilling to drop its normal entry level requirement of high school graduation and previous work experience, the company wouldn't have unlocked the potential of the large labor pool Joyce, Janice, and her colleagues, the ladies in the backyard, represent. By 2004, UPS had hired more than 60,000 people from the welfare rolls nationwide.

As awareness of this potential labor pool grows, my guess is that employers will drop the high school graduation and previous work experience barriers when they know they have communities and government standing behind the welfare recipients making this crucial transition. UPS found, with the community support and the initial insurance provided by the self-sufficiency coaches, that hiring women like Janice and Joyce had turned from a "reasonable business risk" into good business.

Clearly, from the examples of Janice, Joyce, and many others, several keys to success have emerged:

First, the redeployment of state or state-financed workers to newly created self-sufficiency coach positions—broadly based caseworkers who, in addition to connecting clients with a full range of services in one stop also ensure a successful placement, keeping track of the employee and his/her family *after* the employee is on the job. This is now being done statewide in Illinois, and Delrice is leading in the retraining effort.

Second, where there is a group of welfare recipients with an individual employer, the assignment of an experienced employee as a part-time mentor on the job, or in a smaller organization, the designation of someone to take a personal interest in helping the new employee adjust to the dramatically different nonwelfare environment is important.

The self-sufficiency coach idea was created primarily *by the community,* and is a crucial missing piece in most job training and placement programs. The community leaders believed that the many training programs funded by the government over the years have been largely ineffective, and that the more important need was in the area of the "soft skills" required for *retaining* a job—punctual attendance, willingness to work hard and take direction, and personal crisis problem-solving. They also knew that their people could do it, but needed transition coaching and mentoring. They were right. Washington and Springfield were likely to throw money at Janice, Joyce, and her colleagues the rest of their lives if the community did not step in.

Joyce and Janice have school-aged children, so their child care requirements are limited to after-school needs. They also have the advantage of a work location in the city, reachable by bus. However, child care and transportation are two of the most prominent challenges to be met in the welfare-to-work effort.

The ladies in the backyard, Joyce, Janice, and others taught us that the overwhelming majority of women on welfare care deeply about their children and want to do what it takes to help them toward a better life. The sensational cases of child abuse, usually drug-related, are the exception. There isn't enough room for an entry-level worker to pay for child care in the initial move from welfare to an entry level job, and it's very much in all of our interests that the move take place. To help put this issue in perspective, it's important to know that the average cost of day care for a child under two in Illinois is $34 per day.[1] This adds up to 83 percent of the $206 per week earned by a minimum wage worker. Informal care by neighbors is likely to be less, but the economic message is similar. Illinois has substantially increased its child care budget for just this reason, and it includes a provision for unregulated care by friends and neighbors. As a teenager I was a paid baby-sitter for kids in the neighborhood for a few years, and it was a sort of starter job. The parents made the judgment that their kids were safe with me, though I doubt that I provided them with much intellectual stimulation or personal growth.

We read the debate about licensing of child care workers and facilities, paying them more, etc. Care by neighbors makes particular sense since most welfare-to-work candidates don't have cars to drive to a day care center. Care by neighbors also provides jobs in the heart of disadvantages areas, putting cash directly in the hands of working poor people, rather than middle-class providers. In Illinois, child care by seniors is a growing idea with considerable potential and important cultural side benefits. To me, most mothers are more effective evaluators of the care their children are getting than government inspectors, and the key is to make sure that there is enough child care money available to poor people so that they can go to work responsibly and stay on the job. In Illinois this means eligibility for child care help, whether on welfare or not, until a certain income level is reached.

Some conservatives will say, "If they can't afford child care, they shouldn't have had the kids in the first place," but we have to face up to the fact that there are still 5 million recipients on the welfare rolls,[2] and we need to get a member of most of these welfare families a real job. Conservatives should be happy that the family cap limits any monetary incentive to bringing additional kids into the world, and the time limit on welfare ends welfare as a way of life. Child care helps clean up the mistakes of past policies and practices, both personal and governmental.

Transportation is a tougher issue, and many of the answers do not come from overall policy changes. Usually, creativity has to be applied on a case-by-case basis. The jobs tend to be in the suburbs, and the preponderance of chronically unemployed are in the central cities. Policy wonks call this "spatial mismatch," and there is general agreement that it is a serious problem, and one that was not much thought about until welfare reform. Since most really poor people can't afford cars, and we want them to work, it makes sense to help them come up with some public transportation options in order to get started. Imagine not having a car and being unable to afford a cab! Joyce lost one of her only jobs in ten years on welfare because it was not realistically accessible by public transportation, as did Kathy, one of our ladies in the backyard. In fact, the jobs of some of the UPS night-sort workers were threatened when a late-night bus schedule was cut back. The company and the community intervened to preserve the bus schedule and the jobs. Repairing this part of the ladder of opportunity isn't rocket science, but it often requires collaboration among parts of government, employers, and the community.

Transportation is a welfare-to-work barrier in all of our major metropolitan areas, and it is especially acute in rapidly growing car-dependent cities like Atlanta and Los Angeles. The issues are often bus schedules and routes and the linkages between various transportation modes. If an employee takes the Metra commuter train from downtown Chicago to Palatine, will the train connect with a bus that will go by the factory? And can this happen early enough to get to work at 7:30 A.M.? What about going back to the city after working overtime? This challenge requires new thinking across administrative boundaries by governments, within the new paradigm of workers reverse-commuting. As part of the Illinois human services reform effort, a state planner shaded a map of Chicago's communities to show the areas where the most welfare recipients are located (Figure 2, page

88). The high density areas are often isolated and the need to modify transportation systems for the previously unrecognized requirement to get poor people out to jobs in the suburbs is clear.

Along with the longer-term systemic improvements, shorter-term "hand-crafted" transportation solutions must be developed by communities, government, and employers. The Springfield Federation's arrangement of transportation for workers after 6:00 P.M. when public transportation shut down is a good example. In Chicago, United Airlines made a major commitment to hire welfare workers for an expansion in Elk Grove Village out near O'Hare Airport. After working for United for a while, most workers will be able to afford a car, but that doesn't help in getting started, especially since many people on welfare have no savings and make decent housing a higher priority than a car. A large number don't even have a telephone.

This problem was addressed creatively by the state's Welfare to Work Clearing House when they pinpointed for hire welfare recipients on the northwest side of the city who lived within walking distance of the Chicago Transit Authority Blue Line to O'Hare. Also, the airline has persuaded public bus systems in Chicago and its suburbs to extend services so city workers can reach United's reservation call centers scattered throughout the suburbs. United hired more than one thousand workers formerly on welfare in the Elk Grove Village/ O'Hare area and elsewhere for such jobs as ramp workers and reservation agents. Gary Jefferson, who headed United's welfare-to-work program, stated that "the issue that overshadows everything else is transportation."

There are many reasons why it usually makes no sense for employers to move to the inner city, even with tax incentives. It is also clear there are important reasons why people on welfare find it extremely difficult, economically and culturally, to move to the suburbs. They can't afford it, don't want to leave family and friends, have no car, and know that racial discrimination is still an issue in some suburban housing and in other ways.

However, the transportation barrier is fixable and it doesn't take rocket science. It simply needs to be addressed the old-fashioned way: by every community in every state on a job-by-job, employer-by-employer basis. Government hasn't thought much about this in the past, but now that transportation is central to the welfare-to-work challenge every governor faces, somebody at a high level of government needs to take on the responsibility of working with employers and local transportation systems to solve this puzzle on a case-by-case basis. Some of the money saved by reducing the caseload can be redeployed to financing vans, modifying routes and times of public transportation, subsidizing welfare transportation passes, or even taxis. Trains from suburbs to the city can modify schedules and fares for inner-city workers commuting out, not just office workers coming in. When earnings get up to a self-sufficiency level, subsidies can be eliminated and/or a car can be afforded. Some broader solutions are possible, such as better bus service geared to employment in rural areas like the Southern Seven or sprawling suburbs like those in our DuPage test site, subsidized to some degree if necessary.

Another good example of creative problem-solving in the transportation area is the highly successful partnership between United Parcel Service and the Southeastern Pennsylvania Transportation Authority (SEPTA). This partnership created a bus route to the Philadelphia airport—helping welfare recipients overcome one of the major barriers from gaining employment at the airport. The route, which was begun in 1993 by UPS and then transferred to SEPTA in 1995, has grown from four buses to eighty. Over 500,000 riders have used this service. The lesson here is that transit authorities need to open their eyes to nontraditional uses of their systems—connecting distressed neighborhoods that haven't traditionally been well served to jobs, and providing fast-growing employers with a supply of workers. Metropolitan transit systems should play a key role in correcting the geographic mismatch between people and jobs, and as the UPS/SEPTA experience shows, the demand and economics will be there if the routes are thoughtfully chosen. Since most transit systems were set up before the shift of jobs to the suburbs, it's not surprising that considerable adaptation is required. It is easy to forget that most people on welfare, especially in the inner city, don't have cars.

Continued thoughtful work on eliminating the transportation barriers will be an important part of the next phase of the welfare-to-work challenge both in Illinois and nationally. We *know* the answers, even though they can't be put neatly into a one-size-fits-all, top-down government policy.

The DuPage Federation had a different, but related, situation as it addressed family self-sufficiency. Despite severe unemployment in the welfare population, there was only 2 percent unemployment overall in this booming county. Entry-level jobs were available, but transportation was a major barrier, and the child care providers, able to raise their prices to meet private demand, had raised prices beyond the reach of the state-subsidized vouchers—another example of why one size does not fit all. The DuPage Federation adopted a goal: "Eighty percent of DuPage families who need it will have child care that is affordable, accessible, available, and of high quality within four years." Among other actions, the federation held a workshop for churches on child care, and now five church-based centers are accepting subsidized children, and several other congregations are providing after-school care or help in other ways. Of one hundred families in the first group taken on to pilot the new integrated one-stop approach to human services, sixty have found employment with a wide variety of employers, and postemployment follow-up is provided.

Among the creative federation projects with employers is a joint project with the DuPage YWCA and ServiceMaster, a janitorial services supplier. A private building owner awarded a contract for janitorial services to the DuPage YWCA. The YWCA provided training, case management services, and other supports, and became the owner of the janitorial business. Over twenty welfare recipients got jobs, and several of them went on to higher-paying jobs with other ServiceMaster contractors. Taken together, DuPage is another good example of the all-too-rare practice of government working together with a broadly based private sector community collaborative to achieve real results. Again, this is a very different and much more productive process than the common practice of government funding private nonprofit organizations.

To help generate employer interest and to get the governor some press exposure on the overall welfare-to-work issue, Governor Edgar asked me to help put together the Governors CEO Welfare to Work Summit at the Hyatt Hotel in Chicago. About forty CEOs attended, representing a wide range of employers, including Sears, United Airlines, Marriott, Commonwealth Edison, Spiegels, Dominicks (a big regional food chain), big hospitals, and the like. After describing some success stories to them and outlining the major changes the Illinois state government was making, we asked them to share their ideas and concerns. Interestingly, they too conveyed the strong message that their primary requirement for their entry-level jobs is people who 1) show up for work every day and on time, 2) are willing to work and take direction from their supervisors, and 3) get along with their fellow workers. No one mentioned a need for GED or special training— if the "soft skills" of reliability are there, they will take care of the rest. Tax incentives weren't on the list.

The CEOs were much encouraged by the movement to involve communities in selecting and supporting welfare-to-work candidates and by the self-sufficiency coaches, figuring that these steps would enhance the odds of workers showing up with the requisite soft skills. They committed to a meaningful number of hires on the spot and suggested the state set up an 800 number as a clearinghouse for when they needed entry-level employees. The historic disconnect between welfare offices and employers showed up in sharp relief—each was aware of the other's existence, but they inhabited, up until now, different worlds. The 800 number would help. The follow-through was sincere, and the summit led to hundreds of jobs for welfare recipients in addition to increased employer awareness statewide.

The governor's CEO summit was helpful, but it brought together primarily larger employers, and the majority of this country's job growth in recent years has been with small to medium-sized companies. For years we've been reading about the giants downsizing, restructuring, and eliminating thousands of jobs. Then the unemployment numbers come out and they are low—small- and medium-sized companies are absorbing the workers. This means that just signing up the big employers won't do the job. As the Springfield test site showed, a network of smaller employers can be put together by the local federation/collaborative to connect those on welfare to jobs they might not know about or be able to obtain without help. To help communities and local welfare offices build these networks, the state of Illinois provides each community group and each local welfare office with a Dun and Bradstreet list of local employers with twenty-five or more employees. The listing is by zip code and by type of business, with the general manager's or owner's name and phone number. As with raising money, the greatest success occurs when a personal visit is made by a state employee bringing along someone else who has successfully employed former welfare recipients. The key is local small businesses—retailers, hospitals, restaurants, and the like—and the community-based collaboratives can provide major help to the small businesses and people on welfare.

Soon after the five communities established welfare to work as their top priority in one form or another, I invested a considerable amount of time traveling around the state meeting with employers. I saw it as part of my job to convince employers that the state was getting its human services act together, making it *enlightened self-interest* and *a reasonable business risk* for employers to work with the state to hire people from the welfare rolls. As a former business-man, I was heartened at the response from employers of all sizes. The fact that the state was coming to them and explaining how these prospective employees would be assisted and coached by the community and state working together was impressive to them. I explained how, in our test sites, we had stayed with the workers *after* they had been hired to continue the caseworker support and problem solving that is necessary for people with no role models, very limited work experience, and low levels of education. Most employers were willing to try, since the universal concern for entry-level hires almost always related primarily to work habits and reliability, not training in specific skills. To reap the rewards of opening up this new labor pool, I made it clear that employers had to be more flexible, as UPS has been, in their hiring rules—especially in employment history requirements and education. In some parts of the state employers are worried about labor shortages limiting their ability to expand. Expanding the available state labor pool is starting to make sense to them.

What do the academics have to say about all of this? A recent University of Michigan study[3] says: "A sizable [number] of recipients are unable to keep jobs and cycle between work and welfare . . . Evaluations of [two projects] report that a major reason recipients lost their jobs was that they failed to understand the importance of punctuality, the seriousness of absenteeism, and resented or misunderstood the lines of authority and responsibility in the workplace."

A typical response of average Americans, thinking they are putting themselves in the welfare recipient's shoes is, "How can people not know these things?" Of course, the typical middle American can't begin to know what it is like to be in Janice's and Joyce's shoes—a world where nobody they know is a role model for the culture of work, and severe problems make the pressure for tardiness, absenteeism, and antisocial behavior almost overwhelming. As Joyce and Janice have shown, these background limitations can be overcome *on the job,* with some help. As the UPS successes show, we now know what to do to get long-term welfare-dependent people on the road to self-sufficiency. The challenge now is to replicate the self-sufficiency coach/mentoring model economically nationwide—to the great benefit of taxpayers, employers, and most important, newly self-sufficient human beings.

Critics worry about putting people like Janice and Joyce directly to work. Shouldn't they get their GED first? Go to a community college and study nursing or computers? Suppose they get stuck in an entry-level job? There is, of course, value in getting a GED and further training, and Janice and Joyce are being encouraged by their self-sufficiency coaches to do these things along the way. However, the people on the front lines, both community leaders and those on welfare, believe work should happen *now.* Sitting in classes is an act of faith that there is a job on the other end, and often there has not been. When no one in your family has worked, a decent entry-level job is a huge breakthrough. Once this is accomplished, people like Janice and Joyce start thinking about what is next. A good work record at a place like UPS is something other employers look at—a base has been established, in addition to giant leaps in self-confidence.

Once employers have a good worker, tuition reimbursement, on-site training, and part-time school opportunities often open up. Strengthening the capabilities of present workers—promoting from within—is thought by most employers to be preferable to new outside hiring. At the end of the first year, one of the UPS Grand Boulevard workers was promoted to supervisor. There are cases where promotion from within is not a likely or an attractive path for the employee, but many of us can look back at our very first job—such as mine pumping gas and cleaning restrooms—and see it as a valuable learning experience, a bottom rung on the ladder, even though not part of a direct path to a long-term career.

The discovery that welfare recipients can succeed with a "work first" approach is not limited to our Illinois effort. In Riverside County, California, caseworkers also did the unthinkable—telling recipients to take a job, any job, and forego long-term training and education for the present. Riverside's Work First approach raised work rates and income levels and reduced welfare costs far more impressively than any other county in California, and five years later, 72 percent still had jobs.[4]

Critics can be counted upon to assail this approach. People on welfare need "good-paying jobs, jobs that will support a family of four"; "hamburger flipping won't do it"; "people must be trained for the high-tech economy," etc. To these people I say, we can have it all, but not on day one. Listen to the employers tell us what they want— the "soft skills" punctuality and a willingness to work at the entry level. *The way to begin to learn about work is to work.* It's just not good judgment to keep Janice and Joyce out of the workforce with the dream of a first job that will support a family of four in a self-sufficient manner. We can't let the perfect be the enemy of the good. Very few of us had a first job that could meet that test.

The Russell Sage Foundation funded a study of McDonald's workers with tough backgrounds from distressed areas. Interestingly, the study[5] shows that a surprisingly large percentage of the subjects experienced the McDonald's job as a first step in a progressively more successful career path, and a very high value was placed on the work habits learned there. McDonald's picked this up with commercials spotlighting individual workers as "future air traffic controller, future orthodontist," and the like. None of this denies the eventual need for Janice and Joyce to get more education and training either on or off the job if they are to maximize their potential.

Community colleges in Illinois, another undermanaged area of government, need major overhaul (not necessarily more money) if the potential of entry-level workers is to be maximized over the longer term. A handful of states, including Texas, Oregon, and Maryland, are tapping the community college potential by making direct connections to the human services systems. The community college system in Illinois and in many other states is highly political, and much work needs to be done to capture this potential in the next phase of reform. Some legislators, together with Linda Mills, an energetic activist for the poor, and I made a preliminary pass at measuring the community colleges' job placement performance, but were met with fierce resistance. A bipartisan hearing called to request performance information produced piles of paper, but very little performance information, and individual system leaders strongly resisted getting measured. It's just not human nature to volunteer to be held accountable publicly.

With help from Linda Mills, Representative Mark Beaubian, a forward-thinking legislator from the suburbs, sponsored an "accountability bill" in the state House of Representatives that called for measuring the various job training and placement programs against the purposes for which they were established—nothing more. The bill had passed the Senate, but was opposed in the House by the community-college lobby. Mark, Linda, and I set up a meeting with the powerful chancellor of the Chicago community colleges, Dr. Wayne Watson. Dr. Watson, a slight, intense-appearing African-American fellow, had a reputation as a shrewd political operator.

As we sat down in the big conference room adjacent to Dr. Watson's office, we were joined by several members of his staff and one of the community-college presidents. They listened as we tried to explain the harmlessness of being measured against the objectives the various programs were set up to accomplish. Mark, a former owner and CEO of a suburban bank who recently entered politics, and I both figured we should be on solid ground. How can you be overtly against accountability?

It was clear by body language and the icy cordiality that we were not on friendly turf. After twenty minutes of our futile efforts to find common ground, Wayne cut to the chase. "Look, we don't want to get measured. If we get measured, people will see how poor the numbers are, and we will lose funding," he said. Wow! Mark, Linda, and I couldn't believe our ears. Once he laid that heinous truth on the table there wasn't much more to say, and the meeting ended. With only days left in the legislative session, the bill died. Needless to say, a logical future step in the next phase of welfare reform is harnessing the untapped community college potential.

As states work through the pool of welfare recipients, the job gets tougher, but it is still very doable. In particular, three important issues emerge, none of them easily measurable, that can become barriers to self-sufficiency for significant portions of the welfare population: drug and/or alcohol dependency, convicted felon status, and mental illness.

As we get deeper into the welfare population, drug use becomes widespread. Just how widespread is hard to measure. With a special effort the state can compare its list of those receiving drug treatment with the welfare rolls, but this would represent only a small fraction of actual drug users. Based on estimates by peers of the ladies in the backyard, drug use in the public housing projects may be close to 70 percent, with about 25 percent having become seriously dependent. Widespread recreational use of drugs, though short of dependency, can be a major barrier to employment and self-sufficiency, since traces show up in pre-employment testing. Joyce will tell you that if there was a belief that real job opportunities existed, most residents would abstain from recreational use to avoid failing the employment test. This sort of catch-22 is successfully dealt with by UPS, where there is no front-end pre-employment drug screening, but employees are warned that they are subject to special testing if there is suspicion of drug use. This allows for a successful transition period and has worked well. Cherry Electric, in Waukegan, has 100 percent pre-employment testing, and this has made it more difficult for the Waukegan Federation to make placements with their largest employer.

Caseworkers often need a sort of sixth sense to detect the more serious drug dependency situations. Minnie Howsley, manager of the welfare office in the very tough Austin neighborhood on Chicago's West Side, tells me of an attractive, articulate woman on welfare with a better than average education and work history who couldn't seem to hold onto a job. The caseworker would connect her with an employer and she would get the job. Everything would be fine for a few weeks and then she would get fired. Minnie decided to put her to work in the Austin welfare office for a while to observe her more closely. Once again, she did very well for a while, but then her behavior became erratic, and it became clear that she had a serious drug problem that she had kept from her caseworker. She was put into drug treatment as a condition of continuing on welfare, and she will be connected again to a job as soon as an employer can be looked in the eye and told that hiring her is a reasonable business risk. As the caseloads come down and more home visits are made by self-sufficiency coaches, these situations will be harder to hide. The interdependence and need for a hand-in-glove linkage between welfare-to-work efforts and drug treatment is a major problem in fragmented systems. When drug treatment is completed, a job should be available right away, improving the odds against recidivism. Based on my personal experience with people on welfare, I strongly believe that *most people on welfare want to work,* even to the point of giving up drugs if there is a work alternative.

Another big issue that we're wrestling with in Illinois is the substantial portion of the inner-city welfare population with a felony record, often incurred in their teens in connection with gangs and drugs. Remembering again vividly the day Charlene and I spent at Stateville Prison, a discussion with "Bill" comes to mind. "When I get out I can't get no job because the form asks if you have a felony record. I don't know what I can do." Or Julius, the young fellow at the Austin office I met in the caseworker interview: "I had to join the gang or get shot on the way to school." Of course we first ran across this problem when we met Maxine, the recent parolee and one of the ladies in the backyard. When they get out, should these people be sentenced to a street corner for the rest of their lives? For large numbers of ex-offenders in their twenties, that's a long time. Where will that lead?

Although most male ex-offenders get food stamps but not welfare, they are commonly the noncustodial parents of kids on welfare. Enabling them to earn a legitimate income bears directly on the self-sufficiency of welfare recipients both from child-support and family stability perspectives. As human services reform integrates services into one stop shopping and works toward self-sufficiency for whole families, a focus on noncustodial parents of welfare children is essential. This means the next phase of welfare reform must also include fathers. This inexorably leads to a stronger paternity establishment process, fierce child support enforcement, and employment of ex-offenders.

In Illinois an effort has begun to work with ex-offenders to find a responsible way out of the ex-offender employment dilemma. Once again, with community involvement and the support and watchful eye of a self-sufficiency coach, selective hiring of ex-offenders becomes a reasonable business risk for appropriate entry-level jobs. The Safer Foundation in Illinois has considerable experience in ex-offender employment, and they have been valuable in helping give employers confidence to participate. Safer works with both men and women ex-offenders on interpersonal and employment attitudes and connects them to participating employers. A key to their effort is the assignment of a "lifeguard," similar to the Grand Boulevard self-sufficiency coaches, who work with the ex-offender, the ex-offender's family, and the employer for the first ninety days to deal promptly with any problems that may arise. If necessary, the lifeguard will stay connected for as long as a year.

In the first group of Grand Boulevard ex-offenders, a particularly interesting example was Edward Jones, a Grand Boulevard fellow who served time in prison almost twenty years earlier and had since become a part-time minister and community leader. However, he had been prevented from getting a mainstream job all that time and was eager for a shot at a UPS job loading packages. Some employers have observed greater energy and leadership ability on the part of ex-offenders compared with normal hires.

Having spent most of my life as an employer, trying to build the highest quality workforce, I find this a tough one—consciously bringing a known troublemaker into my company. However, the forty-years-on-the-street-corner alternative results in all of us paying a price, one way or another. We shouldn't be surprised when the need for survival pushes people who can't get legitimate jobs into crime. Atlanta recently experienced a rash of armed robberies in large homes in its very upscale Buckhead section. Many of the people who live in those homes are successful businesspeople and other leaders who need to think about making a difference by coming up with noncrime alternatives for those who would rob them. I can't say that this cause and effect relationship is morally right, it's just the way things are. Legitimate work, child support—rejoining the world as we know it is the answer for ex-offenders.

Good numbers are lacking, but we know there is a disproportionate share of mental health problems in the long-term, undereducated and problem-plagued welfare population. Joyce mentioned her depression to me, as did others. Studies have documented high levels of depression symptoms among welfare recipients,[6] often traceable to what amounts to life in a war zone. I've had a number of women express their fear of the father of their children. In a study of welfare recipients in New Jersey, 22 percent reported having been raped, 55 percent experienced domestic abuse, and 20 percent reported having been sexually molested as a child.[7] As we know, some problems, such as some types of depression, can be treated if there is access to the proper advice and drugs. These kinds of problems must be under control if employment success is to be achieved. Illinois self-sufficiency coaches spot these issues and arrange for treatment. The integration of mental health services with the welfare-to-work effort becomes increasingly crucial as the more challenging cases are addressed.

Also in the welfare recipient group with no work history and grade school education levels, we find some cases where the problem of a very low IQ or a major physical handicap may also be a barrier. The severely mentally (and physically) handicapped have probably already been identified and are receiving direct government support, often through the federal SSI program. Not included in any of the figures I have given for Illinois's spending on the poor is the federal Supplemental Security Income program. It operates as part of the Social Security system, and provides a monthly payment of $579 per month for a single person.[8] This program was designed as a safety net for the mentally retarded, the blind, and other handicapped individuals. As we get deeper into the welfare pool with smaller caseloads per caseworker, the process of identifying and fairly handling people with disabilities will improve.

The mentally and physically disabled should be, and often are, actively encouraged to reach the highest degree of self-sufficiency that is realistic—with jobs that can be performed despite limitations. It is well known that there are large numbers of jobs, such as some types of eldercare, restaurant work, and the like, where people with limitations are often more conscientious, and more likely to stay on the job if the supporting arrangements are solid. Meticulous matching of capabilities and job requirements is required. Megan, a pleasant woman in her twenties who waited on my parents in a dining room at their Pennsylvania retirement complex, is very limited mentally, but wonderfully conscientious and dearly loved by all. The welfare-to-work process involves matching lots of different-shaped pegs with lots of different-shaped holes, but there are clearly—despite dire warnings by critics in the last few years—enough holes to go around. As an example, the restaurant association in Illinois, facing a shortage of workers for its members, has undertaken a major effort to prepare welfare recipients for jobs in that industry.

Warnings about the inevitable economic downturns have not deterred us from our task. In the event of a downturn, those who get pushed back out of the workforce have gained work experience and self-esteem, and we can then go to work helping them find another job. They will then be getting unemployment insurance benefits—a totally new and healthier experience compared to welfare. When and if all the job slots are filled, we can then think about other volunteer and public service options, such as the workforce program that was successfully created by Governor Tommy Thompson in Wisconsin. Everyone does some work in return for benefits, a transaction that, for the most part, avoids demeaning individuals and is fair to taxpayers. Meticulously matching individuals with specific private sector jobs, solving the transportation issues, and postemployment follow-up takes time, and workfare can fill some gaps in some communities.

Workfare has met union resistance as union leaders object that some of the work being done by workfare participants might be done by union workers, creating more union jobs. Union leaders always have to speak out against activities that may reduce future union dues, but in my opinion, they have to remember that unions started out speaking for those less privileged, and attacking welfare workers won't help them much with the public. By the same token, those advocates who attack workfare and criticize welfare-to-work for "low wages and benefits" have to remember how much progress for each individual that big step into the workforce really represents and that they are seeing only the first step on the ladder. People not on welfare who are theoretically displaced by welfare workers who receive extra consideration for a job opening will often have a stronger background and therefore a better chance of finding another job.

In addition to the massive human services spending, this country spends a huge but little-talked-about $7.8 billion[9] on various programs for job training and placement. Like a giant ocean liner, this big spending ship sails on little-changed, even when unemployment hits levels as low as the 4.3 percent experienced in 1999. There is over $700 million being spent each year in Illinois alone on job training and placement. These are, for the most part, "second chance" programs for people who didn't get the skills they needed when in school or find themselves at a point where they can't get today's jobs with the skills they have. This spending is in addition to the billions now spent annually on the public schools. Most of it is federal money, but it is administered by the states in accordance with myriad federal regulations. Governor Edgar summarized this one day by saying, "At least 70 percent of our problem in this area is the federal bureaucracy." However, there is quite a bit a state can do to squeeze some value out of this big basket of lemons. In Illinois, this money is being spent through ten different, largely unconnected agencies, ending up in over fifty individual programs statewide, another Rube Goldberg design (Figure 9). Community colleges are big users of this money, as is the Workforce Investment Act (WIA).

For the most part, despite the fact that the world has changed, leaders of these programs often do not see themselves as having a major responsibility to play in the welfare-to-work effort. The legislation under which many of these programs were established focuses on other populations such as "displaced workers," and on training the workforce at large to meet program administrators' views of employer needs. These programs are usually not linked to each other, their connections to welfare caseworkers are largely nonexistent, and the ties to employers are usually (though not always) marginal. It is not unusual for a given community to have as many as a dozen disparate government-funded jobs programs. Perhaps most important, their effectiveness in terms of placement and job retention, or whatever their original purpose, is not measured. Activities (e.g., number of sessions, number of students enrolled) tend to get measured, not outcomes.

I didn't have enough foresight to include the heads of the job training and placement bureaucracies on the task force, but we did put together a job training and placement subcommittee that included some of the key stakeholders, such as the governor's administrator responsible for WIA. This group came up with some good principles (Appendix A) and recommended rationalizing the job training and placement bureaucracies, seeing this as the great opportunity to redeploy some existing funds to help those on welfare achieve self-sufficiency. There are other people who can be helped by this river of money, but thoughtfully established priorities and local flexibility should free up funds to help our most disadvantaged citizens. Some small steps were

Figure 9. Rube Goldberg II: Massive Fragmented Taxpayer Investment in Job Training and Placement Programs
(Simplified)

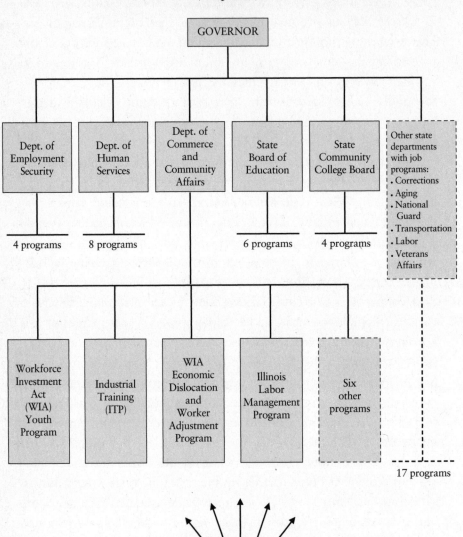

Note: 25 of 49 programs originate at federal level

Total annual funds: ≈ $700 million+

Potential trainee

taken in this direction with the Workforce Investment Act, passed in 1998, but that only scratched the surface. We know the necessary ingredients: integrated services, self-sufficiency coaches, child care, transportation, and connected employers. A whole series of agencies not normally associated with human services and welfare-to-work should be involved, and undoubtedly some laws will need to be rewritten, at the federal level as well as the state level. This situation is understandable, since these programs have been added over many years by well-intended legislators in Washington and in state capitals, and unlike activities in the business world, they rarely get reviewed as to their relevance and effectiveness as conditions change. Once again, we know the answers. Connecting the appropriate portions of the giant job training and placement bureaucracy to the communities like Grand Boulevard and to the human services offices and caseworkers can put almost everyone in the welfare population in even our toughest cities at least on the bottom rung of that ladder of opportunity. Properly harnessed and prioritized, the job training and placement bureaucracies could give a great jump-start to the next phase of welfare reform.

No discussion of jobs and welfare-to-work is complete without a discussion of the huge job potential represented by the government itself. It would be relatively easy for most states to encourage their own subcontractors, particularly in the human services area, to hire welfare recipients. The billions of dollars in human services contracts awarded annually by the state of Illinois represents lots of jobs, and a systematic effort to hire welfare recipients could have a big impact. A welfare hire with taxpayer dollars has the double value of obtaining a worker and reducing the state taxpayer burden. The nonwelfare worker not hired for a given spot is likely to have a more traditional resume and be more easily hired elsewhere.

No one knows how many people will be left and who they will be after a legitimate path to self-sufficiency is opened up to all. I share the view of caseworker Roy Hobbes, Janice, and Delrice that a large majority of the remaining caseload, perhaps 70 percent, will move into work enthusiastically. Another 20 percent, seeing the example of others, and seeing no attractive alternatives, will join in. Undoubtedly there will be a few malingerers, as there are in any population, who will have to be dragged kicking and screaming into the workplace. Part of the process for them may even be homelessness and/or hunger. In my view, once we reach the point where we know there are better options available to these malingerers, we can walk by their outstretched hands with impunity. They have made the *choice* not to work or receive treatment, and we are not obliged to incentivize them to remain on the street corner. Tough love is sometimes what is needed to change behavior.

The experience of connecting employers and people on welfare is personally fascinating. I see it as Martians and Earthlings, without any judgment as to which is which. The response from employers has been heartening, and though there is a long way to go, I believe that the model established in Illinois can be widely replicated. I was deeply affected by the enthusiasm of the welfare-recipient workers ("I want my kids to see me working") despite unbelievable obstacles such as the gang shootings and many other challenges. A visit to one of their apartments in a public housing project will drive deep into your soul a feeling of just how tough it is, and how great the distance is to join the mainstream America we know. Conservatives are right to say that Janice must do it herself, but liberals have a point also—there is a role for government to help people get started up the ladder. Most now agree that self-sufficiency is the goal, and the old dependency model (whether intended or not) must be junked for those who are not disabled. There are those legislators, worried about the employability of those deep in the welfare pool like Janice and Joyce, who are busily crafting exemptions for those with problems—domestic violence for example. This could really work to the disadvantage of the welfare recipients, employers, and taxpayers. A barrier that can probably be overcome would be replaced with an entitlement. My experience, supported by research,[10] is that it is the *number* of barriers that reduces chances of employment, and the chances of overcoming two or three barriers is pretty good. To fall back into that top-down mode and exempt people facing certain individual barriers is to revert to that same old approach that got us into trouble in the first place. We need to keep working until almost everybody is employed, then look at who is left. I believe we'll be very pleased with the results—but not as happy as the former welfare clients themselves.

The principle purpose of the five statewide community test sites was to find out what really works in achieving self-sufficiency, and this purpose was largely achieved in all areas. Employers didn't need tax breaks or other incentives to take an interest, merely reliable employees. The limitation was not available jobs, but rather the state and the community filling in the necessary pieces to overcome the barriers to work. In recent years we have been fortunate to have remarkably low unemployment rates and lots of help-wanted ads, including those for entry-level jobs. Some exciting answers grew out of the Governor's Task Force work in each of the five test-site communities. The employers will be fine, we just need to know how to work with them responsibly. These successes are replicable—there is no question that they will work in other states—and inform the national debate. We truly have the tools in our country to help the 5 million people remaining on welfare turn their lives around, as well as those of the noncustodial fathers who are such an important part of the picture, without new spending. This will dramatically change the face of this country. I heard then Governor George W. Bush of Texas say, "Societies are renewed from the bottom up, not from the top down." This spoke to me. We know the answers, now let's make a difference by implementing them.

Janice, Joyce, and many others previously thought unemployable are now working with pride, and a wide range of employers are now actively involved in hiring both men and women from the "hard core" unemployed. The next phase needs to involve more employers and the remaining tough cases, both from the welfare rolls and the fathers. On a very tangible microlevel, I think back to my mugging in New York. The connection is obvious. My work with the Governor's Task Force has convinced me that the odds are that if these youths had a chance for decent jobs they would have taken them. Further, my efforts have convinced me that the odds are that if they had those jobs, I wouldn't have been hit on the head and had a big fist smashing my nose. Think about it.

PRINCIPAL POINTS

1. Most people on welfare really want to work.
2. Historically, connections between employers and human services systems have been virtually nonexistent, yet self-sufficiency is the goal of human services systems—big changes are required.
3. Approached in the right way, with the right transition supports, most employers see hiring welfare recipients as a reasonable business risk, and enlightened self-interest.
4. One stop support, such as a self-sufficiency coach connected to the community resources and government services for a period *after* the job is started, and help from an on-the-job mentor is normally necessary to achieve success.
5. U.S. job growth is with small and medium-sized employers (the local store, nursing home, etc.) so the importance of community involvement in identifying and working with these employers is crucial.
6. As reform integrates services into one stop shopping and focuses on self-sufficiency for whole families, reconnecting noncustodial parents of welfare children to their families is essential. This means the next phase of welfare reform must include fathers, fierce child support enforcement, and employment of ex-offenders.

8

Collaborating at the Top of the Bureaucracies— An Oxymoron?

EMPLOYEE: *"Mr. Edison, please tell me what laboratory rules you want me to observe."*
EDISON: *"Hell! There ain't no rules around here. We're trying to accomplish somep'n!"*

W e're human services, we don't do transportation," said Governor's Task Force member Mac Ryder, the slight, owlish, bespectacled Springfield lawyer and bureaucrat, when confronted with the problem of getting clients to work. Mac became a member of the Governor's Task Force when he found himself head of the giant ($1.2 billion annual budget) Department of Children and Family Services upon his predecessor's departure to take a higher-paying job with a private provider doing business with the state. He had moved up from his job as the agency's general counsel and brought with him the not uncommon lawyerly view of state agency leadership. There are, understandably, lots of lawyers in Springfield and in various state agency management positions. Agencies in most states, especially human services agencies, are frequently sued, and it is not uncommon for an agency to be forced to operate under a court order designed to remedy some mistake or neglect. The lawyering approach reflected much of what happened in human services in Illinois. The primary focus is staying within the law and making sure the letter of the law is upheld. From this perspective, the system is at its best when all the laws are upheld. When this narrow view crowds out the opportunity to achieve real self-sufficiency, both clients and taxpayers get shortchanged.

We were sitting in a sunny state of Illinois building conference room at our regular bimonthly meeting of the Governor's Task Force on Human Services Reform, and Mac's depressing statement shot through me like an arrow and made me wonder if I was wasting my time. He still doesn't get it, I thought. Technically he was right. I supposed that there was no legislatively approved line item for transportation to jobs in the budget. My mind flashed back to a UPS board of directors meeting in Minneapolis some years earlier where I showed up armed with data on the inroads the brand new upstart Federal Express was making in the delivery business. "We're a ground company, air delivery is not our business," said a wealthy old-line director. UPS finally changed and became outstanding in the air business, and dammit, the state of Illinois was going to get good at whatever was necessary to help people become self-sufficient. Mac was right, there was nothing about transportation in the federal or state legislation or regulations that set up and governed these big agencies. Top-level bureaucrats breaking out of the old paradigm and focusing on real outcomes are almost an oxymoron, yet this would have to happen if we were to succeed. *We would have to change the rules!* They would also have to give up turf and work collectively.

From the time the task force first began to meet in early 1993, we were setting the stage at both the community level and at the state level to pursue the self-sufficiency vision and move ahead on the principles established at the task force retreat. Central to that vision was one stop shopping. Someone who wants help shouldn't have to go to and be processed by as many offices as there are state agencies. And at the local level, services available and how they can best be delivered should be more influenced by the community than by Springfield. We needed successes implementing these ideas in our five test sites, and success in spreading the word and persuading all the stakeholders that the task force vision and principles were the way to go—statewide.

To prepare for the changes in both structure and policies that I hoped would come, we set up subcommittees of the task force that would broaden the base of those involved and provide needed expertise and support. We had to make ourselves act like an increasingly larger pebble thrown into a giant pool, with rings radiating outward in concentric circles of increasing amplitude. People used to, and often wed to the status quo, would begin to notice the rings, and we could then, hopefully, get them involved. The governor was a cautious soul, a bit of a loner, and not much of a risk taker. We had to reach out and bring as many players as possible into the fold.

Though not as personally transforming as work with individuals on welfare and with local communities, work at the top level of the state was a great opportunity for insight and was a crucial piece of the puzzle. Intellectually, it became ever easier to see why government is so slow to identify and act on things that seem so obvious to us as outsiders. I slowly developed a great respect for the difficulty of getting things done in government—even when you are the governor. Although there were some battles and a few halfhearted participants, it was heartening to watch most (but not all) state administrators eventually agree to give up turf and work together as they began to share a vision of effective reform. My message to them was essentially, "Would you rather have your children remember you as someone who fought for a larger budget for your agency, or someone who was a key player in historic reform?" However, top state administrators, family advocates, media, and others were initially highly suspicious: What job do you have *your* eye on, Gary? Do you want a state contract? What is your *real* agenda?

Typical was the reaction of Department of Mental Health and Developmental Disabilities (DMH/DD) director Jess McDonald. Jess is a very bright agency director with energy and vision and a shrewd sense of politics—in a class by himself. If he has a weakness, it is a tendency to be a one-man gang at the expense of creating a strong and deep management team. He was an advocate of community involvement and community-based decision making even before the GTF started moving down that path. Although he had political problems with the senate president and didn't get along with the state budget director, I saw Jess as an informal leader of the state director group, and someone I should stay close to. I made sure we had periodic one-on-one visits where I would get his view on how we were doing and any suggestions he might have.

One day, to my amazement, he volunteered a personal assessment: "People in my department, myself included, found it very hard to believe that someone like you would spend most of your time working without pay in the trenches on welfare reform, without some personal agenda. However, we now trust you and believe you care about helping people." Hooray! It was hard to be greeted with initial suspicion by the countless people encountered in an effort like this, but it was understandable.

To ensure involvement of the day-to-day operators of the state systems, we formed a senior policy council consisting mostly of the deputy directors of the various human services agencies and the state budget office. In the business world, if the boss (in this case the agency director) is involved, that would be enough. However, the agency directors on the task force were all appointees of the governor. It was at the next level, the deputy directors, that one found the senior career civil servants who would likely be there long after the directors left. We needed their buy-in. In addition the frenetic schedules of the agency directors made it risky to assume that information coming out of the task force was effectively passed along.

One of the senior policy council members was a former next door neighbor and friend of the governor. He became a champion of the task force principles and change, and an important ally. Springfield is a small town, and Jim Edgar lived there for twenty years prior to being elected governor. Everyone seems to know or be related to everyone else, and we needed to be on the network and in a positive way if possible. Dramatic cultural change required a critical mass of believers. There is no way a major reform effort can be designed and implemented without the support and involvement, or at least acquiescence, of the key executive branch leaders—key staffers, department heads, and others. Without some visible support and commitment at this level, passive resistance prevails in government. The irony here was that if we ended up consolidating departments, there would be no need for six or seven heads of such departmental functions as finance, audit, legal, legislative liaison, inspector general, minority affairs, and the like. Yet high-level support is particularly important in convincing longtime midlevel administrators that change must happen—even for the B team. Elective politics and low pay produces constant churning at the top, but the middle, protected by civil service, stays.

Task force member and state budget director Joan Walters led the senior policy council. Under her leadership, the council became a principal source of financial and other data, and some new advocates for change emerged. Joan really committed herself to the work of the task force, utilizing her background working in human services for the city of Seattle. She was particularly interested in measurable results. She was dearly beloved by many who worked for her, but intensely disliked by many who had to deal with her on budgetary matters. With close-cropped hair and a nice smile, she was warm on the inside, cordial on the outside, and had no problem being tough as nails. The fact that Joan of Arc is her personal hero is revealing, I believe. Joan was the first woman to hold the powerful director of the Bureau of the Budget position, with a stately paneled suite of offices in the ornate capitol building guarded by a huge walnut door. Governor Edgar trusted her implicitly, and with good reason. Unlike the federal government, which prints money when there is a shortfall, state budgets must be balanced each and every year. The governor cannot possibly understand the budgets of the scores of agencies and other entities which report to him and his small staff. He provides broad political guidelines identifying the major areas he wants to emphasize, leaving enormous discretion and power to his budget director. She is also his point person on his negotiations with the legislature. When there is almost no discretionary revenue, as was the case when the task force was formed, both the power and the pain associated with the job are extreme.

With strong leadership from Joan, we set up a number of key task force committees, further deepening the involvement of the state agency directors. Each committee had co-chairs, one state agency director, and one nonemployee GTF member with expertise in the area.

We formed a management information systems subcommittee headed by the computer savvy director of the Public Health Department, Dr. John Lumpkin, and GTF member Steve Singer, an MIS expert and partner of Andersen Consulting. An inevitable future need was an integrated management information system—something no state had—to bring together all the information on an entire family from all the state agencies to a caseworker's personal computer, along with an inventory of helping services available to clients. In the age of automated tellers and the Internet, state human services systems, almost without exception, have both feet firmly planted in the Dark Ages of computers. As a new head of the Internal Revenue Service in Washington said about the huge government computer operation he inherited: "We are an absolutely first-class example of a museum of 1970s technology." Jim Dimas, a wonderfully energetic, visionary full-time staffer, was recruited from a Washington, D.C., public health association to staff the MIS committee, and work commenced on an integrated case management system dubbed Pathfinder. Injecting "outside" perspectives was important. All other states were consulted to avoid reinventing this obvious wheel, but no state had an integrated system. The Pathfinder design, updated as technology advanced, was to become the basis for integrated systems design in Texas, New York, North Carolina, and Arizona.[1] One of the Illinois team members, with seed money from the Casey Foundation, went on to form a national nonprofit management information systems consulting firm to help transfer know-how. Unlike the business world I came from, having "competitors" adopt your ideas is an exciting, positive development. Integration of the myriad human services management information systems will be a potent tool for caseworkers like Roy Hobbes, and management information systems reform needs to become part of the national reform movement.

Over time I came to get a somewhat better understanding of why government management information systems are so terribly behind the times, often lagging business by a decade or more. First, legislators and political leaders tend not to think like managers, but rather like the lawyers that most of them are. They've grown up in an environment where lots of money and people swirl around amid incredible complexity, so the vision of a management information system that gives hard data on real outcomes and one stop for client services instead of reporting on compliance with federal and state regulations may seem naive or idealistic—they've never seen one. Secondly, appropriating large sums of money to install a state-of-the-art computer system isn't a vote-getter compared to a bricks-and-mortar project in the district or a new program or a tax cut with benefits for voters. In addition, installing new systems tends to be longer term, raising the question, "Will I be in office when the payoffs from the new system happen?" Finally, the systems aren't easily understood, and new systems installations are notorious for delays and budget overruns—bringing the risk of some bad newspaper stories. Add to all this the political games with contractor/contributors that must be navigated and the difficulty of finding top technical people to work at government pay levels, and it's easy to postpone biting the new computer systems bullet. Business is easier. Nevertheless we knew a new management information system would be an important reform element, and we were determined to move ahead as effectively as possible. I've entertained a fantasy that as part of the settlement of the huge Microsoft antitrust case, Microsoft would agree to develop and install a state-of-the-art human services system for a large state, and do it in a way that it could be economically replicated by the other forty-nine!

We knew that state employees and those who received state funds, like nature, abhorred a vacuum. If we didn't provide them with information, the rumor mill would. We formed a public relations committee to ensure that word of the Governor's Task Force and the communities' activities were communicated to the 26,000 employees of the human services departments and to the outside world. A regular newsletter, *Illinois in Reform,* was produced, with lots of space for questions and answers. Editors were identified representing a cross section of employees, and a spirit of openness was established. Considerable work was done to reach out to as many of the state's twelve million citizens as possible, to ensure that we could begin building a critical mass of believers as well as comfortably assert the openness of our effort to critics. Some longtime critics of the state human services systems such as Jerry Stermer, head of the advocacy group Voices for Illinois Children, had spent years pounding the table for more money and new programs. They were understandably suspicious of an effort that asserted that more money wasn't the issue. Besides, systems change is not a very emotional hook, compared to, say, a new program for abused children that could drive the many fund-raising appeals these organizations require in order to stay viable. Other critics, like Jimmy Lago and the alcohol and substance abuse providers, worried about the impact of change on their organizations. Our communications aimed at rising above these interests, focusing on the need for change to help disadvantaged people become self-sufficient.

I wrote a *Wall Street Journal* editorial page piece[2] that led to national television and radio appearances and gave added credibility to local public relations efforts. Although initially I found it awkward, and I'm sure I didn't look relaxed, I soon got reasonably comfortable going into a small room, looking into a camera and answering questions from people in New York I couldn't see. Because the reform principles were truly nonpartisan, these public relations efforts generated little opposition. The opposition that existed was relatively quiet and behind the scenes, because it was more personal. I had some fun with the public relations part of the effort, for example guesting through phone lines on One-Eyed Jack Jackson's 7:00 A.M. drive-time radio talk show in the Springfield area. One-Eyed Jack didn't know much about welfare/human services reform except that welfare was a big problem that needed fixing. He seemed rather amused that I thought it was fixable, and I think he was genuinely pleased at the high level of interest in the subject—so much so that I was invited back several times. I answered a number of questions from Springfield bureaucrats in the systems, some of whom cheered me on, indicating that some of the problems, such as clients cheating the system, were worse than I thought. I have never met One-Eyed Jack, and always wondered whether he really only had one eye. My suspicion is that the rakish card-sharp image the nickname evoked was designed to establish a persona to go with the rapid-fire, hard-edged patter. It took some doing, but I finally learned to boil my answers down to one or two sound bites even though the reality was much more complex. Not surprisingly, the most thoughtful dialogues were almost always those on National Public Radio and public television.

One of the cochairs of the public relations committee was Terry Mulvihill, a Goldman Sachs partner. I had been looking for community-conscious businessmen willing to invest some time to help change human services, and Terry was suggested to me for the GTF by a top businessman who wanted to help but felt he couldn't do it himself. Terry, a handsome, silver-haired, upbeat ("Unbelievable" is his trademark enthusiastic response to anything resembling good news) sixty-year-old, was always on the lookout for ways to make a difference in other people's lives. A great communicator himself, Terry was the legendary Omaha billionaire Warren Buffett's stockbroker, among other things. His many activities also included heading up the fund-raising for St. Joseph's home for abused children, a place for especially troubled, sometimes-violent kids. When the Casey award for $2.5 million to the state came through, Mike Lawrence, the governor's communications director, was worried about the appearance to a dirt-digging reporter of using any of that foundation/welfare reform money to hire public relations help. It would look like the governor was using money intended for poor people to promote himself with voters. I was stuck, since public relations was a core ingredient of the reform effort. After I talked to Terry, he quickly wrote a check for $30,000, which enabled us to hire energetic part-time P.R. consulting help that resulted in the *Wall Street Journal* placement, among other important contributions. He wrote another big check the next year. Terry's life was dramatically changed by the accidental death of a wonderfully accomplished daughter, inspiring a reassessment of his priorities that has benefited an untold number of people.

While I don't believe we were successful in reaching even a majority of the state's twelve million citizens with our message of reform, I do believe we reached the majority of those concerned about disadvantaged people and those with a stake in government. National opinion polling shows a long-term decline in public confidence in government doing something right, so my guess is that large numbers saw our effort as worthwhile but, like Bishop Conway, were doubtful that anything would come of it. However, we reached enough people that I started regularly running into stakeholders and other interested people who knew about the Governor's Task Force effort and much of what we were trying to do, even though we had not met before. This was a good test, I thought.

A particularly crucial subcommittee was the employee involvement committee, where we met with a cross section of the massive employee group, and obtained the active involvement of the leaders of the three main employee unions. Union involvement was a principal objective of this group—I was determined not to give Henry Bayer, the AFSCME head, and his associates any ammunition that they could use to stir up the troops, and involvement and openness is the best prophylactic. Union leaders need causes to legitimize the monthly union dues, and we needed to convince the union employees that the reform was about self-sufficiency, not privatization. I subsequently learned that the unions have been very active communicating among the states, and that Michigan's aggressive privatization of human services sounded an alarm bell nationally and a determination to dig in suspiciously against change.

From my Mark Controls experience, I knew employee involvement was very important. During my eighteen years as CEO, I and my top managers spent lots of time leading what we called rap sessions with employees at all levels around the world. We would invite groups of employees, usually no more than fifty at a time, to meet for an hour or so, often for beer and pizza after work. I would do my best to explain what we needed to accomplish, and then spend most of the time opening up the dialogue asking people what they thought, identifying problems and getting their advice. Employee involvement generates good ideas, and I have long believed it is a good use of top management time.

Chairing the employee involvement committee was Robert

Wright, director of the giant Department of Public Aid and a task force member. A very smart young manager with a masters in public administration from Syracuse University, he had an amazing recall of department statistics that impressed legislators and the governor's office. However, I never saw him get enthusiastic about anything, and I always sensed in him a skepticism that anything would ever change. He always cooperated, but never got on board enthusiastically, perhaps sensing—correctly as it turned out—that his job would disappear if we were able to pull off the reform.

We used to have lunch in a small diner near his office in Springfield, and he would stoically agree to whatever I needed at the time. While munching french fries he would make notes of whatever data I needed, or what I needed him to say to one of his many managers. It was as though he didn't see it as his job to have a vision or to push anything—just cooperate when asked by someone you don't feel you can say no to. He assigned some good staff people to the employee involvement effort, and this group did a terrific job of creating the climate for employee acceptance of the big changes to come. Unfortunately, Robert had the misfortune to be the director at the time a contracting kickback scandal occurred in the Public Aid department, and though not charged with anything, he resigned. I doubt that he benefited personally, but rather was in the wrong place at the wrong time. Springfield is full of people who care a lot more about making money from government one way or another than they care about good government. They equate making big campaign contributions to an entitlement to contracts without competitive bids. Many problems for which government contracts are drawn are often complex, and a greedy political "friend" can often be found sucking dollar bills through a loophole. Sometimes a midlevel bureaucrat ends up with a few bucks in the process.

As the test site communities were organizing their collaboratives, establishing their priorities, and beginning to develop relationships with the state, the elected community leaders joined the task force. This was a big help in task force discussions, since it shifted the dialogue even more in the direction of bottom-up, community-based problem solving—"Here's what we need to do in Waukegan if we're going to get folks self-sufficient." The directors of the big departments were outnumbered and were exposed regularly to what was going on out on the front lines. They listened carefully and generally provided constructive support.

As the Governor's Task Force work proceeded, the focus of the meetings increasingly turned to the activities in the five pilot communities. For the state to connect all six of the human services departments involved, each of the five communities ended up with six state liaisons, employees of the state designated by each department head/GTF member at each monthly community meeting. The need for six liaisons to have complete state representation was obviously very labor intensive and was symptomatic of the fragmentation frustrations of the ladies in the backyard and the caseworkers writ large. The six state departments on the Governor's Task Force grew to seven with Maralee Lindley, the energetic director of the Department on Aging, asking to join. She saw useful potential ties between community-based programs for seniors and human services reform. To me this was another piece of evidence that we were where the action was.

After about twenty months of task force activity Jim Edgar's first term ended. The Governor's Task Force was functioning well, with well-established reform principles and very active community organizations coming together in the test site communities. The current fragmented organization was increasingly seen as a problem, and an expectation of change was growing. Dr. Preister, the independent evaluator said, "The leaders of the major human services departments, together with other persons who brought different and unique perspectives (business, researcher, public officials), were *required* to collaborate as *the Governor's Task Force on Human Services Reform.* In interview after interview, participants said that even if the task force produced no other positive effect, the fact that the state human services began meeting regularly and working together collectively for the first time is, in itself, a monumental achievement." He went on to say, "The combination of both a state-level collaborative and community collaboratives has produced . . . interesting results, mostly by requiring both the state agencies and the communities to do their business in a new way. Moreover, this combination seems critical for successful reform, based on the reform experiences of other states. States that have attempted only a state-level collaborative have had difficulty implementing reform at the community level, and states that have attempted community-level reform have met bureaucratic resistance at the state level.[3]" Dr. Preister goes all over the country evaluating reform efforts, and he says our path is the best one. I know he's right—our direction is logical but lots of the tenacity that Harvey talked about will be required if we're really going to change the system and maximize our ability to make a difference in people's lives. I remind myself that tenacity was always in the top group of characteristics he would look for in someone.

We were off to a good start, but a new worry emerged—one that I frankly hadn't thought about much—a built-in challenge of all government reform efforts. How do we operate during an election campaign, and what are the risks of a new administration? Suppose we get a new governor and a whole new staff? At the state level it is important to keep the momentum for change going even though the governor's staff is focused on the campaign and there is a tendency to slow down while the bureaucracy wonders who will win and whether or not there will be a new direction. They did know that there was a good chance they would face much the same cast of bosses after the election, and this was helpful. In the meantime, as insurance I hoped I wouldn't need, I had some democratic friends make contact with opponent Dawn Clark Netsch's policy people to persuade them that the task force effort was bipartisan and she'd be smart to continue it if she won. Any statewide reform effort is likely to have to bridge a gubernatorial election, and the trick is to get word to the opposition camp that the effort is bipartisan and effective, and therefore hard to attack successfully. There is even the prospect of *losing* poll points.

Life was made easier by Governor Edgar's reelection, but Felicia Norwood, one of the two key governor's office representatives left to work as a lawyer and manager for Aetna. She was offered more than twice her government salary for a less stressful job. The governor assigned her responsibilities to Howard Peters, a deputy chief of staff, and a major new player emerged on the scene.

Howard Peters is a tough guy's tough guy. Built like a cement block and able to bench press over four hundred pounds, he made his name early in the corrections system as someone who could walk into a juvenile detention facility and gain instant respect from all the gang members. He worked his way through an historically black college in Tennessee and went on to earn a master's degree in Illinois in order to prepare himself for greater responsibility in the Illinois Department of Corrections. He worked his way up, becoming warden at two prisons before being called to the Pontiac maximum security prison, one of the most violent in Illinois, after an assistant warden and friend and a superintendent were killed in a riot. He straightened the place out and was selected by Governor Edgar to be the director of the Department of Corrections. He successfully managed a large increase in the number of inmates statewide and established a reputation as a tough, smart manager. Governor Edgar then selected him as one of two deputy chiefs of staff in the governor's office with responsibility for twenty state departments and another twenty-three authorities, boards, commissions, and the like. These responsibilities represent approximately two-thirds of the state's $35 billion budget and about 60,000 employees. In addition to human services, his portfolio included such challenges as the environment, state police, the state bonding authorities, the Departments of Transportation, Revenue, and Insurance, and much, much more. A deputy chief of staff obviously can't manage all these activities, but he or she needs to be a good firefighter and problem solver, keeping the governor out of trouble. How was he going to get time to come to task force meetings, let alone help us reform human services? Would he be interested? Was he a risk taker? I was worried.

With thoughtful notes and my most sincere demeanor, I went up to the big sixteenth-floor office down the hall from the governor in Chicago's Thompson Center for my first meeting with Howard. Even though I had a good relationship with the governor, if Howard wasn't on board, change would be very difficult. We sat down at a round table in his stark office, and after brief pleasantries I said something like, "I want to help make you successful in your new responsibilities." He stopped me right there and said, with a suspicious tone of voice and expression, "Why would [read: a rich white guy like] you want *me* to be successful?" His suspicion was palpable—he suspected I had a personal, probably monetary agenda, I subsequently learned. Howard didn't move to the top of the bureaucracy without being able to sniff out what was really going on, and a pure volunteer interest in good government just didn't fit with his experience. I persuaded him to come to the GTF meetings, and to everyone's benefit, he got very interested and involved. Almost immediately he became an important force for change. At one of his early meetings, he pushed each community to get on with the process of changing people's lives. "Pick a project that fits with your community's top priorities and that requires a change in the way the state operates in your community. Let's review them in the next few task force meetings and then get started." He was saying we'd spent enough time organizing and planning—the time had come for action. Howard had come up to speed fast and was ready to take some risks in our test communities.

Within the next few months, each community came forward and presented their ideas for welfare reform experiments in their community. All of them focused one way or another on providing a broad range of services to a whole family on an integrated basis, with the goal of removing barriers to self-sufficiency and getting people sustainable jobs. Springfield came forward with their Lee Center idea and Grand Boulevard with the self-sufficiency coach concept for fifty workers. Waukegan kicked off its pilot project to organizationally and geographically restructure service systems that were currently located in a county office not easily accessible from Waukegan. DuPage launched its effort to move fifty families from welfare to work by bringing together previously fragmented systems and solving important transportation problems, and the Southern Seven embarked on their transportation-focused welfare-to-work effort.

Policy as well as organization structure problems were highlighted. For example, the leaders of Focus, the Southern Seven Counties collaborative, in one its many reminders to GTF members that their rural area combines disproportionately high poverty and unemployment with great distances to any job and almost no public transportation, suggested a policy change. They brought to the task force the policy problem of the welfare rules effectively *preventing* car ownership, the problem being that owning a car with a value in excess of $1,500 made a person ineligible for government assistance. Picture a forty-five-mile drive each way to a job with a $1,500 car. The GTF worked to identify those areas where government policy had in effect put a moat between the job aspirant and his or her job. The car limit was eliminated by the state.

Other Illinois policy changes were made concurrent with the efforts of the Governor's Task Force. Unlike structural changes, policy changes often have an ideological political component. The two most important early policy changes related to the incentive to work and the availability of child care.

A number of states still have policies that leave people worse off financially after they get an entry-level job than when they were on welfare. We'd all be tempted to stay home and have a bigger income. A careful calculation of paycheck deductions, transportation and clothing costs, child care cost gaps, and loss of occasional cash income from the huge underground cash economy often leaves people less well off with a real job. Illinois' Work Pays policy gradually reduces the monthly welfare payment ($1 for every $3 earned) until the welfare check is eliminated. A whopping 40 percent of those remaining on the welfare rolls in Illinois were working or in work-related activity. This group was on the road to self-sufficiency, they just weren't fully there yet. In addition, if the employer does not provide health insurance, the welfare recipient is allowed to retain his or her coveted green health card. Before the policy changes were made it often didn't make economic sense for welfare recipients to move to entry-level jobs, now it does. It is true that other employees in comparable jobs at a given workplace may have less family income for a period if they did not come from the welfare rolls, but this has not been a significant problem. Most conservatives and liberals alike, when made aware that moving to work is a step back financially, support this phase in approach.

A second major policy pillar was the broadening of child care eligibility while incorporating a small co-payment provision, which increases with the recipient's income. In Illinois, child care assistance is available to all families whose income is below 50 percent of the state median income of about $33,000 per year. Working parents can choose home child care or a child care facility as they see fit. Over 143,000[4] children were given assistance in 1999. If you are a single mother with two children, haven't worked before, and get a $6 an hour job, the $12,000 per year wages just won't let you go to work if decent child care takes $3,000 to $5,000 of it. Conservatives may lament the fact that there is no working father allowing the mother to stay home, or the fact that the kids came along in the first place, but here we are, and we must move ahead. While progress is being made in tracking down fathers for child support and in establishing paternity, the movement from welfare to work is a huge step forward in changing the culture. Liberals lament the sometimes less than ideal home child care and fear the strong push directly into work, but some are now acknowledging that those who have made it to the bottom rung of that ladder are closer to self-sufficiency than they have ever been.

A 1998 study by the Tufts University Center on Hunger and Poverty[5] ranked Illinois in the top ten in the nation in terms of implementing *policies,* independent of the also crucial *structural* reform, that would improve the economic circumstances of the poor. Only thirteen states were deemed to have policies that actually improved chances for self-sufficiency. The ranking was not determined by spending, just sensible policies. Removing policy barriers one by one is tough work, and most states have a long way to go.

One class of government policy barriers relates to regulations that limit entrepreneurs like shoe shiners and independent taxi companies among the poor. A classic case of government interfering with people's right to earn a living is Faith Carey-Proctor's hair-braiding business in Canton, Ohio.[6] She has been operating illegally for seventeen years, working from her home without a cosmetology license. Obtaining the license is expensive, with 1,500 hours of training required. Capability is required in perming, cutting, and tinting, which braiders never use, and requirements do not include the skills black families have passed down for generations—twisting, braiding, and weaving in extensions. Ms. Faith Carey-Proctor was told to close her business and was threatened with a misdemeanor charge for operating without a license. She wanted to remodel and expand her business, but was afraid. Enter one of my personal heroes, Clint Bolick, leader of the Institute for Justice in Washington, who is helping her sue the Ohio Board of Cosmetology. Clint is a very smart, very committed white lawyer who has passed up a high-paying corporate law career to take on economic justice cases that help poor people fight government. The institute is a nonprofit that is partially financed by the Casey Foundation. Clint is removing barriers standing in the way of the creation of jobs for poor people.

As each community group discussed their hoped-for changes in policies and programs for poor people in front of the task force, everyone was well aware that the decision makers for many of these changes were right there in the room. Howard Peters has since told me that a big turning point for him occurred when he observed that the state employees assigned as community liaisons had become so deeply involved with their communities that they had become advocates for the community. They were often arguing for changes at the public task force meetings on the side of community leaders, taking on their department director bosses sitting around the table as members of the task force. They argued for redeploying people to support the community initiatives; they argued for transportation, flexibility, co-location of services, and whatever else made sense to get results in the community. It was impressive and exciting. The idea of learning from communities was taking root, even with Howard, a fellow whose whole managerial life was spent running the ultimate in top-down authoritarian organizations—prisons!

The community experiences, knowledge gleaned from the ladies in the backyard and their peers, caseworkers, employers and others as the pilot project unfolded in the initial five communities, reaffirmed in a very valid way why the existing organizations, policies, and culture should not survive in their present form. Fragmentation was out; working together was in. Caseworkers in the pilot projects started helping to solve whatever problem became a barrier to self-sufficiency. This initial group of caseworkers had access to all available services, regardless of department, or whether the services were public or private. The community efforts were getting real results. People's lives were changing. The principles developed early on were validated—the need for integrated services for the whole family, community involvement, and measuring outcomes—the bottom line: how many people really ended up getting and holding a job?

The challenge of changing the culture of these giant bureaucracies was both daunting and crucial. It was one thing to change the mind-set of workers in five communities, something else to change the whole state—perhaps one hundred and fifty communities.

It became clear in many ways that the people in the management ranks of these big government departments had not been seeing their mission as problem solving to enable their clients to climb to self-sufficiency. Instead, they saw their job as it had been for the past thirty or forty years—meticulously administering programs that were slavishly designed to carry out centrally designed legislative mandates. Much of this can be traced back to the welfare rights movement of the sixties and seventies and the success of that movement in the courts. That success in the courts was fueled by some social workers who overstepped the bounds of decency, rifling through clients' purses looking for assets and the like. The court victories gave birth to a new sense of entitlement on the part of recipients and federal regulators that denied discretion to social workers as an intrusion on the dignity of those in need and made the rules and regulations paramount. The welfare cases rose from 803,000 in 1960 to 1,909,000 in 1970, 3,574,000 in 1980, and exceeded 5,000,000 in the early 1990s before welfare reform reversed this trend.[7] Most of the cases are, in fact, single mothers with children, so the actual number of people on welfare is much greater.

Understandably, the motivation of most of today's workers whom

I met in my work was to avoid rule violations, for which they would be punished. They were not rewarded or evaluated by the number of clients who exit the system by becoming self-sufficient, so why take a risk, even if it would solve a problem? My eyes were further opened—no wonder these billions are being spent without real progress. Taxpayers who don't want to see their taxes go up in order to increase spending on social programs have a good point. What's the return on this investment?

On the national level, after we had been at work in Illinois for almost two years, we received an unexpected but very welcome boost from the Congress passing and President Clinton signing the Personal Responsibility and Work Opportunity Reconciliation Act of 1996—the famous welfare reform bill. Congress seized the issue, marketed it well, and made it very popular. The focus was on values, specifically the work ethic (you shouldn't get something for nothing) and good government—if you spend billions, you should be able to show results. The emphasis on state flexibility and responsibility, combined with the emphasis on work, really added momentum to the idea that the state systems must change in order to be successful in the new environment. Aggressive governors like John Engler in Michigan and Tommy Thompson in Wisconsin began seeking and getting publicity for their welfare reform activities as part of their vice presidential efforts. All of this was very helpful, even though many of these activities only scratched the surface of truly fundamental reform. The new law ended the entitlement to benefits and introduced time limits. The rules are complicated, but basically there is now a five-year limit for an individual receiving benefits, creating a major incentive for work. Janice, Joyce, and the others got a head start.

This federal attention added force to the badly needed cultural change in Illinois's huge state bureaucracies. The new law helped make emphasis on work the overarching purpose of the state human services systems. It would now be easier to make the case that all the human services agencies should function as a seamless system so that those who need to find work have the full mobilization of all the state-funded services, as they would in an integrated system. This new sense of purpose that was coming out of our community test sites was now on the national news. The selling job was made easier, and the new five-year limit on welfare became a topic of conversation in every welfare office in the state. A welcome urgency was added to our reform effort. Revolutionary as this new law was, it primarily dealt with the welfare check, and did not address at all the problems of the fragmented state systems and many of the barriers that still confronted the ladies in the backyard. Though the new welfare money gave the states more freedom, it still came with lots of federal regulations. An additional plus, however, was the requirement of specific measured outcomes—a series of percentage targets for people in work or work-related activity in each of the next five years, building up to 50 percent of the welfare rolls in the fifth year. These targets gave states, from the governor on down, much needed focus.

It is important to remember that governors in most states have been reelected for years without ever solving, or even focusing upon, the human services/welfare problem. Getting a cautious Governor Edgar's commitment was a challenge. He had to be convinced that pursuing good government was also good politics. Why take the risk when your approval rating is already 72 percent? In working in the '88 Bush campaign and with the Bush White House I learned that political leaders tend to pay more attention to newspaper stories and editorial pages than to staff memos. I remember well a discussion at lunch in the White House with Jim Pinkerton, deputy assistant to the President for policy in the Bush administration. I was bemoaning the lack of interest and effort on the many domestic policy challenges, and Jim, a good friend and brilliant, prominent policy guru from the campaign, seemed to be in a position to make a difference. "How can we deliver on the 'kinder and gentler nation' commitment that he made? Let's work on some ideas and try to sell them," I offered. Jim said, "Bush will pay attention if the ideas are in David Broder's *Washington Post* column. A memo will just get lost in the pile." This advice stuck with me. Keeping the governor on the train was key, and the media would have to play a major role. There were several media milestones.

Early in the life of the task force, I managed to stimulate a page one, lead story in the *Chicago Tribune*,[8] the most important newspaper in the state (circulation about 700,000), on part of our proposed reform approach. I didn't clear my *Tribune* discussions with the governor's office for fear they would get nervous about what would be said. "State's Troubled Families May Get 1-Stop Welfare," the headline blared. The extensive article talked about "one-stop shopping" (a perfect, simple, sound bite) for human services. It went on to explain and illustrate that this meant that services from all the presently separate departments (Mental Health and Developmental Disabilities, Public Aid, Alcohol and Substance Abuse, Children and Family Services, Public Health, and Rehabilitation Services) could be available at single locations around the state, instead of myriad separate locations. Detailed examples describing the existing, fragmented, uncoordinated approach were included, along with my statement that "Illinois could become a national model." The $2.5 million Casey Foundation grant was also mentioned.

My sources told me that at the next day's staff meeting Governor Edgar was quite surprised and very pleased that his initiative got this kind of positive attention. Aha! I'm sure he thought, A way to *keep* my approval rating high.

Similarly, one day I got on a plane to New York and happened to see Jim Edgar and his wife, Brenda, and he said, "Gary, I saw your *Wall Street Journal* op-ed on our reform effort." I was a bit nervous about this article, since I hadn't cleared it with anybody except to say that it was coming, and had gotten out ahead of him, stating, "Illinois governor Jim Edgar looks forward to rolling out his community-based approach statewide." At the time he was being mentioned frequently on a short list of possible vice-presidential candidates.

I asked him what he thought of the article, and he said, "It was great—I've been getting good calls on it from all over." Whew! Another step in shifting the political calculus against retreat. A major unstated goal throughout was to reach the point where the political cost of turning back exceeded the political cost of going forward. I also wrote a *Chicago Tribune* op-ed piece at almost every critical juncture in the process.[9]

We also arranged a number of television events in communities as a way of reminding him of his public commitments, and getting the word out. I saw the events as a way of selling him what we were doing, and he saw them as a way to keep his poll numbers and visibility high—a fair transaction. To him such phrases as "one-stop shopping," "build the system from the bottom up, involving communities," and "no one size fits all," became shorthand for our complex reform effort.

Governor Edgar had a very distant management style, working closely with a very small group of the top people on his staff. I would hear back periodically that he was happy, and through his deputy chief of staff permission would come back to go ahead and do something that I felt he should be aware of. Once I got a copy of a letter he had sent to the National Governor's Association nominating me as the Illinois candidate for some sort of community service award. Periodically, considerable time would go by without my seeing him or getting from him the publicity boost that the reform effort needed to assure potential critics that the governor was still behind the effort. As a former CEO, I couldn't imagine being so passive on a matter that was one-third of my annual budget and potentially one of the two or three major accomplishments of my time in office. At one point I had a list of items that I felt needed his personal attention, and I found myself getting the runaround from his scheduler. I decided to review the situation in a letter to him and end the letter with the not-so-subtle message that said in effect, "Either we meet or I'm out of here." Parts of the letter reiterated the message he needed to carry:

> I was . . . told by Joe [Khayyat, the scheduler], that you . . . felt that a meeting was unnecessary.
>
> A year ago, when you and I . . . met, you used strong and persuasive words to underscore how important you felt it was to carry out a major, fundamental overhaul of the system, moving from the present system to an integrated, community-based system with a strong focus on outcome measurement. I then further stepped up my time commitment to the reform effort, to the point where I am very close to being a full-time vol-

unteer (approximately three days a week in the task force office, and a considerable portion of the rest of the time on the phone or on related work). This has been very difficult (and personally costly), but to me it is well worth it if we can really reform the system(s), in the truly major way envisioned by the task force.

I told Joe I was very unhappy with the decision not to meet, and gave him several reasons . . . There are some important aspects of this reform where modestly increased personal involvement on your part can make a major difference. We haven't talked about this for one year, and a one-half hour investment after one year is extremely modest given the overwhelming importance of major human services reform.

Governor, my fear is that your second term will go by all too quickly, and we will not have taken full advantage of a truly historic window of opportunity to improve the life outcomes of thousands of disadvantaged people. The systems are a mess and we can make a huge difference—leading the nation. Some of your best/top people are especially committed and dedicated to this major reform effort—Joan Walters and John Lumpkin, for example. I felt a need to connect with you, and therefore am unhappy with the way things turned out. I'm sure you realize I need to evaluate how to best use my time in this coming year.

I got a call back right away, we had a productive meeting, and I was able to move ahead confident that the governor was still on the train. With all the noisy public issues and crises (floods, competing gambling interests, refereeing sports stadium financing battles) a governor faces, it's possible for steady longer term efforts like systems reform to get lost in the shuffle. Since I didn't have a hands-on governor to work with, I had to stimulate his participation. To this day I believe he missed a great opportunity to use this reform work to establish a national reputation for innovation. Other governors got much more national attention with less fundamental accomplishment. My only possible explanation is that a heart attack he experienced at the end of his first term caused him not to take the health risk that pursuit of higher office might entail.

Working with his speechwriters, I also made sure Governor Edgar discussed our task force activities in his annual State of the State addresses. In his 1996 address, for example, he stuck his neck out by saying, "The Casey Foundation, a nationally recognized innovator in the human services area, liked our willingness to innovate and make better use of existing services. So, in 1994, the foundation gave us a 2.5 million dollar grant to launch a one-stop shopping initiative as a fresh, sensible approach to delivering human services effectively, efficiently, and compassionately. Troubled families often need services that cannot be supplied by a single state or community agency. We found that too often they have difficulty obtaining services and when they do, there is duplication, confusion, and conflicting approaches from different agencies dealing with the same families. So, with the help of the Casey Foundation, we are testing a brand-new approach in five communities throughout Illinois. In those communities . . . the people closest to the problems are being empowered. Neighbors. Community groups. Churches and synagogues. Civic and business leaders. Local officials. They are custom-tailoring and implementing remedies that they believe will work in *their* communities."

In his 1997 State of the State address he invited Rosetta Dunbar from the Grand Boulevard/UPS welfare-to-work effort to sit with his wife, Brenda, in the Capitol State House chambers. During the speech he asked her to stand, and he described her success to virtually the entire government as well as a television audience. He went on to say, "What Rosetta Dunbar and UPS have done together with community leaders in Grand Boulevard and the state of Illinois is precisely what needs to be done throughout the state if welfare reform is to succeed." Someone on President Clinton's staff saw this on C-Span, and Rosetta was then invited to play the same role in President Clinton's State of the Union speech. Airline tickets to Washington were arranged and child care provisions made, but she was dropped out of the speech at the last minute. It would have bothered me if the President took credit for what we were doing in Illinois, but the extra attention would have been worth it.

Rosetta, a twenty-five-year-old welfare mother with a tough background—Robert Taylor Homes, nine years on welfare, high school drop-out, four kids, and enthusiasm for her new job—became a sort of poster woman for reform. She did well on television and was featured in Pulitzer winner Clarence Page's column[10] syndicated in fifty newspapers around the nation.

For their part, the enthusiasm of caseworkers having success in the five test site cities and counties was being regularly written up and passed along in the newsletter *Illinois in Reform* and in speeches to the various groups of human services employees statewide. A typical caseworker quote, this one from Waukegan: "I don't ever want to go back to working the old way again," referring to her new freedom to help solve problems, no matter what they might be, on the way to family self-sufficiency.

With all this attention the climate was right and the time had come to *change the system,* consistent with the principles we had adopted two and a half years ago. The Felicia Norwood/Rube Goldberg chart had to go, rational integration with its one stop shopping had to become a reality. One day Howard Peters said to me, "I think something can happen now. How *should* we reorganize? What are your thoughts?" We talked about the principles and especially the need to have a field organization that brought together all of the departments and services and worked with communities, building on the success of our test sites. These needs pointed to a single integrated department of human services—realizing the worst fears of some providers, department staffers, and union leaders. The important objective was to give the front-line caseworkers the power and the tools to be real problem solvers, not just gatekeepers to benefits. The dependent client with substance abuse and mental health problems needs a rational path to the bottom rung on that self-sufficiency ladder that includes a job, child care, transportation, and a self-sufficiency coach. What goes on out in the field, in the communities, counts more than who reports to whom in Springfield. However, we needed a new organizational framework to make all this happen, otherwise we would lose too much time coordinating between and among separate bureaucracies.

There are those fiscal policymakers who feared integration, thinking that easy access to needed services would result in too much demand, increasing costs. For example, if everyone on welfare who needed substance abuse treatment got it, we couldn't afford it. Fragmentation is good because it keeps costs down, the thinking goes. I was sure there would be some increased use of services, but we had to face it. The alternative was continuing to waste billions, ensuring that self-sufficiency was unattainable for large numbers of people because of barriers that are left in place. All the barriers must be out of the way for the ladies in the backyard to move down the path and get off the taxpayer's dole. We needed to make a difference.

I knew we had reached our long-sought point of no return at a lunch at Harry Caray's in Chicago with Steve Schnorf, about two and a half years into the process. Steve, a large, rumpled, laconic man in his mid-forties, was an assistant to the governor. He is a lot smarter than first impressions would lead you to believe. Steve grew up with Jim Edgar in Charleston, Illinois, and is one of his closest confidants. One of Steve's main functions was to deal with the myriad special interest groups, an important element of which are the billions in contracts and other payments that go to the many private groups that provide human services (alcohol treatment, foster care screening, etc.). He was a pro at dealing with the highly paid lobbyists who are the source of big gubernatorial campaign dollars. At a much earlier Harry Caray's lunch (his favorite place—noisy, marginal food, but great baseball atmosphere), Steve had told me, "Don't expect any major changes out of this governor. He's been successful his whole career without making any big waves. He is most comfortable with people around him like me who don't push any sweeping visions." Very depressing.

We had a second Harry Caray lunch date as we were approaching the moment of truth—the time to reorganize. I had heard that Steve was telling legislators and providers, "We'll just be moving a few boxes around on the organization chart—don't worry about it."

I went through with Steve at considerable length the momentum generated by the communities, some legislative leaders who wanted the changes in front-line service delivery we were proposing and statements made in the media. I explained that the governor's speeches *required* truly major change on the front lines if we were to deliver on them. Then I looked Steve in the eye and said, "You know, Steve, the political cost of moving forward, at this point, is a lot less than the political cost of turning back."

He looked very thoughtful for a while and replied, "I think you are right." Steve got in a state car to catch the plane for his return home to Springfield, and I walked back to my office in the state of Illinois building with some extra bounce in my step. I felt we were reaching some kind of crescendo. I privately talked with a number of the Governor's Task Force members to let them know our work was paving the way for big changes. We knew what to do, the moment for major action was approaching.

On January 10, 1996, at about 4:00 A.M. in Panang, Malaysia, where Charlene and I were headed to a vacation destination on Langkawi Island, I got a call from my secretary informing me that an executive order had been issued calling for an integration of almost all of the seven human services departments into a single Department of Human Services. She read the executive order to me on the phone, and it said very little about front line services, communities, and measuring outcomes. Somehow, with the many hands governor's-office documents pass through, the blood was drained out of the description of the reform.

To their great credit, Howard Peters and Joan Walters had become potent advocates for change within the governor's staff inner circle. I give them great credit for pushing an inherently cautious governor to embark upon a high-risk major change. The Governor's Task Force and the communities had been laying the groundwork for over two years, and I had periodically reminded the governor that we "can't go on this way," using the Felicia Norwood chart as a prop. He used the words "one stop" for services often in speeches and became a believer. In addition there were enough tangible examples around the state (the Lee Center, DuPage, Southern Seven, and Waukegan successes, the UPS pilot, and more) that the reorganization had, in many respects, been road tested. This would be the biggest reorganization of state government since 1900.

Things had gone quiet from my perspective for about a month while, I subsequently learned, the governor and his staff wrestled with what I regarded as the inexorable momentum and need for change. Then they gave birth to a government device called an executive order, calling for the combining almost all of the main agencies which primarily served disadvantaged and poor people. The seven agencies (Aging, Public Health, Rehabilitation Services, Public Aid, Alcohol and Substance Abuse, Mental Health and Developmental Disabilities, and the Department of Children and Family Services) represented about $10 billion in annual spending, or almost one-third of the state's annual budget. This was a huge change, and though all of the reorganization was in the executive branch under the purview of the governor, and both the house and the senate were led by the governor's party, it was clear that the executive branch of government could not do this unilaterally. Much more legislative involvement would be needed and besides, embedding the change in law was more permanent than an executive order.

The executive order was a big chunk of my hopes and dreams, but some pieces were missing, and it needed to be done right. There was nothing in the way the executive order was worded that didn't line up with our task force work and the federations, but there were some holes. It looked too much like the emphasis was on moving the boxes around. I was sure that the executive order would scare Jimmy Lago at Catholic Charities and Henry Bayer, the union president, and many others. They would wonder what was behind it. I suspected they would put pressure on their legislative friends to oppose it. Sokoni Karanja and the other federation leaders would wonder how I felt about it and what it meant for the federations.

In prior years a law, sponsored I'm told by young State Representative Jim Edgar, was passed giving the General Assembly (house and senate) the right to stop a governor's executive order if they so vote within ninety days. A flurry of activity commenced, and Steve Schnorf and the legislative liaisons in the governor's office were pressed into service. No one from the governor's office asked for my help—they either didn't think of it, or they were more comfortable doing things the way they had always done them.

Meanwhile as my secretary read the executive order to me on the phone in Panang I was angry they had moved ahead without me—this was my baby! My pride was injured, and I was kicking myself for letting too much time go by without meeting personally with the governor. On further reflection, I reminded myself that I was an unpaid, part-time volunteer and the governor wasn't obliged to clear things with me. Besides, he was a career politician—maybe he knew something I didn't know. It turns out he didn't—we were headed for a mess.

PRINCIPAL POINTS

1. Moving ahead to dramatically change the myriad state human services systems consistent with the new principles requires new structure, new policies, new laws and, perhaps most important, a new culture.
2. National welfare reform is only part of what is required to move long-term recipients to self-sufficiency.
3. A far-reaching internal communications effort involving all levels of employees is essential to foster internal cooperation and minimizes resistance to change and union opposition.
4. Outside help from committed volunteers, foundations, and other private organizations can provide surprisingly crucial leverage.
5. A major public relations effort is an essential element in effecting major change in government.

9
The Role of the Legislature— Messy Democracy

Politics is like football. If you see daylight, go through the hole.
—JOHN F. KENNEDY

That sorry son of a bitch hasn't got a friend in the world; he's so insecure he only surrounds himself with second-rate people. I'll be damned if I'll let him combine that human services mess into one big department. Then no one will ever know what is going on. My guys plan to kill that executive order in the first fifteen minutes we go back in session." These were the words that greeted me when I walked into the office of Illinois State Senate president Pate Philip, for many years one of the most powerful political leaders in the state. I had known Pate for a number of years and had walked into his office with the opening line, "Let's talk about our friend the governor."

Pate, a tough, shrewd Republican leader from large and rapidly growing DuPage County, about an hour west of Chicago, is a big, brusque, cigar-smoking, former marine. A longtime Pepperidge Farm bread salesman in his sixties, he's an arm-around-you, locker-room man's man with more than his share of biases—almost a caricature of the image we might have of a statehouse politician. Extremely powerful from many years of running the Republican party in by far the biggest Republican county in the state, Pate seems to enjoy picking fights. His targets of choice included Chicago's Mayor Daley ("We'll pass a law to take O'Hare away from the city of Chicago"), whoever happened to be governor, or almost anyone else.

An example of Pate's clout is that DuPage County regularly delivers close to 10 percent of the statewide Republican vote and is the most important Republican county in a state where voter registration was very close between the parties. Statewide political offices go to both parties, often with small percentage differences. Nationally, Illinois was one of a handful of crucial swing states, serving as a defining presidential battleground. Republican presidential candidates are expected to show up on Pate's carpet hoping for his blessing.

I agree with a number of his biases—a skepticism of big government and bureaucracies, for example—and in 1990 I was fortunate to be able to secure his support in my quest for the Republican U.S. Senate nomination. I had kept in touch over the years, often seeing him at Republican events and contributing financially, sometimes in response to a personal phone call. I benefited from a strong bias he holds for successful businessmen, so we had a pretty good relationship.

In January 1996, when Governor Edgar decided that he was willing to take the risk of reorganizing the entire complex of human services systems consistent with our principles and pilot sites and decided to issue the executive order, he and his legislative team, led by Steve Schnorf, focused their sale to the legislature on moving boxes around on the state organization chart, downplaying the scale of what was proposed. The real changes, the one stop shopping, the role of the community, and measuring real outcomes, apparently didn't come across in their pitch. But in downplaying the scale of change, they increased legislators' suspicions. The legislators were too smart to buy a pig in a poke. I had previously made Pate and his chief of staff, Carter Hendron, aware that I was helping the governor on human services reform, but I had not focused them sufficiently on what we were doing—a major mistake in hindsight.

Earlier in the year, Pate had raised his profile as a perceived enemy of human services, especially in Chicago, by saying that the large number of black employees in the Department of Children and Family Services meant that there was a poor work ethic. This racist comment, not surprisingly, was good for statewide headlines and stories over several days. But the political harm from comments like that from Pate is limited, since there has often been an underlying feeling on the part of some suburban voters that their hard-earned tax dollars were being wasted on inner-city welfare programs—Chicago's problem, not theirs. On the positive side, his protégée Gayle Franzen, DuPage County board chairman, was working with the Governor's Task Force through the DuPage Federation test site, and that was going well.

The alarm bell went off when I returned from Malaysia and was shocked to see a headline screaming: "Republicans Fighting." The story featured big individual pictures of Governor Edgar, Pate, and House Speaker Lee Daniels on the front page, each with a very angry face. The story described Pate and Lee's disagreements with Governor Edgar on education funding and human services reform, together with unpleasant personal comments. The primary battleground was education funding, where Jim Edgar had gotten behind the work of another task force which had concluded that more money should be raised for the public schools by increasing Illinois state income taxes by a whopping one-third. Pate and Lee concluded, probably correctly, that voters would quickly move them from the majority to the minority if they supported the tax increase.

Swept into their anger was my human services reform and reorganization which, it turns out, came at them without much warning or thoughtful rationale, despite its impact on one-third of the state budget. Human services reform and reorganization had also become a possible bargaining chip to use with the governor in the more politically potent education fight. I was regretting going on vacation. In my gut, I feared three years of work going down the drain, but more important I was letting down all the people who need help to change— the ladies in the backyard, caseworkers, and all the others. And, of course, I was letting down Harvey. It was clear that the governor and his staff hadn't been very persuasive on the reasoning behind the reform, and the legislative leaders felt that the executive branch couldn't be trusted. Why didn't I do a better job in managing this part of the process?

I picked up the phone and called Pate's district office, telling Nancy, Pate's assistant, I wanted to talk to him as soon as possible about the executive order. A few days later I was on my way out the tollway to Pate's suburban Elmhurst district office in DuPage and a 10:00 A.M. meeting. To be safe I allowed extra time, arriving a half hour early and using the extra time to make notes in a coffee shop near Pate's modest district office. Pate thinks like a businessman and distrusts the bureaucracy. My notes stressed accountability—measuring outcomes to get a return on the taxpayer's investment. Involving communities should appeal to him—DuPage knows best. Fixing the fragmentation by integrating services in one stop would make sense to him as a former salesman out with customers. Putting myself in his shoes, I had to come up with a way to give him some oversight of this big change process. I made another note—"create a role for Pate and the senate." *I had* to persuade him to change his mind—this was it.

After absorbing the opening blast against the governor, I sat down at the foot of his desk and started talking. "We agree that the human services bureaucracies are a mess, and here's a chance to do something about it—we *can* get results and accountability. We can hold the bureaucrats accountable for self-sufficiency. He settled back in his chair and started to listen. I gave him a copy of the principles that formed the backbone of the reform, and we talked a few minutes about the most important ones. He looked at the Rube Goldberg chart, and quickly grasped the one stop shopping idea. Though I hadn't yet reached the point of making him smile, it was clear the idea of being able to determine the return on the taxpayers' investment in human services pleased him. He listened carefully as I talked about the successes in the five test sites, especially DuPage. I could see one of the reasons he was regularly reelected senate president—he was a good listener. I continued, "We have longtime welfare recipients with almost no employment history successfully working!" I suggested he call his close friend Gayle Franzen or Margo Schreiber, the energetic DuPage County Federation chair whom I knew was a friend of his.

After about forty-five minutes he said, gesturing to the papers in front of him, "Me and my guys have had twenty-three meetings with the administration, and already you've given me more information about why we should do this than in all of those meetings put together." I felt like leaping up from my chair with a cheer, but I wasn't there yet.

Putting myself in his shoes I said: "Pate, if I were you I wouldn't sign off on a huge reorganization of one-third of the state government budget without some oversight. Why don't we set up some kind of legislative oversight group, where your people could work with the governor's office to make sure things are done right? It'll take at least a year to put the pieces in place for a change and do it right. To ensure checks and balances we could do it legislatively rather than through an executive order." He didn't come right out and agree, but it was clear he liked that idea. I was excited about embedding the reform and reorganization in legislation—a much more permanent approach than an executive order. However, it brought with it the problem of figuring out how to withdraw the executive order without the governor losing face publicly—a manageable problem, I felt.

Serendipitously, he then said he felt that this proposed merger of several large organizations required the involvement of someone from the private sector with merger experience. I mentioned that I had led the worldwide merger and acquisition practice for McKinsey & Co. and would agree to stay involved. His eyes lit up and he asked if I would consider running the newly combined Department of Human Services. I said I thought I could be more effective behind the scenes, but would help ensure that we found someone very competent. Besides, I thought, if I were to indicate that I was open to taking a job in state government I would lose much of the support that I had built. "Aha!" some would say, "he *does* have a personal agenda." He then talked about who *couldn't* run the new department, stating that if the governor was going to choose Joan Walters to run the department, he would make sure the reorganization didn't happen. I told him I'd make sure the Governor understood those views, and chose not to ask him why he had such strong feelings.

He then said "If we do this we've got to keep that Medicaid mess out of it until it gets fixed—I want to keep my eye on it directly, also DCFS." Medicaid (medical benefits for the poor) had been prominent in the media with payment scandals, and the foster care part of the Department of Children and Family Services periodically earned notoriety for incidents of child abuse and neglect. Even with the exceptions of Medicaid and DCFS we had most of what we needed to integrate human services, and upon reflection I thought it would be a plus if our reform effort initially was not vulnerable to the public criticism that the next abuse incident among the 44,000 kids in state-supervised foster care would undoubtedly bring. I said that I believed we could get most of the value of the reform with this compromise, and before I could figure out what to do next, he was on the phone to Springfield with his chief of staff Carter Hendron, outlining our understanding and telling Carter he thought this was the way to go. He then said he wanted me to go through it all with Senator Steve Rauschenberger, his respected head of the senate appropriations committee. He then called Steve, who happened to be in Chicago in the state of Illinois building office that senators use when in Chicago on business. Pate outlined our discussion to Steve and told him to meet with me. Steve and I agreed to meet as soon as I got back to Chicago that day.

At one point near the end of our meeting, Pate asked me if there was a single one of the human services department heads that I would hire as part of the management team for my former company. I dodged the question, not wanting word to get back to the governor that I agreed with Pate that his team was weak—but he had a point, given the huge stake in terms of human lives and the billions involved. The management team should have been stronger.

But isn't the legislature a big factor in restricting pay levels of top people in the governor's office and agencies to the $60,000 to $90,000 range? These are huge responsibilities for which compensation is one-third to one-half the levels for comparable managerial responsibilities in the private sector. Of course Pate would reply, "If we raised the pay, he would still surround himself with the same group of weak people he feels comfortable with, they'll only cost the taxpayers more." As a taxpayer, I believe that higher salaries—if used properly to attract competent, experienced managers—would be an excellent investment. I've found that often good, younger managers feel they cannot justify to their families the salary cuts required for service in state government. However, I can't fix the pay issue now; my plate is full enough with human services reform. Despite Pate's critical rhetoric, I became convinced his primary objective was to come up with a plan that would really have a positive impact on the human services systems reform.

I thanked him for getting things moving again and reiterated my promise to stay with it. He put his arm around my shoulder and walked me to the door, asking me about my family. He said, "You're my kinda guy." We said good-bye, and he said, "Thanks for stopping by, *pal*."

As I was making the now one and a half-hour drive back down-town, I was exhilarated. Today I really made a difference! We're going to make it happen—Rube Goldberg is history! Though there were important steps left, we were on a clear path to reforming the system.

In reflecting on my meeting with Pate, I realized that he listened to, understood, and appreciated my coffee shop points, but he also placed heavy weight on personalities. Who was going to run it? Who was going to be involved in making sure it got set up properly? He was as much businessman as policymaker. Setting aside the inflammatory rhetoric, he was pretty good at cutting through complex issues and getting to the bottom line. Hopefully the inevitable pressures from providers wouldn't cause him to waver. As a Republican, Pate was used to opposing the unions, but some members of his caucus in swing districts could be peeled away, shrinking Pate's majority. Hope-fully our work with the Employee Involvement Committee and with some of the providers would take the passion out of those who would normally be opponents. If the unions and providers were neutral or only mildly opposed, we'd be okay. If we became a primary target, there would be trouble. As I approached the Loop, I reminded myself that right after my meeting with Rauschenberger I had a 4:00 meeting with Howard Peters—maybe that would be the moment to start getting the warring factions together.

Senator Rauschenberger is a colorful character. An energetic, mid-forties fellow with a black, gray-flecked goatee, one of his favorite descriptions of himself is "a failed recliner salesman from Elgin." He did own a furniture store in Elgin that was rumored to not be doing very well when he ran for the $47,000 theoretically part-time job of state senator. The self-deprecating humor masks a very sharp intelligence that catapulted him over a large number of more senior senators to the powerful ($36 billion budget) appropriations job and possible heir apparent to Pate. We discussed the framework of a deal, and I decided I had to strike while the iron was hot. "Steve, Howard's waiting for me upstairs. He's the governor's top guy on human services, I think it would be good if you came along." He said he would, Howard agreed that I should bring him, and what followed was fascinating to me.

After the handshakes I described my meeting with Pate. I went through it in some detail, because I wanted to make sure that the case for what we were doing was clear in their minds. I knew each would have to go out and persuade many others, particularly the stream of legislators and provider lobbyists they both would be talking to in the coming weeks. Then I said, "Now it's up to us to put a plan together to move forward." To their great credit, they started by openly clearing the air—each sharing their suspicions of the other and the other's colleagues and the ensuing misunderstandings. The senate thought the governor was not being open and might have a hidden agenda. The senate understandably was insulted that such a huge reorganization would be done unilaterally by the executive order—an insult to the institution and to Pate personally. The governor's office thought the senate might have some other agenda, unrelated to the merits of the human services reform, and feared the senate was reflexively negative on anything relating to human services—a hopeless mess in the senate's view. Why was one big mess any better than six smaller messes?

After a thorough clearing of the air, a spirit of new resolve emerged, with both Howard and Steve sensing a real window of opportunity to make a difference. The outlines of a bipartisan Legislative Task Force on Human Services Reform were hammered out. It would have appropriate membership from both sides of the aisle in the house and senate and be equally balanced between the two bodies. The governor's office would appoint the chair, but the legislature would have more votes, and therefore could limit or slow down the reorganization if it found the developing plans unsatisfactory. We established a timetable that called for implementation of the new organization one year after the law was passed and signed.

I suggested Phil O'Connor, a knowledgeable and well-respected friend, as chairman. Phil, a Ph.D. and partner in the consulting arm of one of the big accounting firms, is an expert on the economics and politics of the electric utility industry. Trim, balding, and intense, he has a casual demeanor that accompanies a quick, very creative mind. Most important, Phil is a former top official in state government known and liked by the house speaker, Pate, and the governor, and someone I had worked with before in campaigns and on reform projects. I had been keeping him informed and getting his advice on my human services reform quest. He is a loyal Catholic and cares about the less fortunate. His interest in the Governor's Task Force was a natural, and in retrospect I probably should have recruited him as a member. The suggestion of Phil was enthusiastically accepted by Steve and Howard, adding momentum to our effort. The next step was to draft the law and get it passed by both the senate and the house.

House Speaker Lee Daniels was also very angry with the governor, but I had done a better job of keeping him informed of our reform efforts, periodically visiting him in his downtown Chicago law office and talking with him at various events around town. Lee was also in touch with and personally sensitive to the role human services plays in government, and was influenced, some believe, by his having a disabled daughter. He had also developed a passionate commitment to government accountability during his years as a legislative leader and as a business lawyer in downtown Chicago. Lee was convinced taxpayers don't believe they are getting a return for the huge amount of money now being invested in human services, and for him to remain speaker in a swing state like Illinois, he must show results. Lee became speaker in 1994, and for just two years, on the basis of a majority of just a few seats. He also believed strongly that his members, for the most part, are elected in districts by voters who strongly oppose taking more of their income by raising taxes. Voter polls clearly supported his view.

Lee's anger centered on Governor Edgar's announcement, without clear communication with Lee, of that education-funding plan that included a 33 percent state income tax increase. I had invested time with Lee earlier, so I was sure he understood and agreed with our reform plans. I had convinced him that he would get more accountability, both at the caseworker level and at the top management level. Lee told me, "Your human services/welfare reform plan is fine, but you've got to understand that when there is a war going on there are other casualties." Translation: he was using the governor's need for approval of our welfare reform and reorganization plan as a bargaining chip in his effort to keep the governor from raising taxes. It pained me to think he would let human services reform be a casualty of politics unrelated to what we were doing, but there we were. It wasn't right, it wasn't fair to have years of work jeopardized. Of course to think that politics has to be right and fair is naive to the extreme, I thought. I was learning more about politics than I wanted to.

Lee and his small, young staff must also deal with myriad other issues such as utility deregulation, riverboat gambling, gay marriages, the $36 billion budget, etc., etc., all in a relatively short, very rushed legislative session. State representatives are paid $47,000 per year, drive hours to Springfield on Monday night, and back home on Thursday night, dealing with hundreds of issues in three session days per week—almost guaranteeing lack of depth and often lack of interest. There are 1,700 registered lobbyists swarming over Springfield, putting pressure on and "educating" the 59 senators and 118 representatives—a real zoo. I had developed a relationship with the chiefs of staff of both the senate president and the speaker, and over the preceding year or two had sent key members in both bodies articles about the reform, met with them in their offices, and talked briefly with them at political events. However, for the most part, the only legislators who show real interest tend to be those on the committees relevant to human services. The scope of legislative activities is too wide and the issues too complex to expect anything much different.

Lee and Pate, despite tremendous pressure from the governor, the press, and the education lobbies, defeated the tax increase (the state ran a large surplus the very next year) and found other ways to add to the education budget. Lee then signaled his troops to let the human services welfare reform proceed.

We were extremely lucky to avoid showing up in the crosshairs of one or more of the most potent lobbying organizations. Perhaps some were distracted by the education battle. The influence of major lobbyists over certain legislators is legendary. For example, Representative Shirley Jones,[1] chair of the House Public Utilities Committee, receives the largest portion of her campaign funding from Commonwealth Edison and other utilities, and obtained State of Illinois scholarships for the daughter and stepson of the Commonwealth Edison lobbyist.[2] No one bothers to try to get Representative Jones to do anything inconsistent with the interests of Commonwealth Edison. Henry Bayer's AFSCME always shows up as one of the top twenty political contributors in legislative elections, along with top-twenty teammates the Teamsters, United Autoworkers, teachers union, and AFL/CIO, who often work together. We are fortunate that Henry chose not to try and shut us down. By far the largest political contributor in Springfield, the Illinois State Medical Society could have stopped us in our tracks. As I started to learn the ropes in Springfield, I became amused by how interested all those doctors were in good government—contributing hundreds of thousands of dollars in each election, more than any other group! The teachers and trial lawyers followed them at the top of the big contributor's list for a recent election—I wonder why! Springfield is arguably worse than Washington in purchasing influence because there is no $2,000 individual contribution limit.

The law was drafted by lawyers from the governor's office and both chambers and approved by a committee in each chamber. Further negotiations resulted in adding parts of the Department of Children and Family Services to the new Department of Human Services and leaving out parts of the Department of Public Health that relate to concerns like health inspections, certain kinds of licensing, and the like. Aging, though a logical part of the new organization, was pulled out at the last minute due to pressure from the American Association of Retired Persons (AARP). There wasn't enough time to get AARP in the boat, and a delay would not have been worth it. At some point we should be able to convince AARP and other special interests that they will get more mileage from this small department if it is integrated with and leveraged by the other family efforts.

The final welfare reform/reorganization product was the Department of Human Services Act (HB 2632), a 956-page law about one foot high. I was told that its size was due to the necessity of changing language in scores of existing laws that governed the work of the six predecessor agencies. It contained most of the important elements necessary to implement our now tried and true Governor's Task Force principles. The combined organization broke down bureaucratic barriers and gave us the framework and flexibility to take our ideas statewide, subject to the Legislative Task Force approval of our specific implementation plans.

May 2 was the big day when HB 2632 came to the floor of the senate. Steve Rauschenberger would have to carry the mail as the sponsor of the reorganization effort. He introduced it correctly, saying "it provides an organization for a single front door into the human services . . . in the state of Illinois and provides the potential for consolidated case management. I would urge its adoption." Senator Earlean Collins from Chicago, later to become a Democratic member of the Legislative Task Force, rose in opposition, complaining that "no service providers, people that really know about service delivery, will be involved" on the Legislative Task Force. There was considerable discussion about what the providers thought, with the Democrats implying that the providers were against the bill, but the Republicans implying that the provider's voices had been heard, and they were going to be alright. After considerable discussion, mostly about whether the process leading to the bill was open or not, Senator Rauschenberger responded: "Let me try to reassure you . . . the Governor formed a task force on human services more than two years ago . . . they've worked with people from the . . . University of Chicago, Northwestern University. Much of the emphasis—the whole beginning of this in the governor's executive order and his State of the Senate [address] comes from Gary MacDougal's [Task Force] on Human Services."[3]

Then Pate stepped up to the plate in his role as senate president to wrap it up. "I rise in support of HB 2632. And I want to compliment Senator Rauschenberger on all the long, hard work in his committee putting this together. Now let me just say this: I think the key to this whole consolidation is the task force that we're going to create by resolution today. Three from the house; three from the senate; the governor picks the chairman . . . So everybody is going to have their input. Under the governor's executive order, that would not be true. So we have changed the circumstances. This is a step in the right direction. We ought to have one stop shopping . . . a person could go to one person for their help . . . it'll do away with duplication."

The vote was thirty-seven ayes, sixteen nays, two voting present. Senator Barack Obama (D) told me recently that he was instrumental in getting this bill passed—evidence that this kind of human-services reform can (and should) be bipartisan. It was good for my morale that Steve Rauschenberger thought invoking my name would be meaningful to the other senators, especially since I knew I really hadn't done as much prior homework with the legislators as, in retrospect, I should have.

The bill also passed in the House sixty-nine to forty-four, meaning that the new vision attracted votes from both parties in both chambers. The house majority leader Bob Churchill did a very good job describing the bill, putting special emphasis on communities, saying, "It will provide accountability by working closely with the communities to meet local needs. [This will help ensure] that the bureaucracy doesn't take the money out, but that the money actually goes to benefit the people who come in to be served by this state. I truly believe this bill sets in motion a reorganization, the results of which are going to prove one of the best things we've done in this state."[4] In assessing what the providers were up to, I came to the conclusion that most said they didn't like it, but they didn't fight it as hard as they could have. I decided we had done a pretty good job with them. Bob Churchill said he had met with 130 of them, including the unions, and cited some, including Voices for Illinois Children, that approved. A Democratic opponent took the floor and cited a poll of providers he had taken where "86 percent were not in favor of this." Providers' views were mentioned in almost every speech—but fortunately we prevailed. Though it all worked out, the process was too risky and hair-raising. A defeat would have created a black cloud we might not have been able to get out from under.

Charlene and I drove to Springfield to watch the governor sign the bill in that beautiful historic capitol office of his on July 3, 1996, my birthday—the best possible birthday present. The organizational and policy framework was now established to make integrated services for the whole family, connections to communities, and measured outcomes happen statewide. The formation of the new Department of Human Services should accelerate our self-sufficiency mission. I'd had a wonderful birthday party with close friends the weekend before, but it was hard to beat the sense of satisfaction of seeing the task force ideas become the law of the state. The office was full of press and TV cameras, together with about thirty guests, many of whom had very little to do with the welfare/human services reform process and some who had actually opposed it. As Charlene and I watched them crowd in toward the governor for the group picture, I had to work harder than usual to keep my ego in check—it somehow felt as though they were taking credit for my work. But then Harvey's voice told me that scrambling for credit can be destructive. "This is not about your ego, Gary, this is about helping people." I took an available spot in the back row.

The new law gave our reorganization/reform team twelve months to implement the long-sought, integrated, community-based design, incorporating the previously agreed-upon task force principles. Our principles had moved from being a good idea that most observers thought should happen to a law that *required* their implementation—

the first of any state. In signing the bill, Governor Edgar trumpeted "the biggest reorganization of Illinois state government since 1900," involving about one-third of the state budget. As I look back on it, I realize we were extremely lucky that the conflict and chaos produced legislation, a much more permanent change, rather than the original executive order. An added plus is the broad involvement of legislators in the change process.

As I thought about the challenge ahead, the thought crossed my mind: don't pray too hard—you might get what you want! The pressure was really on now, but the rewards of grass roots involvement in helping people to self-sufficiency are great. We're making a difference!

We formed the Legislative Task Force with two Republicans, including Senator Rauschenberger, and one Democrat from the senate; two Republicans and one Democrat from the house; together with Howard Peters, Joan Walters, and Phil O'Connor from the governor's office. I was intensely aware that the legislators had the votes and could greatly limit the reorganization until they were satisfied—Pate's checks and balances. In particular, the committee was required to approve the plan for a "unified electronic management and intake information and reporting system." As a practical matter, both houses had to be kept happy, through their appointed task force members, or any number of legislative barriers could have been thrown up. There were three principal keys to successfully moving the process through the next twelve months: considerable one-on-one relationship-building with each member of the Legislative Task Force; the use of a quality outside group to help manage the design and change process; and getting input from the literally hundreds of people who had a stake in the new organization: providers, advocates, caseworkers, unions, managers, and anyone else who expressed interest.

I knew our vision and strategy was on target. A few months before the Legislative Task Force was formed, Dr. Preister, the outside evaluator, after months of interviews and evaluation, summarized where we were with the following encouraging words in his report: "These, then, are the strengths of Illinois's reform initiative. It is supported by political muscle. Its conceptual design is on target, focusing on state-level interservice collaboration as well as collaboration at the community level. Its scope is comprehensive and inclusive, and [it] focuses on results with a strong emphasis on [self-sufficiency]. The harvest of these strengths is widespread support for the reform effort. In interview after interview, it became clear that while there are some skeptics, the buy-in by stakeholders is very widespread."[5] While approval of academics is not a primary objective, the feedback from dozens of interviews can provide helpful guidance.

One of the house appointees to the Legislative Task Force, Representative Dave Leitch, assistant house majority leader and VP of a bank in Peoria, turned out to be a key figure with a single-minded answer to welfare system problems. He believed the single most important reform step would be the issuance of a "smart card" with which recipients could access benefits, and his interest in systems resulted in his getting appointed head of the task force management information systems subcommittee. Someone from the governor's office whispered to me that a smart card consulting firm was affiliated with Dave or his bank. True or not, it made sense to spend time with Dave, including a lunch and walk along the Chicago River. The discussions were always somewhat oblique and inconclusive, but I came to believe he really understood what we were doing and believed in it. I told him that a smart card might eventually become part of the system, but first we had to rationalize the overall structure in which a smart card could function. In the end he voted to support the reform, despite the absence of a smart card from the MIS plan.

One of the strongest, most engaged appointees to the Legislative Task Force was house Democrat Barbara Currie from Chicago's Hyde Park community next to the University of Chicago. Barbara, later to become house majority leader, is a smart, hard-working, bookish-appearing liberal in her forties greatly respected by her colleagues, especially in human services matters. One day I called Barbara, without first talking to the governor's office, and went out to visit her in her office in a Hyde Park shopping center. We spent and hour and a half going through all the background and reasoning behind the reform and reorganization effort, and she became comfortable that the effort was truly bipartisan. She cautioned me that not everyone could become self-sufficient, and we agreed to make an explicit provision in our mission statement and principles for the mentally and physically handicapped, while still having the overarching goal of maximizing self-sufficiency. She asserted that we were being naive to think that we could do all we wanted without a lot more money. I pointed out that there wasn't any extra money in the budget, and that the Republicans believed that raising taxes was political suicide. She said she was sure they could get away with it, and I delicately shifted the discussion to other issues. All in all it was the start of a mutually respectful relationship that has been very helpful in our reform quest. Her dedication to human services reform showed clearly when, during the course of the task force work, the Democrats recaptured the house and she became majority leader. Arguably task force membership should have shifted to include two house Democrats and only one Republican, instead of the other way around. However, after comments to that effect, she did not make an issue of it and got down to business. The message to me was that she felt we were moving in the right direction. I also felt that the drive out to Hyde Park had paid a dividend.

The other legislative members of the task force were interested, but less engaged, with the exception of Steve Rauschenberger who, as the senior senator, tended to drive the agenda forward. Steve and I would meet or talk before each Legislative Task Force meeting and agree, along with Phil O'Connor, on what needed to be accomplished. We were operating in a bipartisan manner, and it was working. Interestingly, the two Democratic members had spoken vigorously against the bill in their respective chambers.

As a former partner I am clearly biased, but I believe McKinsey & Co. to be the finest consulting firm in the world. Specializing in top management challenges such as strategy and organization design, McKinsey's clients include a very large share of the most important corporations in the world. Partners work very hard, and their compensation is in the range of $1 million a year. A dominant criterion for working with a client is the firm's assessment of whether real change will take place. They try hard to avoid work where the end product is only a report, and as a result they do little work for governments. However, as they go about their intense corporate work, they look for opportunities to be helpful to the communities where they are located, and individually and collectively they donate considerable hours to helping nonprofit organizations. Encouraging this kind of work also helps the firm retain bright, community-conscious younger consultants.

Earning my everlasting gratitude, McKinsey & Co.'s Chicago office donated a team of seven consultants, including senior partners, for seven months—an in-kind contribution well in excess of $1 million. They took over a large office in Springfield in a building next to the capitol and commenced work on the design of the new organization, consistent with task force principles and experiences from the five test sites. They interviewed those involved in the test sites and throughout government. They also spent time with providers and legislators. They did everything necessary to ensure that the emerging organization design was sound, including extensive client file reviews to validate assumptions. They also spent much time facilitating the resolution of conflicting views on organization design with the myriad involved stakeholders.

As an example, McKinsey reviewed 365 client files gathered from eighteen existing programs administered by both the state and private providers. The team identified the overlap among departments and gaps in services. Representative families were described and discussed, and the written reports and presentations evoked, for me, thoughts of the ladies in the backyard. These were, in effect, the ladies' case files, and we were in the process of changing the system so it would work to help them become independent. McKinsey went on to illustrate the improved outcomes in those few circumstances when services were coordinated and complete. Within the framework of integrated services, they developed a number of alternative organization designs to explore and get comments from the many stakeholders within and outside government. They visited communities, all of the Governor's Task Force test sites, and interviewed welfare recipients. By the time they made their reports[6] to the Legislative Task Force or the governor's office, they had done so much homework that they knew more about the issues than almost anybody. The fact that the firm was volunteering their time and had no aspirations to obtain the state of Illinois as a paying client enhanced their credibility. They achieved buy-in and commitment at every stage of the process, and then pulled together all of their findings with thoughtful documentation—an operational blueprint for the new Department of Human Services, now required by law to open its doors July 3, 1997 (Figure 10).

Governor Edgar picked Joan Walters to head up the reorganization process and, working with McKinsey, she involved hundreds of people inside and outside of the government on seventeen committees or teams, with titles such as Program Consolidation, Rate Setting and Performance Contracting, Management Information Systems, and Service Delivery Redesign. Everybody got a chance to get their ideas out on the table. This totally inclusive process made the implementation of the reform effort very hard to criticize, and some good ideas resulted. Howard Peters and I chaired a committee of providers who told us what they would like to see changed. Among other things, they were receiving an inordinate number of overlapping audits and reviews from various state agencies, and egregiously slow payment for their services due to unnecessary bureaucratic delays, often resulting in severe cash flow pressures and unmet payrolls. One small provider told of mortgaging his house to meet a payroll. Commitments were made to make changes under the new structure, and providers who might have opposed the reorganization now hoped that integration of separate departments offered the prospect for a more rational relationship with the state. There were times when I thought Joan had gone too far with her endless schedules of meetings stretching over most of that transition year, but having survived it, the value of inclusiveness was great. The climate was sufficiently positive that the duplicated staff and management positions (e.g., public relations, legislative relations, department director, etc.) eliminated at the top levels of the various departments happened smoothly without a big dip in morale, despite the fact that many of those affected had leg-

Figure 10. The New Integrated Community-Connected Human Services System
(Illinois)

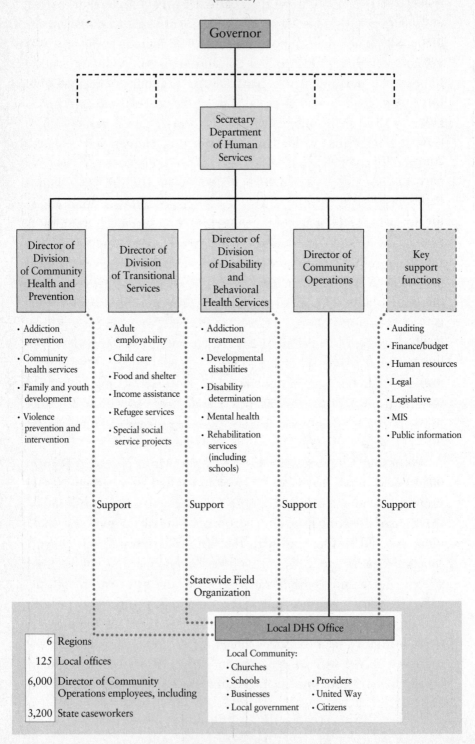

Governor

Secretary
Department
of Human
Services

Director of
Division
of Community
Health and
Prevention

Director of
Division
of Transitional
Services

Director of
Division
of Disability
and
Behavioral
Health Services

Director of
Community
Operations

Key
support
functions

- Addiction
  prevention
- Community
  health services
- Family and youth
  development
- Violence
  prevention and
  intervention

- Adult
  employability
- Child care
- Food and shelter
- Income assistance
- Refugee services
- Special social
  service projects

- Addiction
  treatment
- Developmental
  disabilities
- Disability
  determination
- Mental health
- Rehabilitation
  services
  (including
  schools)

- Auditing
- Finance/budget
- Human resources
- Legal
- Legislative
- MIS
- Public information

Support   Support   Support   Support

Statewide Field
Organization

Local DHS Office

6	Regions
125	Local offices
6,000	Director of Community Operations employees, including
3,200	State caseworkers

Local Community:
- Churches
- Schools
- Businesses
- Local government
- Providers
- United Way
- Citizens

islative sponsors or relatives and friends elsewhere in the bureaucracy and in the provider community. Administrative cost savings in the first year were $4 million, a nice plus, even though this wasn't the reason for the reorganization.

Another crucial piece of any state's reform is the management information systems that are needed to provide the information on individual and family histories to front-line caseworkers. It is clear that it is really not possible to rationalize the existing sprawling, fragmented computer systems (usually a separate, older mainframe for each department and program), without something like the new Illinois Pathfinder management information system and its one stop shopping for human services, utilizing community-based personal computers. A personal computer at the fingertips of a caseworker is connected to a rationalized state "data warehouse" containing all the information on the client and the client's family obtained in previous contacts with the various state systems. The PC also contains an inventory of private community supports in addition to government services. The technology to carry out the necessary integration economically— linking to, but not junking the older base systems—has only been available in recent years. Ironically, this means that advances in technology, often cited as a reason the disadvantaged are left behind in today's economy, make system reform more feasible than ever before.

Illinois' new law calls for a flexible, community-connected system, one that is clearly focused on helping people like Janice and the ladies in the backyard become self-sufficient. The new system is expected by experts to be a model for the nation—most of Rube Goldberg is history. The five community test sites, spread across the state, clearly showed the value of pulling together the many human services programs and services at the community level, helping make the governor's sound-bite one stop shopping a reality.

Profound differences in the nature and culture of legislative districts, short attention spans, pet causes, tremendous pressures, some racism, and probably occasional corruption make dealing with the legislature one of the most challenging aspects of human services reform. There are also some potentially very useful lessons for other states, some of them stemming from a mistake I made in not involving some key legislators early enough. There is also more work for Illinois. A logical next step would be to rationalize in similar fashion the sprawling job training and placement bureaucracies, discussed earlier, and productively link them to human services. Integrating the job preparation activities at the community colleges with other job training and placement programs and holding the community colleges more accountable for results would be a big political challenge. Many legislators have community colleges in their districts, and each is a political force. The steps taken in human services reform would be a good model to follow in pursuing this parallel project.

In terms of my personal journey through the process of reforming a massive welfare/human services system, the legislative challenge was among the most fascinating and difficult. It became clear very early that, even though all of the relevant agencies were part of the executive branch, reorganization and reform could not be achieved without changing laws. I had never been involved in changing laws before, and the experience gives new meaning to the old saw that laws are like hot dogs—you don't want to see them being made. Most states have not integrated their human services systems, and as they get deeper into their welfare pool, the urgency of creating an integrated, community-connected system will grow—a chance for community and state leaders to *make a difference*.

PRINCIPAL POINTS

1. For the reform to be institutionalized it should be embedded in legislation at the state level, allowing it to better survive changes in key players and administrations.
2. "Self-sufficiency" and "accountability" are bipartisan mantras that can facilitate the process of bringing large numbers of short-attention-span legislators with widely varying backgrounds into agreement.

3. Building personal relationships with the influential legislators is critical.
4. The systems change process is very messy, but truly open and inclusive planning will maximize chances of success.
5. An impartial third-party outside group can make a huge contribution to the design of a new organization.

10

Pulling Together
"All the Pieces of the Puzzle"

One never knows what will happen if things are suddenly changed.
But do we know what will happen if they are not changed?
—ELIAS CANETTI

The newly restructured system, with all the pieces of the puzzle pulled together, made its debut when the new Department of Human Services opened its doors on July 3, 1997. Things began to change immediately. The 6,000 employees in the 128 Department of Human Services field offices went back to the same offices they had occupied the day before when they were the public face of the Department of Public Aid, the first line of assistance for people who wanted help from government. The day before, they were administrators of an income maintenance system, focused on filling out forms and applying the state and federal definitions of who is needy to their circumstances. In that system there was only one overarching focus: eligibility. Either you were eligible for welfare, food stamps, or medical assistance, or you were not.

On July 3, caseworkers began the process of becoming something else: the front line of a system focused on solving problems and achieving results. A monthly check would be only one arrow in the worker's quiver. Their arsenal of help moved toward including such things as clothes for job interviews and payment for auto insurance to keep the car on the road and give the person a way to get to work. Caseworkers were to be given new training, so that they could become the focal point for the delivery of all services, not just welfare checks, food stamps, and Medicaid cards. Though it would take considerable time to fully implement all the needed changes and create the new culture focused on problem solving and results, we were on our way to realizing the potential that the new system and structure allowed. A single state caseworker, augmented by specialists when needed, now has direct responsibility for almost all services for a given family, helping clear the way for Janice, and thousands like her, as they move to self-sufficiency.

The new law frees most front-line caseworkers from narrow restrictions on whom in the family they can serve and with what services. The structure was now in place to connect welfare with services for job training and placement, alcohol and substance abuse, mental health, developmental disabilities and rehabilitation, together with food stamps, and Medicaid at a single point. Over time, the goal of seamless, coordinated services was now possible. However, training the 3,128 caseworkers, only 31.6 percent of whom are college graduates, is a formidable task that cannot be accomplished quickly. I kept remembering that "it took thirty years under the old system to get into the mess we inherited, so it will take some time to turn it around," to quote a phrase I became fond of using.

The new $4.5 billion department employs about 20,000 people, and a dramatically new management structure was installed that made integrated services and communities the focal point. As Pate requested, the $5 billion Medicaid bureaucracy and the child protection functions of the Department of Children and Family Services (DCFS) are not in DHS. However, Medicaid eligibility is still handled by DHS workers in DHS field offices, a fact that makes little difference as seen by the recipient. This means Medicaid is still part of the one stop, even though the payment processing bureaucracy still reports separately to the governor. Though not crucial, over time, management logic points toward eventually folding the rest of Medicaid in with DHS. The Department of Children and Family Services works closely with DHS, and further improving this connection is important. As an example of the common sense consolidation of programs that took place in the new DHS, eight previously separated child care programs, four under DCFS and four under the old Public Aid department, were combined under a single division in the new DHS. Each program previously had different policies, payments, and entry points. Now there are consistent eligibility requirements and payments, with one entry point into the system.

The combining of departments and programs, and previously separate administrative costs for such things as public relations, legislative liaisons, and the like produced $4 million in savings which was applied to direct self-sufficiency services. This wasn't a major reason for the reorganization, but it was a nice plus and got things off to a good start.

The field offices of the new DHS became the Division of Community Operations under the leadership of first-time government employee B.J. Walker, the energetic Governor's Task Force staff leader. B.J. brought along some other GTF staffers to help provide the critical mass of leaders to change the culture. As has been done in much of American industry, among their first moves was a major reengineering of the field offices, installing processes and training to reflect the new focus on self-sufficiency. These changes had to be done with sensitivity to union issues, but often the larger obstacle was the state's own Central Management Services bureaucracy, a virtual museum of antiquated rules, regulations, and systems which apply to the more than 150,000 state employees.

I was pleased that Governor Edgar named Howard Peters, the former prison chief, secretary of the new department, since he had a strong belief that most people on welfare *could* be self-sufficient if they found there was a ladder to climb. He is also smart enough, strong enough, and committed enough to change things. Howard's speeches often include a statement that I love to hear: "Welfare isn't good enough for poor families, they deserve to be able to work." One of Howard's first moves was to make college graduation a caseworker prerequisite, and with retirements, turnover, and a modest increase in the number of caseworkers, the percentage of college graduate case-workers increased 20 percent to 37.3 percent by the end of 1998. In the short run, requiring a college degree was a good way to increase the capability of the organization to do the many new things that were required, as caseworkers were expected to think on their own and become problem solvers. However, over time it would be good to develop sufficient training, personnel system sophistication, and union cooperation, so that pure merit—independent of seniority and creden-tialism—could govern promotions to caseworker. A degree require-ment could become a barrier to some capable people, including former recipients, obtaining jobs they could do well. At UPS there are very capable senior managers with responsibility for thousands of people who lack a college degree, but their competence is unquestioned. Illi-nois needs an equally agile personnel system. Because there were no layoffs of unionized workers, union problems during this period were minimal, as Henry Bayer and his associates watched attentively. At the management level, to avoid excessive trauma and to get moving quickly, most positions in the new DHS were filled with redeployed administrators from the previously separated departments, subject to later review.

In addition to the statewide DHS field organization being able to speak for almost all human services, the department was staffed with community liaison workers whose sole function was to work with communities to link employers, churches, and schools to those enor-mous state resources. Some other states had a single human services department, but usually it was not unified in a single field organiza-tion, and there were none we were aware of that also connected as in-tegrally with communities as in Illinois. All of the pieces of the puzzle are necessary for real success, and the Illinois reform, for the first time in any state, had the integrated framework to bring the essential ingre-dients for success together under one roof. This was to become espe-cially important as we got deeper into the caseload, dealing with more complicated problems.

Measuring self-sufficiency outcomes—a crucial and overarching ingredient in winning the confidence of voters and a primary focus of legislators and the governor—was built into the new system in a way that was as important to the ladies in the backyard as to anyone else. For the first time managers at all levels were held accountable for outcomes, not process, and self-sufficiency is the number one outcome.

Are lives really changing for the better? Getting good outcome data from government systems is extremely difficult, since most of the data requirements have historically been federally driven and until the recent federal welfare reform, *real* outcomes were not the focus. One of B.J.'s early moves was posting bar charts of individual office performance results on a prominent bulletin board in each local office. These charts measured key progress indicators such as number and percentage of clients working (the first step), total cases closed, cases closed due to work, and cases returning to the rolls. Office managers now had a bottom line, and some nonperformers have been removed or retired early. Current employees who are thriving in the new culture are being promoted, and active recruiting is underway for new talent.

A big part of measuring outcomes is changing the standards of performance for the many multimillion-dollar subcontracts to service providers. Instead of the value of their contracts (and therefore the size of their organizations) growing based on the number of dependent people they have found to serve, many are now being paid based on their success in helping people become self-sufficient by getting jobs, retaining those jobs, and exiting the system. The better providers welcomed performance-based contracting, but some were clearly uncomfortable with the idea of being measured.

As the management team moved through the major changes of the first year, Dr. Ira Barbell, the Casey Foundation professional deeply involved nationally in state-level systems change said, "No other state in the nation is pursuing fundamental reform on both the state level and at the community level. Illinois leads the nation in implementing a structure that pulls together almost all the crucial elements necessary to deal with the toughest cases in the self-sufficiency challenge. Other states have received more publicity, but when the easier cases have left the rolls, fundamentally integrated services and committed community involvement will become crucial, especially in those states with the tough big-city problems."

So how is Illinois doing on the bottom line? Great! The welfare caseload dropped an amazing 22 percent in the first year of the new DHS, 31 percent downstate and 18 percent in the city of Chicago.[1] The welfare rolls reached a thirty-year low. The percentage of welfare families in which at least one member worked rose from 27 percent in July 1997 to over 50 percent, about 50,000 families, in June 1999.

Illinois' impressive 86 percent reduction in the rolls by June 2003 (Figure 1, page 9), despite a soft economy in 2000, gives comfort that these vulnerable people, for the most part, didn't lose their jobs as the boom economy of the nineties weakened. The reduction in Cook County (Chicago) has been 85 percent—outstanding results for one of the toughest challenges in the nation. I can't prove (though someone probably will) that the kinds of entry-level jobs available to those just getting started on the workforce are still there when the economy weakens, but these results fit with the strong continuing interest that hotels, restaurants, farms, and other businesses have in ensuring that the flow of immigrants continues. There is work that needs to be done, and most of us initially learned about the world of work in basic entry-level jobs.

Fascinating to me was the description by Dan Miller, Associate Director of the Illinois Department of Human Services (IDHS), of what happened as the first recipients faced the five-year cutoff. Amazingly, only *six* cases remained out of the thousands that started the five-year process. These six were subjected to an intensive case management review, with experts in alcohol and substance abuse, work training, and the other relevant services around the table. IDHS was determined to do whatever it took to give these recipients the help they needed to get into the workforce. It turned out that most had a backup plan for relatives or others to provide help but they had decided to stay in the system receiving benefits as long as they could. In several cases the reason for not going to work was a legitimate concern that they be home to provide support and supervision to their children who had problems.

The nationally mandated five-year time limit for receiving welfare (TANF) payments means that of those now on the rolls in Illinois (and nationally), most are new since federal welfare reform was passed in 1996. Unfortunately the flow of young women onto the rolls has not stopped, and this accounts for most of the 90,000 recipients in Illinois and the roughly 5 million nationally (Figure 1, page 9).

The national reduction of 60 percent, or over 7 million recipients, is very impressive, given the fact that almost all states are not yet organized in a way to provide integrated services to families and have not taken much advantage of the opportunity to leverage state and federal resources by linking their efforts to communities in a meaningful way. Think what can happen when states tap these sources of further strength! We must be mindful of the fact that going off the rolls does not necessarily mean that the person is working. Some cases are closed because the client stops showing up, moves, or notifies their caseworker that they have a job. A client who has left the rolls may not want to be tracked, and presumably there is no need for the government to track them, but Illinois and some other states have been doing sampling to see where things stand.

Another important benefit of the accomplishments to date is the reduced caseload for the caseworkers, which gives the caseworkers more time to focus on the increasingly difficult cases remaining. Eighty percent of those who left the Illinois rolls in the first eighteen months of the new DHS did not return.

It is incorrect to characterize most people on welfare as abusers of the system but, as with any group of people, some people *were* cheating. To avoid detection, some working poor give false Social Security numbers to employers, and many work for cash, outside the economy that files reports with the IRS. Based on my interviews with caseworkers, it would be fair to guess that 5 to 10 percent of those who were on the rolls were already working, mostly in the nation's huge, multibillion-dollar cash economy. This ocean of money serves as the payroll for countless maids, laborers, unregistered taxi drivers, beauticians, shoe shiners, carpenters, roofers, prostitutes, sellers of drugs and stolen goods, baby-sitters, and on and on.

Of course, illegal and unreported economic activity is a notoriously difficult thing to measure, but based on reasonable ratios of the amount of money in circulation versus reported transactions, illegal and unreported activity is estimated to be about 19 percent[2] of the country's entire gross domestic product and climbing. The poor undoubtedly represent a small fraction of this huge number, but even a small fraction is likely to be a significant source of income in poor communities. Studies have shown[3] that these activities have long been used to augment welfare checks and often are necessary for survival, and we learned about it in listening to the ladies in the backyard, especially Lavon. Though no definitive study exists, it is certain that a number of the people performing these activities will overlap into the welfare system. The closer attention by caseworkers, required job-seeking activities, and the like has forced a choice: give up the $377 per month welfare check and part of the $315 monthly food stamp benefit, or give up the other income. The result is that a meaningful number of cash economy wage earners drop off the welfare rolls.

Typically people ask to get paid in cash primarily to avoid income taxes. But with the Reagan tax cut that eliminated income taxes in the lower brackets and the recently expanded earned income tax credit (EITC), there is effectively no federal tax on income up to $23,000 per year ($11.05 per hour)[4] for a single parent with two or more children. This makes payment in cash largely unnecessary for tax avoidance. However, the 7.65 percent FICA/Social Security tax and state income taxes in some states are still required at these low levels, cutting into valuable income often needed for survival.

A huge and not well known federal incentive to "make work pay" is the Earned Income Tax Credit or EITC.[5] This $25 billion benefit is a huge help to those who have entry-level jobs, essentially adding thirty cents to each dollar of earnings. For a low-wage worker with two children, this "negative income tax" adds $3,000 a year in tax free income at the $11,000 earnings level and is obtained by filing with the IRS. Unfortunately, despite intensive nationwide campaigns by the Casey Foundation and others, there are still many low-wage workers who don't know about this benefit and don't file for it. The EITC is a largely bipartisan effort that, augmented in many cases by state-level EITC's, increases the incentive to work. Also enhancing the transition from welfare to work, the Illinois Work Pay[5] program only gradually reduces the welfare check when work income starts, a very enlightened approach.

Because employers are required to turn in payroll lists, which are then matched against the welfare rolls to catch cheaters, there are still reasons why it is going to be hard to break the "can-you-pay-me-in-cash?" habit. Researchers Kathryn Edin and Laura Lein[6] extensively studied the survival strategies of women on welfare, estimating that on average the welfare check and food stamps cover 60 percent of living costs, with the rest being made up by other sources. Eight times as many mothers engage in unreported work as reported work. Edin and Lein reported that in addition to payments in cash, there is common use of false Social Security numbers to keep wages from counting against the welfare check. More women received cash from men than from any other source. The absent father was the most frequent contributor, helping out 33 percent of the women. Not surprisingly, three times as much money is given covertly as through formal child support. All of these circumstances enter into the decision on whether or not to try to keep qualifying for a welfare check.

While it took us thirty years to get into the situation we face and it will take years to get fully out of it, the great strides made already have even surprised me. Some exciting progress has been made, and the new system has produced a whole new way of thinking on the part of many managers and longtime employees of Illinois human services and some exciting milestones. In nine Illinois counties, the welfare caseload was reduced to *zero*. Spectacular—beyond our dreams!

Michelle Hare has worked for the state Department of Public Aid and then the new Department of Human Services for twenty-three years. A pleasant, middle-aged, unpretentious blond woman with considerable energy, Michelle started as a clerical worker and had worked her way up to office manager for Sangamon County by the time the Governor's Task Force launched the Springfield Federation in 1994. She worked very closely with that community collaborative on the establishment of the Lee Center one stop, which became the locus of integrated services under the leadership of the federation, and was very effective in responding to other community priorities. She also called on the Springfield Federation to tap into their job network as they placed the DHS clients.

Michelle took to the new way of doing business in human services with gusto, and is now central Illinois region manager with twenty-eight offices reporting to her. The region has an office in each of the twenty-eight counties stretched across central Illinois, and includes such small cities as Springfield, Decatur, Quincy, and Danville, each with their own smaller-scale version of inner-city poverty, and smaller towns, such as Rushville and Clinton, that seem to exist only because they are a county seat. Her central region is largely flat prairie, blanketed by rich corn and soybean fields and divided by the occasional river flowing toward the Mississippi. Michelle got me a cup of coffee in her busy office complex in downtown Springfield, and we sat in a spare conference room to take stock of what was happening. The new organization structure with its dramatically changed mission had been in place about a year and a half.

It was exciting to hear her talk. "To me the last twenty months have been a world of difference. Now it's truly different work—now the family is clearly the important piece and we are free to solve whatever problem shows up as a barrier to self-sufficiency. For most of my career before this, the job was to ensure timely and accurate dispensing of benefits. If the client presented a problem, we'd have to say 'we don't do that here.' As part of the bureaucracy we weren't able to think the way we do now." Michelle cited lots of examples, as if she remembered each and every client. "Before, if a pregnant sixteen-year-old client came in, all we could do was set her up for benefits. She could be lacking prenatal care and have substance abuse problems, and there was nothing we could do. I felt like I was leaving the job undone. My job then was to get her correct address, make sure she was categorically eligible, and make sure the check was cut for the correct amount. That was it. Now we send her over to the public health prenatal care worker for immunization and other care, giving us a chance to avoid low birth weight and other damaging and expensive problems that can result. Before we had no ties to public health— didn't even know anybody over there. Now we keep track of her and, two days a week, we have a substance abuse treatment specialist on site in the Sangamon office from Gateway, the private provider, who will help get her the treatment she needs." She periodically referred to the larger systemic changes. "Before the big reorganization the substance abuse people were off on their own—they weren't connected with us. I didn't even know who they were. We've made some good progress in co-locating services, but there is still a lot of work to be done." She moved her story back to the pregnant teenager. "After the baby is born we can get her back on track with child care, transportation, and a job. She knows welfare is time limited. One of the best sources of jobs in Sangamon is the Springfield Federation and the job network they have set up with the Springfield Chamber of Commerce and a private job training and placement contractor. They've found hundreds of jobs. The Springfield Federation is so strong now that they can successfully challenge the bureaucracy. This is the way it should be. It's all very exciting—everybody in the community is working together. I feel more successful the last twenty months, more fulfilled," she said. To me her words are like a dream come true. The community federation, with all the key local players is working hand in glove with the state, and the state is linking together its previously fragmented services—just like the dream vision laid out by the Governor's Task Force back when we started our reform effort!

In reflecting on Michelle's comments and her story about the pregnant teenager, I reviewed in my mind how far we had come toward implementing the basic principles developed at the Governor's Task Force retreat. While teenagers will continue to get pregnant, hopefully the rates will decline as more of them grow up in self-sufficient families which offer them more hope and alternatives to early childbearing. Once this girl showed up to get a welfare check, the fact that previously fragmented services were *integrated* made a difference. *Prevention* of dangerous and costly neonatal problems entered the picture right away. It was clear from the beginning that *self-sufficiency* was the goal, and permanent dependence was not an option. The *community* and its *volunteers* are now part of the system, and *public services* work closely with *private contractors*. The federation has been acting as an honest broker among providers, connecting them and minimizing the dysfunctional rivalry that occurs when each acts independently, pursuing its own pipeline into state funds. Michelle talked about the big change in working with the *whole family* if necessary, not just individual clients, and at the state level, millions in overhead were redeployed into direct services (*fewer administrators in relation to caregivers*). Michelle came close to validating our entire effort before I had even finished my cup of coffee. However, I was also aware that central Illinois, though containing plenty of poverty and problems, was not the size or texture of Chicago's inner city. I do believe, though, that it helped show us the way. I knew that we had a formidable challenge in front of us to fully implement these things statewide.

The whole process made me think of what happened at Mark Controls when we were trying to turn around our biggest division, Powers Regulator, a marginal operation which had fifty building controls contracting and service offices spread around the country. We developed a new strategy emphasizing after-sale service, changed the organization structure, and put the best people in the company in the toughest field offices. Visits to the offices told me we were on the right track, and after an understandable but anxiety-producing time lag, the momentum built until a loser turned into a winner.

I asked Michelle how things were going in her other offices, and she told some interesting stories. "When we started to work in the new organization in the new way, I met with the office managers, and we brainstormed for new ideas. One of the things we came up with was the idea of what we call 'front door money.' Before putting a client on the rolls and having them dependent, we look to see if there is a better way to get her into the work force or keep her there. In rural Illinois car trouble can easily jeopardize a job or the ability to get a job, so small investments in things like tires, auto insurance, and shocks can prevent the bigger costs of getting back on the rolls. In addition, those clients who are working and on the rolls at reduced levels often need help on a one-time spot basis to keep them working. We have to know the people and be sure we don't get taken advantage of, but it has worked well so far." Aha, flexibility at the local level—terrific! She showed me a memo from the Montgomery County office manager asking for $1,000 to replenish his "front door money" fund, listing seven people who received a total of $858.46 in amounts ranging from $83.75 to $196.55 over a two-month period. Items listed included tires, water hookup, car insurance, dental, work clothes, and gas money. The memo ended with the statement that these people "would not be working unless this money had been spent."

Front door money takes some political courage. Inevitably there will be someone who lies to a caseworker, or an office manager who makes a mistake. The client then gets some clothes or dentistry that she shouldn't, making a "gotcha" newspaper story. The story is unlikely to refer to all the jobs found or saved using front door money, or the very small percentage of misuse, since it would diminish the scandal value. It is clear to me that government has to take these manageable risks, doing what makes sense instead of letting fear of a press story drive policy. Any business that made decisions based on keeping visible mistakes as close as possible to zero would soon be passed by competitors willing to take risks.

Michelle said that all the offices now have the flexibility to provide bus tokens and cab fare as needed to get clients to work—a service Delrice found she occasionally had to provide as a self-sufficiency coach in Grand Boulevard. She said they commonly provide clothes so that when they send clients over to an employer they will look presentable. Before getting into my welfare reform quest it was hard for me to imagine people living so close to the line that they had absolutely no savings or cushion of any kind, but I learned that this is the reality for many, and the reasons are endlessly varied. This is the bottom of the ladder. This modest flexibility for spending at the local office level might not sound like much, but prior to the focus on outcomes, this degree of local flexibility was unheard of. If community leaders came in for coffee, there was no place in the budget that would allow for doughnuts. Office managers made decisions about dispensing millions, but bus tokens and doughnuts couldn't be authorized, even though these managers might be part of the process of cutting office spending dramatically.

Michelle said she was making progress "marketing what we are doing to the local communities. We've got lots of community involvement, and it often starts with networking around employment. In Macon County [where Decatur is located] they've formed the Macon County Federation that is much like the Springfield Federation." She told me about a senior citizens van in Edgar County, across from Terre Haute on the Indiana border, that now doubles as transportation taking welfare clients to work, and about the Kumler Ministry that has volunteered to provide transportation for welfare clients. It sounded like she'd made good progress in involving communities, but it takes a few years to really develop the kind of capability and influence that the Springfield Federation has achieved.

I'm reminded of a statewide boost that was given to the offices when each was asked to submit ideas on how they might use modest grants, averaging $15,000 or so, to stimulate community involvement. Churches were heavily involved as partners in these efforts, along with local schools and businesses. The activities made sense, most being work related. A local car dealer in Lasalle County helped provide reliable used cars on an affordable basis to allow transportation to an entry-level job; a local community college in Chicago helped train clients in household painting and repair, allowing for self-employment (in the cash economy?); in Will County, just south of Chicago on the Indiana border, used cars were bought, repaired at the local high school and the community college, and then sold to DHS clients on an affordable basis; some version of the used car assistance idea showed up in half a dozen communities. A number of others were for transportation vouchers or subsidies to make work economical. In Sangamon County the project was a Web site that allowed potential employers to prescreen clients for jobs. In the very distressed East St. Louis community the effort was to "help clients who have felonies, misdemeanors, bench warrants, or suspended driver's licenses which prevent them from passing police clearances that many employers require, to have certain felonies removed from their record. Many juvenile offenders that have already served time do not have the money or knowledge to [pursue the legal process that allows them to] have their record cleared." After the grants were awarded, the offices were given consulting help to assist local office managers with their implementation. These projects further identified local barriers that could be removed quite inexpensively if the community pitched in. It's the new culture of the Illinois human services system, and can easily become the culture for the nation.

My happy discussion with Michelle Hare was moving to a close, but she had another piece of news that really made me smile. "You know we now have an office with no welfare clients—the caseload is *zero* in the Schuyler County office! I had no idea where Schuyler County was and I was sure it was a long way in every conceivable respect from Cook County, but I wanted to learn more about it. The map in her office showed that it was in the western part of her region on the Illinois River. I scanned a memo describing how the office worked with the last five cases, and it was an interesting display of versatile hands-on coaching by state caseworkers. Those working but still drawing partial welfare payments were mailed job ads and pushed toward a GED. Assistance was rendered in collecting child support in several cases, and the final case, a mother with three autistic children, was helped to apply to a state rehabilitation center for her children and for Supplemental Security Income. This final case was an example where the special needs were so great and the awareness level on the part of the client so low that the extra caseworker attention now available due to reduced caseloads got her the financial and other support that she needed. This help allowed her to leave welfare and focus on the needs of her kids—driving to her psychologist appointments, spending time at the special school, and other requirements. The Schuyler experience gave me some confidence that when we got to the very bottom of the welfare pool we would find the right answers—and in a few cases the right answer might not be traditional work. However, I'm sure the woman with the three autistic children is working as hard as any of us. With no welfare clients, what does the Schuyler office do now? This is a small office, and there are still other functions and services, such as food stamps, as well as a maintenance function as new clients come along. Over time it may be possible to do some downsizing through attrition, but it is important not to act precipitously. When the economy turns down, we'll want experienced caseworkers—in addition we have to be careful about the example it would set rewarding successful people with the loss of their jobs. Good people can also be transferred to places of greater need, and it will be a while before the whole state runs out of welfare cases—though this should be an objective!

As I said good-bye to Michelle and left her office for my next appointment in the capitol building, I thought about how great it would be if I could get the legislators I was about to see to experience what was really going on. The Legislative Task Force, satisfied with the plans for the new department, voted unanimously to move ahead on the reorganization without limitations. The LTF then went out of business as specified in the law. In hindsight, it might have been a good idea to keep it going as a way of ensuring good communication with key legislators. I knew legislators heard grumbles from providers who want more money. People whose lives have been changed and are now working aren't likely to call, and they don't have lobbyists. There was a rumor that the alcohol and substance abuse providers were lobbying to get their own separate department back. I also heard rumors that some big providers including Jimmy Lago were quite worried about the funding coming to their organizations since the caseloads were coming down. There was increasing competition for "referrals," as cases assigned to providers are called. Maybe it was time for another lunch with Jimmy. One would think downsizing in human services was *good,* since it meant less human misery. We've got to reassure the legislators that they are on the right track. Most of them are happy, and the good numbers make the reform hard to attack, no matter what your relationship to the lobbyist providers. With the growing community involvement across the state, they ought to get good reports when they go back to their districts.

With the passage of time, the federations and other community collaboratives seem to get stronger and stronger. Greg Washington, Sokoni Karanja, and the Reverend Martin are as active and determined as ever in Grand Boulevard. Giving that crowd in Stateville some hope for a life, the ex-offender employment effort is off to a promising start. This is a crucial piece of the puzzle. In a large number of cases, ex-offenders are the fathers of the kids on welfare. Reduced recidivism and higher marriage rates should follow. The joint efforts with the job training and placement contractors are coming together well, and employment of hard-core welfare recipients continues to grow. The Grand Boulevard Federation took a leading role in managing 325 neighborhood welfare cases with multiple barriers to employment, and a subcommittee was formed to develop a strategy for some of the tough housing issues. Some downtown foundations have taken a strong interest in working with the Grand Boulevard Federation. Like Springfield and the others, the Grand Boulevard Federation has accomplished all we might have hoped for and more.

With all the success to date and promise for the future, the challenge ahead for Illinois and the nation continues to be formidable. Some may look at the fact that welfare rolls nationwide have been cut almost in half and declare victory, pronouncing the people remaining on welfare, with their drug, mental health, crime, and housing problems as beyond help. "In any civilization there is always an underclass, and we just have to live with it," I heard an otherwise sophisticated New Yorker say the other day. It is easy to adopt this view—a combination of declaring victory based on the major success to date and finding the remaining challenge hopelessly tough. In Springfield the other day, someone whispered to me that some racist legislators feel "there isn't much more we can do, the group willing to work is now working, and those left are disproportionately inner-city blacks, and they won't work." We, of course, know better than that, and I am eager to prove them wrong.

It is clear that an important test of government and communities working together, both nationally and in Illinois, is what happens from here on. The seamless array of problem-solving help must be put together by both communities and government so that we can take advantage of this unprecedented opportunity to make a difference. Trekking in Nepal, I did not really dream of being at this point where our prospects could be so promising—a unique window in history.

The best way to look at the situation is to appreciate how relatively quickly and easily the first phase of dramatic progress was accomplished, and look at the many important reforms yet to be accomplished as reasons to be optimistic about the next phase of the effort. Besides, some of the ladies in the backyard are in the group remaining. We know, having met them and some of their contemporaries, that most of them very much want to become self-sufficient, and we have learned that with some help they *can* be. The social cost of not moving ahead, in the form of crime and wasted lives, is still enormous, and the cost to taxpayers in the form of prisons, foster care costs, welfare checks, and the like are still huge and largely unnecessary. The achievements to date should give us more confidence that we can be successful in this second phase—the task that remains.

In Illinois, future effort, which I think of as the "Next Frontier," calls for building on our accomplishments to reach for "new higher ground." Particularly challenging is the extremely complex, heterogeneous group of remaining welfare people for whom we are trying to facilitate self-sufficiency. How fast we can move is dependent upon having a deeper understanding of factors no state has measured, such as the number of drug users in the remaining welfare population, number and degree of mental health problems, and number with a felony record. Some will have two or three of these challenges. Our friend Janice who works at UPS sticks with her estimate of drug use at 50 percent or more among unemployed inner-city welfare mothers. A good, state-supplied self-sufficiency coach, an effective connection to drug treatment, and an employer willing to take a reasonable business risk are required for those mothers. Experts have estimated that about 10 percent of the welfare population has prison records.

Self-sufficiency coaches have a special challenge with this remaining group on welfare, and it is safe to say that more resources will be required for each case, especially for drug and mental health treatment, to get many of these people employed and keep them employed. However, when they become successfully employed, experts say the mental health and substance abuse problems are likely to be more manageable. This extra support costs money, but it is being paid for by the savings from the reduced welfare rolls. For the taxpayer, the long-term savings from getting most of this last group off the welfare rolls are tremendous. It is also a smart investment to focus redeployed resources on self-sufficiency efforts directed toward the non-custodial parents—the fathers of the welfare children. Instead of just handing out food stamps as we did with Julius, we should tie the food stamps to legitimate work and family reunification and child support. Further flexibility from Washington will be helpful in moving resources to address local requirements.

The challenge is to manage these problems in an integrated, effective way that can create the chance for self-sufficiency for tens of thousands of ladies in the backyard and their partners. The "Next Frontier" stage is set, and *we know how to do it*. There are several elements in the next phase for Illinois—and much of the nation:

1. Complete the integration of the hundreds of Department of Human Services contractors, especially the alcohol and substance abuse contractors and welfare-to-work job training and placement contractors, into a seamless DHS case management process. Ensure that all new contracts are structured with incentive based on clear outcome measurements. The incentive can result in no future contract if performance is poor, and extra funding for the agency if success is achieved. Payments should be made as benchmarks are achieved.

2. Continue to integrate and link DHS case management with relevant non-DHS government entities such as the famous Chicago Housing Authority and various city of Chicago entities that are also trying to put disadvantaged people to work, such as Mayor Daley's Department of Employment and Training. One weakness of welfare-to-work efforts nationwide is a disconnect between the state effort and the efforts made by bureaucracies that report to the mayors in major cities. Even if the mayor and the governor are of differing political faiths, given the bipartisan nature of the solution, it is a win-win deal for both to work together. They need each other, and the increase of work among disadvantaged people has a particularly big payoff for the mayor in terms of the high likelihood of concurrent reductions in crime as people become legitimately employed.

3. Get to work connecting or consolidating the huge, fragmented array of job training and placement programs, establishing priorities that include welfare to work, and linking them more effectively to the human services system, communities, and employers.

4. Ramp up the number of communities (including schools, churches, United Way, local employers, community-based organizations, local governments, etc.) closely connected with DHS at the local level, and broaden their involvement in DHS problem solving. Begin to institutionalize the tracking of outcome data, organization of programs, and the tracking of funding *by community.*

5. Further strengthen the ties between DHS and employers, especially smaller community employers. Get DHS front-line workers to think increasingly of community employers as their customers, learning about their businesses and their employment needs.

6. Come up with additional creative answers to the transportation barriers in addition to building on and replicating the successes achieved so far.

7. Complete the management information systems work necessary to link all elements of the system, including nongovernment community resources, to the individual computers of caseworkers. No state in this great high-tech country has a first-class computer system design that can tie in all of the governmental and nongovernmental resources and related information at the caseworker workstation. The first state to create such a system should make it available to the other forty-nine. This is a great opportunity for a foundation to leverage its resources.

8. Gain a deeper understanding of the makeup of the remaining 93,000 people in the welfare pool, especially as to the incidence of alcohol and substance abuse, mental health problems, and ex-offender status, and redeploy the resources to develop the capacity to deal with those problems. Over the longer term as leases expire, correct the mismatch between the locations of welfare offices and the people they are trying to help. Use newly located offices and the payrolls they contain as spurs to community development.

9. Connect the unmarried males not on welfare who are often the noncustodial parents of welfare children, to their families and to work by a tough paternity identification process, tough child support enforcement, and helpful ex-offender employment programs.

The vision for the "Next Frontier," both for the state and the nation, is clear—nothing less than rationalizing the myriad well-intended but often fragmented efforts, continuing to redeploy the required resources, and maintaining the sharp focus on outcomes. This leads to a state and a country where everyone has a ladder of opportunity that they can climb to self-sufficiency and a better life. Anyone who wants to be connected to work can do so. Those who are limited because of mental and physical handicaps can achieve the maximum level of independence possible. Solving the poverty problem doesn't mean that there won't be a single person in poverty. It *does* mean that everyone has a viable route to escape poverty. Those who are mentally and physically able to work and who choose not to work can be ignored with a clear conscience, since we will *know* they have the opportunity. The vision includes more viable inner-city and "poor side of town" economies and infrastructure as increasing incomes attract retail stores and services. In addition, further substantial reductions in crime will occur as additional legitimate sources of income are opened up to disadvantaged people. The bad public housing will be vacated as people can afford to move out. Blighted areas will be cleaned up and rejuvenated as families come back together, safety is enhanced, and people can afford plants and paint.

There will always be legislative threats on the horizon, as well-intentioned legislators try to "help." For example, in Illinois a group of legislators is trying to advance legislation to exempt victims of domestic violence from work requirements. Of course, one of the reasons that women get trapped in domestic violence situations in the first place is that they are often dependent on their abusers. Opening the door to exemptions for domestic violence could rob many women of the incentive to break out of their dependence and not be victims of domestic violence in the coming years. Other well-intended exemptions would clearly follow. Some states have already wandered too far down the exemption path.

Another challenge for Illinois and the nation is rationalizing the myriad job-training and placement efforts. To maximize the muscle of all relevant federal, state, and local resources behind the effort of connecting our ladies with their ladder of opportunity, a big portion of the over $700 million in job training and placement can be brought to bear. This money in Illinois goes through ten different departments into about one hundred programs. A joint bipartisan hearing held by Senator Chris Lauzen (R) and Representative Jan Schakowsky (D) asked for outcome measurement data from each program. They merely asked program leaders to report results against what the program was set up to do (which may not necessarily be getting recipients into a job). Chris asked me to come down to Springfield to listen and help him sort it out. The hearing produced big piles of paper and lots of words, but little outcome measurement.

Much of these dollars flow through the community college systems in each state—often highly politicized bureaucracies with strong antipathies to accountability. Chris and Jan moved on to other activities, as did another panel member, Barak Obama, who became a U. S. senator. This political mobility is something the bureaucrats and providers may have counted on. Rationalizing the job-training and placement systems will require the same kind of focus, tenacity, and leadership we used to reform the human services systems. This represents a real opportunity to make a difference.

Rationalizing the myriad job-training and placement programs hasn't been crucial yet, and these programs are providing some help now, albeit awkwardly. Lots has been accomplished without fixing the systems; imagine the potential if they were made logical! Considerable federal help will be needed to unlock the potential of these dollars, and doing it will become extremely important when the inevitable economic downturns occur. Recent federal modifications in this area were helpful, but not nearly enough. More local flexibility, integration, and accountability are required.

Another real opportunity for the state of Illinois and the nation in the coming phase of welfare reform is getting government and the many large foundations in the country working together in a mutually advantageous way. Annual reports show that many foundations are devoting considerable resources to the disadvantaged and to poor communities. Many of them write checks to the various private charities, and others embark upon their own initiatives, hoping to shed light on some important social problem. Foundations are important not just for their money, but also because of the spotlight they put on programs. Typically they write lots of reports and convene many conferences. Foundation executives often serve on important boards, and they are very popular—honored guests at civic functions. Despite all of the visibility that the ability to write big checks brings, it is all too rare to find a substantive collaboration between government and a foundation on poverty issues.

Foundations are in a great position to fund pilot projects that would be difficult for a state to initiate and finance. Before it is prudent for state governments or the nation to take risks on innovative ideas, legislators and governors want to know: has anyone done this before? What happened? The Casey Foundation funding of the five test sites for integrated services in Illinois is a good example. Their success with integrating services and community involvement paved the way for statewide reform. Most foundation boards, given the choice, would like to see the foundation funds really make a difference. This means pioneering an innovative idea and, if it is successful, facilitating its replication around the state and around the nation.

Howard Peters would like to know more about license-exempt child care in communities and employment approaches for ex-offenders. He's also interested in tapping the resource of competent seniors for child care and mentoring. If such models worked well, he would aim to redeploy the funds necessary to replicate the models statewide. The money is available from welfare savings. Foundations could, in effect perform the research and development work, something most of them like to do, but the R&D could have much more impact. To do this kind of work, most foundations would have to become more focused than they are now.

Reading the annual report of many foundations, such as MacArthur in Chicago, their resources are so scattered that it doesn't seem possible for them to develop a critical mass anywhere. Adele Simmons, the immediate past president, would find a few minutes to expound her views at a meeting on the problems of Chicago communities before running off to dedicate a rain forest in Belize. A nuclear peace conference in Stockholm came shortly after. A retired senior MacArthur Foundation executive told me: "If Mr. MacArthur were to come back from his grave, he would say, 'This isn't working. I've changed my mind. I'm taking my money back!' " A more cohesive strategy and results-oriented sustained effort isn't as much fun, and a more hands-on strategy brings greater risk of visible failure, but the payoff can be great. I fantasize about foundation annual reports that, in addition to the normal financial report and list of grants, have an audit to determine, for those grants designed to help others, the number of lives changed for the better as a *bottom line*. Vague statements about people served or helped need to be replaced by real results—the same hard-nosed accountability to which DHS is now subjected. I also fantasize about improving foundation responsiveness in other ways, such as term limits for trustees and increased spending requirements that will change the atmosphere from one of institutional perpetuity to one of greater time urgency. People need help now.

There needs to be a coming together of the state human services leaders and foundations interested in helping disadvantaged people. I would argue it is not possible to responsibly help disadvantaged people without understanding what the nine-hundred-pound gorilla—the government—is up to and figuring out a way to work with it. With a good dialogue, foundations would learn of the problems confronting the state as it works toward self-sufficiency for the disadvantaged, and hopefully together they would identify needs that might overlap parts of the foundation's giving strategy. The state gets innovative ideas to replicate, and the foundation avoids the common problem of good projects that disappear when the money runs out, leaving only an evaluation report and some canceled checks. To me these foundation projects are more castles in the sand—they look great for a while, the money runs out, and the water returns the beach to its previous state. With more states like Illinois working closely with communities and the private sector, foundations can have greater impact for their dollars. The annual disbursements from even the biggest foundations are a drop in the bucket compared to almost any state human services budget—a foundation's millions versus a state's billions. Making the billions more effective can affect thousands of disadvantaged people—great leverage for foundations that care about helping people.

Having said all of this, I participated in the convening of a meeting of the leading Chicago-area foundations and the top state human services officials. The discussion was interesting, with the foundations seeking information on the state reorganization and reform, and the state leaders suggesting possible R&D projects. Everybody went back to his or her office and—nothing happened! My guess is that the foundations are used to people *coming to them* with proposals for their consideration, and this kind of proactive partnership won't happen without a lot of work by someone who will invest the time to *make a difference* on this opportunity. A smart man once said, "A pearl of great price is not had for the asking." Connecting foundations with both communities and the state can be a big plus as we move the welfare reform effort forward.

Governors have a great opportunity to demonstrate leadership and help thousands of people become self-sufficient by aggressively managing this next phase of the welfare reform challenge. The relevant Rube Goldberg chart for their particular state will identify the pieces of the puzzle that must be restructured to have a cohesive and effective management organization, focusing on a family, not on the boxes at the top of the chart. Most states are not yet organized to pursue the self-sufficiency mission effectively. Each state must carefully design an integrated organization that gives caseworkers all of the tools that they need to help longtime dependents start up the ladder to self-sufficiency.

It is also important that a careful review of state policies be carried out, policy changes made, and needed federal waivers obtained to make sure that it makes economic sense for people to leave welfare rolls for work and to remove other barriers. As Nobel Laureate Milton Freedman said, "If you and I are fools enough to make it to their advantage to subsist on welfare rather than work, they would be foolish not to take [welfare]." An analysis of the remaining welfare caseload should be made to quantify alcohol, substance abuse, mental health, and disability funding needs, as well as special efforts required to deal with convicted felon issues and transportation problems. Then the governor and his team should use the bully pulpit to sign up communities to help, with special emphasis on churches, United Ways, schools, and businesses. Giving regular recognition to communities that are doing a particularly good job is important and can have an excellent political payoff. The governor needs to put a real manager in charge of all this and hold him or her accountable for real results—visible measurable self-sufficiency outcomes.

Each state should get started on an integrated caseworker PC-focused management information system. It will take a few years, but it will be necessary to get the best results. Texas, California, North Carolina, and Arizona have already followed the lead of the Illinois Pathfinder systems design. Governor, pay whatever you have to pay to get the best management information systems manager possible—he or she will save you billions, in addition to saving lives. The right person will not be a nerdy technocrat, but rather someone with vision and people skills who can manage the technology.

In this next phase of welfare reform, it is not too early to begin thinking about what should happen when the welfare caseload is cut in half again, as government and communities work together to help make self-sufficiency happen. Rather than start shutting down welfare offices, lay off caseworkers, or wait around for an economic downturn, governors, mayors, and communities can take advantage of the long-awaited opportunity to move aggressively into reconnecting young fathers like Kenny, a twenty-two-year-old unemployed ex-offender, with their families in a productive way. Truly effective paternity establishment, child-support enforcement, drug treatment, and hard work can be made to happen. We sometimes forget, when we talk about inner-city welfare problems, that the welfare roles are almost exclusively women and children. For almost every child on welfare there is a father out there, like Kenny, not doing his job. How satisfying it will be to free up some capacity in these giant state welfare systems to go after this problem with a vengeance. A huge bonus from this activity will be a corresponding drop in crime, drugs, and other gang-related activities. In fact, the coupling of family reattachment and work may be the only fundamentally effective way of dealing with these problems. Until we help the fathers become legitimately self-sufficient, we'll have to keep building more prisons. The $38,000-per-inmate annual cost does not even include front-end capital construction costs.

In addition to reconnecting fathers and putting them to work, the newly freed-up human services systems can engage in prevention activities, which have a high return on investment to taxpayers. Working closely with churches and schools, these offices could become family resource centers, providing support to alcohol and substance abuse education efforts, abstinence and pregnancy prevention, violence prevention, connections to job training and placement, and other self-sufficiency-focused activities. For example, the drug and alcohol problems that plague our society stretch well beyond the welfare population. As a family resource center, a human services office can reach into an inventory of public and private services to connect anyone in the community with problems to effective help. The mix of activities carried out would depend on the economy and the specific needs of the community. A creative, energetic state should be able to find corporate sponsors for some of the family resource centers.

Key members of congress are hungrily eyeing the welfare (TANF) funds freed up by the success of the states in the first half of welfare reform. Given the fact that the job is far from complete, we know that there are high payoff opportunities for some, but perhaps not all of the money that has been freed up. It makes sense for the feds to look at each state individually, requiring a thoughtful plan for investment in the next phase. Again, one size does not fit all, and the way the formulas were negotiated with the states, the excess varies dramatically from state to state. No investment should be made unless tangible, measured outcomes are part of the deal.

There is a very big job still in front of our states and nation. None of the recommended governor action items require managerial and organizational steps that aren't routinely used in industry, and the management information system needed is not as sophisticated as many already used in industry. The training and upgrading of case-workers is very doable—and most of their clients *really want to become self-sufficient*. We know the answers: involved communities, integrated services for whole families, and measuring real outcomes. The tough part, as we've seen, is the political challenge—providers, lobbyists, legislators, state regulations, federal regulations, and the media. It will be interesting to see which governors emerge to lead the way on this next phase. What a great opportunity!

PRINCIPAL POINTS

1. The state of Illinois has made great progress in implementing the nation's first fully integrated family-centered, community-linked, outcome-driven system, to the degree allowable within federal limitations.
2. Leaders of other states, understanding the basic principles necessary for self-sufficiency, have a great opportunity to use the Illinois model as a prototype for reforming their systems.
3. State policies and laws should be changed to eliminate barriers, ensure that work is financially attractive, and facilitate a smooth transition to work. Communities should be the centerpiece, and top-down approaches should be avoided. Illinois can be a model.
4. Foundation help was very important in the Illinois reform, and foundations can and should play a much larger pivotal role nationwide.
5. All of these steps can be political winners as well as sound government.

11

Lessons for a Nation—
A Win-Win Opportunity

*Organizations are of two kinds: those which get something done and
those that . . . (prevent) something from being done.*
—BERTRAND RUSSELL

I walked into the old-world elegance of the 110-year-old Chicago
Club for a breakfast meeting with a delegation from Washington's Brookings Institution. It seems they have an outreach
agenda to share Washington wisdom with the provinces. I was skeptical, but the breakfast was free, and I always make a practice of checking in periodically to hear what the Beltway is up to. The speaker was
Bruce Katz, a former HUD chief of staff, and a very bright, wiry,
fortyish head of the Center on Urban and Metropolitan Policy at
Brookings. As part of the Washington maturation process, when a
Washington operative has been in and out of government a few times,
a sign of career progress is getting money to create a sort of sub–think
tank to work on a problem that interests you. This keeps bread on the
table between government jobs, and the papers produced sometimes
find their way into government policy, since politicians, their staffers,
and top executive branch officials don't have much time for reflective
thought. Often these Washington talks lack grounding in the realities
of the real world outside of the Beltway. I wasn't expecting much.

Bruce's talk turned out to be a wonderful exception. He talked
animatedly about Washington's severe problem of what he called

the Balkanization or fragmentation of human services. He laid out the complexity of funding streams, congressional committees and subcommittees, executive branch departments, and programs. He described the hodgepodge of conflicting eligibility requirements, purposes, definitions, and reporting requirements as well as the built-in government-inflicted barriers thwarting the effectiveness of well-intended programs. He then went on to convince me that he really understood the problem by describing his efforts to work with and learn from communities and states about what they were doing to try to rationalize the mess handed down from Washington. He painted the picture of states, mayors, and communities struggling against the federal tide as they try to come up with ways to pull together some of the disjointed pieces and make things work.

All of this resonated with me as I thought about the fissures driven into the state human services systems by the myriad separate federal funding streams and their requirements. While we showed in Illinois that much could be accomplished at the state level and on the front lines in the communities, wouldn't it be great to have the feds working in the same direction? I invited Bruce and his team back to Illinois and to Grand Boulevard and they spent a day in Chicago asking good questions and displaying real interest and understanding. We decided to work together whenever we could in an effort to build the critical mass of understanding and conviction needed to start changing things in Washington.

How *do* you change things in Washington? What should be changed? From the ladies in the backyard to the caseworkers with their five hundred forms, from fragmented human services to fragmented job-training and placement programs, it is difficult to know where to begin.

It is hard to stretch far enough to get your arms around everything that is part of the human services systems. It is easier to understand the particular than the whole, but the whole is how people live their lives. And if we are to understand the system, we must understand it as people experience it. To accomplish this, an experiment[1] was carried out by the Institute of Educational Leadership, a Washington think tank, that described the virtual Hernandez family, a family that was typical of those living in the poor City Heights section of San

Diego. The experiment identified and examined the more than twenty federal, state, and local programs that could be helpful to them in their struggle to escape poverty.

The father, Carlos, works when he can as a gardener, and he "has a way with machinery," keeping the fifteen-year-old family car running. Yolanda, born in Mexico, speaks little English, has a job as a housekeeper, and is four months pregnant. Yolanda's sister, Alicia, lives with the Hernandez family in their $450-a-month apartment and takes care of the children while Yolanda is at work. Nine-year-old Jose is in third grade, and eight-year-old Maria is in second grade. Five-year-old Pablo is about ready for preschool. The family does not have health insurance. One-and-a-half-year-old Roberto is deaf, and Alicia's health has not been good. The family manages to get by day to day, and has $140 in a savings account. They have no phone.

In the experiment, members of Congress, policymakers, and journalists played the part of the family, learning firsthand the hurdles they had to surmount to get help. The experiment was focused on how this family could get onto and up the ladder of opportunity. The tools were more than twenty federal, state, and local programs that could be helpful to them. The participants in the program had a head start—unlike the Hernandez family all the programs that might help the family were already identified for the participants. Also, unlike the Hernandez family, they did not have to drive miles between offices and wait weeks for appointments. Not surprisingly, the Ph.D.s, lawyers, elected officials, administrators, and think-tank people could not deal competently with the paperwork confronting the family or the eight-hundred-page workbook of application forms and descriptive materials. Not incidentally, the workbook would have been an estimated six hundred pages thicker if it had included *all* programs.

The participants found themselves cutting corners and selectively giving information to the array of program representatives present—a welfare caseworker, a job training and placement specialist, a child care coordinator, a city housing assistant, a school nurse-practitioner, and the other "helpers" they were required to satisfy. Though these program representatives were, for the most part, not federal employees, each of them was carrying out the will of the federal government, sub-

FIGURE 11: WHO IS IN CHARGE OF FEDERAL PROGRAMS
THAT MIGHT HELP THE HERNANDEZ FAMILY

Program	House Committee	Senate Committee	Executive Branch Committee
AFDC (Aid to Families with Dependent Children	Ways and Means— Human Resources Subcomittee	Finance— Full Committee	HHS— Admin. for Children and Families
Medi-Cal (Medicaid)	Commerce— Health and Environment Subcommittee	Finance— Full Committee	HHS— Health Care Finance Administration
Food Stamps	Agriculture— Dept. Operations, Nutrition and Foreign Agriculture Subcommittee	Agriculture—Nutrition and Forestry; Research, Nutrition and General Legislation Subcommittee	Agriculture— Food, Nutrition and Consumer Services
SSI (Supplemental Security Income)	Ways and Means— Human Resources Subcommittee	Finance— Full Committee	Social Security Administration
Child Care Programs	Economic and Educational Opportunities—Early Childhood, Youth and Families Subcommittee	Labor and Human Resources— Full Committee	HHS— Administration for Children and Families
	Ways and Means— Human Resources Subcommittee	Finance— Full Committee	
Head Start	Economic and Educational Opportunities—Early Childhood, Youth and Families Subcommittee	Labor and Human Resources— Full Committee	HHS— Administration for Children and Families
WIC (Special Supplemental Food Program for Women, Infants and Children)	Economic and Educational Opportunities—Early Childhood, Youth and Families Subcommittee	Agriculture—Nutrition and Forestry; Research, Nutrition and General Legislation Subcommittee	Agriculture— Food, Nutrition and Consumer Services
JTPA (Job Training Partnership Act)	Economic and Educational Opportunities—Early Childhood, Youth and Families Subcommittee	Labor and Human Resources— Full Committee	Labor Employment and Training Administration
GAIN (Greater Avenues for Independence Program)	Ways and Means— Human Resources Subcommittee	Finance— Full Committee	HHS— Administration for Children and Families
Section 8 (Rental Housing) and Public Housing	Banking and Financial Services— Housing and Community Opportunity Subcommittee	Banking, Housing and Urban Affairs—Housing Opportunity and Community Development Subcommittee	HUD— Public and Indian Housing
Free and reduced-price school lunch and breakfast	Economic and Educational Opportunities—Early Childhood, Youth and Families Subcommittee	Agriculture—Nutrition and Forestry; Research, Nutrition and General Legislation Subcommittee	Agriculture— Food, Nutrition and Consumer Services
IDEA (Individuals with Disabilities Education Act)	Economic and Educational Opportunities—Early Childhood, Youth and Families Subcommittee	Labor and Human Resources— Disability Policy Subcommittee	Education— Special Education and Rehabilitative Services
EIC (Earned Income Credit)	Ways and Means— Full Committee	Finance— Full Committee	Treasury— Internal Revenue Service
TOTAL	5 House committees 6 subcommittees	4 Senate committees 3 subcommittees	6 departments and 1 independent agency; 7 agencies

Source: Hearing before the Subcommittee on Oversight and Investigations of the Committee on Economic and Educational Opportunities, House of Representatives, March 27, 1995

ject to and limited by the rules that came with the federal dollars that paid some or all of their salaries. As the table (Figure 11)[2] shows, just the thirteen most important programs for the Hernandez family are generated by five committees and six subcommittees in the House of Representatives; four committees and three subcommittees in the Senate; and six departments, one independent agency and seven agencies in the executive branch.

The accompanying chart[3] (Figure 12) showing the congressional committees and executive branch departments and how they relate to each other gives a dramatic demonstration of how the more than $373 billion[4] federal portion of taxpayer's money pointed toward children and families travels through the Washington morass before the checks and rule books are sent to the states. This hideous arrangement could never be designed on purpose without a conscious, perverse objective to confuse the recipients and ensure inefficiency.

The current situation grew up over many years, fed by countless piecemeal additions thought up by well-meaning legislators, each adding their particular ideas on how to fix a specific social problem. Each program seems to have been written with the thought that the individual who participates in this program will participate in no other program. This means definitions of terms such as *low income, child,* and *youth* are written without regard to how they are written elsewhere. In the real world, a person can be both a youth and a mother. These definitions are important, because they determine eligibility. In four important programs, there were four different allowable eligibility limits for the value of a car. Perhaps not surprising, given the scale of the mess, the list of problems of this sort is endless.

Federal auditors for each of the departments and agencies, usually located in big regional federal office buildings in our major cities, meticulously audit their particular sets of caseworker forms for compliance. The emphasis is all too often on micromanaging the process, and rarely includes assessing self-sufficiency outcomes. Not all programs can produce self-sufficiency, of course, but when properly linked or integrated, each service can contribute in a measurable way to the whole. This federal audit activity, of course, breeds a counterbureau-

Figure 12. The Genesis of Most Human Services Programs–The Washington Octopus

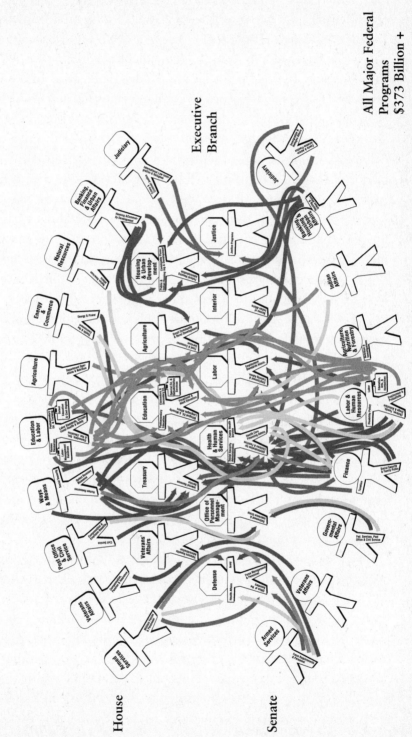

All Major Federal
Programs
$373 Billion +

cracy in each state that prepares for and deals with these burdensome, complex audits.

Fixing unnecessarily wasteful bureaucracy is important, but not the real point. The real point is that this disjointed array of top-down programs reflects the various Washington entities that initiate and control programs, and *does not reflect the holistic and integrated needs of the families attempting to become self-sufficient.* The system needs to be turned upside down, with the families at the top. We learned from the stories of people on welfare, caseworkers, and the McKinsey work that everything must connect on the front lines at the family level to produce a self-sufficiency result. Substance abuse treatment, mental health, transportation, food stamps, job training and placement, and a self-sufficiency coach must all work together—if any one is missing, success on the job won't happen. Drug treatment without a job at the end encourages a return to drug use. A job without needed drug treatment is destined for failure, as is a job without reliable child care or reasonable transportation. There are many examples, and it is easily seen that a missing piece wastes the rest of the money.

Creative states like Illinois, Texas, Wisconsin, Oregon, and Michigan have accomplished a great deal swimming against the federal fragmentation tide, but there is a limit to what even the most aggressive states can do to offset the federal damage. Only the President and Congress can get us beyond that limit—to the point, for example, where the system is strong enough to do the job in the event of an economic downturn. The time to move is now, building on the existing momentum for change, and building in the flexibilities needed to deal with any coming economic downturn.

After a few minutes looking at the chart and thinking about the Hernandez family, the thought occurs: why send all that money to Washington in the first place? There is little doubt in my mind that the states could keep the money and do a better job of helping people become self-sufficient—not to mention helping individual taxpayers. If we didn't already have the knot of Washington-originated money, it would be tough to argue for sending all those tax dollars to Washington. Taxing us in the states, running the dollars through Washington, and bringing a reduced amount back to the states bogged down with rules and regulations usually doesn't make much sense. But these pro-grams already exist. Even Ronald Reagan, a former governor, recog-nized that he did not have the nation sufficiently on his side to sharply pare back Washington's role in social policy. His policy was not "no grants" but rather "block grants." Given the fact that Washington currently *has* the money, what can be done?

Congress and the President must mount an intense effort to break down the bureaucratic barriers, integrating long-separated programs and targeting the whole family, not just individual members. Top-down micromanagement from Washington has failed. Governors and may-ors must be empowered and encouraged to take ownership of the Washington-generated funding streams and pull them together in a way that works for their communities. As in Illinois, the effort must be bipartisan and not be about increasing or decreasing funding. Politically, this reform can have all the right messages: "self-sufficiency," "ladder of opportunity, but the individual must climb it," "family-focused," "accountability/outcome measurement," "return on the taxpayer's investment," "no more one size fits all," "empower communities," "involve churches, mosques, and synagogues," "com-munities and private charities at the table to help establish priorities," "connect with employers at the community level," and many more.

Block grants, devolution, and *flexibility* are the bywords that should guide Congress and the President. Block grants can put together any number of programs on the Hernandez family list to great advantage. Assuming the block grant comes to the states with minimal strings at-tached, flexibility as to the use of these funds is significantly increased. This means that within a broad problem area, the state can decide how to use the money. The Springfield caseworker might not have to tell the distraught mother that she can only help if the mother locks her daughter out of the house (so that the federal funds earmarked for abuse and neglect that pay her salary can be used). If she felt that she could help the mother with some preventative counseling, the cost of that work would not be disallowed, and more money would be saved down the line as a family split-up is avoided. Devolving decision mak-ing through block grants allows states to combine programs and re-porting requirements at the local level.

States can then further devolve various degrees of responsibility to local entities. Depending upon the state, further devolution can involve counties, cities, or other entities. *What makes sense for Illinois will be different than for Iowa.* Since governors now have the responsibility for by far the largest portion of human services dollars, they should have primary responsibility for human services, taking whatever steps are necessary to organize their states in a way that the crucial need to involve communities is done effectively. Just as some large school systems, such as Chicago, have done better when mayors have been given clear-cut responsibility, so will state human services systems do better when the governor is unambiguously responsible for human services. Regional and other issues make it messier for mayors to have primary responsibility, and politics can create gridlock between a governor and mayors if responsibility is split. Involvement of mayors is very important, but someone needs to take the lead.

States should then be encouraged to track outcomes, organize programs, and track funding *by community,* recognizing that big cities are composed of many very different communities. As the initial welfare block grants (Temporary Assistance for Needy Families, or TANF) showed, states used some of the money not needed for benefits to beef up other needed areas identified at the community level. In Illinois this money went to child care, transportation, and ex-offender job training and placement, among other investments.

From Washington's perspective, flexibility in entitlement programs, (those programs where Washington agrees to pay a share of whatever amount a state spends) with no overall limit, means financial risk to the U.S. Treasury. It's the open-ended entitlements that involve the most spending for children and families, the most paperwork and record-keeping requirements, the most restrictions on states, and the most desire for change by states. It is a telling fact that the federal share of Medicaid has risen from $17 billion a year when Ronald Reagan became President in 1981 to over $100 billion a year today.[5] Part of the rapid growth stems from incentives that encourage states to claim that as many state dollars as possible are eligible for matching federal dollars. The worst case of this came in the late 1980s when hospitals "donated" money to states so that states could get a federal match. The hospitals then got multiples of the money back in the form of higher rates. Abuses committed by overly aggressive states have resulted in federal rules and paperwork motivated by the fear that without the rules and record-keeping requirements, states would show up at the Treasury with a Mack truck to take away all the cash they could.

The current balance puts paperwork far ahead of efficacy. Pushing the balance towards efficacy in the current system risks losing some federal funds to state budgets. However, the initial welfare block grants enacted in 1996 show how states can be given flexibility and shed record-keeping requirements while the federal government gains protection from potentially unlimited financial risk by moving from an open-ended entitlement to a program that provides each state a predetermined fixed amount.

Congress could start by creating two block grants, one for children and their parents, a second for the disabled and elderly. Another possibility is to make services for children and families a block grant while continuing Medicaid just as it is today for the elderly and disabled. The transition of increasing responsibility to the states is unlikely to occur all at once, but there are a number of alternative meaningful steps that should be taken right away. Finally, the fear that the next recession will swamp programs that help the needy if an entitlement is turned into a block grant can be accommodated by providing that the size of the grant increases or decreases with the state's population and unemployment rate, or other relevant indicators.

Every entitlement that becomes a block grant moves the monkey to the back of the states for producing results. As with TANF/welfare reform, states must deliver. Hopefully the fears that many opponents had of irresponsible states "racing to the bottom" by cutting supports and leaving citizens "sleeping on sidewalk grates," have largely dissipated, given the fine job done by most governors in welfare reform.

An important byproduct of all this *can* be a large reduction in the federal paperwork that drowns our welfare caseworkers, freeing up valuable time for the tougher remaining cases. If political candidates would join me in a Chicago human services office they would see those endless file cabinets full of paper "for the feds." At the state level there is very little we can do about this horrible waste of case-worker time. Each block grant, if thoughtfully designed (as TANF was), is a step down the road to devolving decision-making to the local level. It also allows the ladies in the backyard to get more help from their caseworker. The increased authority and flexibility that becomes available at the local level should be tied to results, as was TANF. Financial incentives and penalties are valuable in getting the attention of governors and state bureaucracies, and should be included with the next wave of block grants.

Block grants that name broad purposes for which states must use federal funds are the most desirable form of flexibility. However, that flexibility makes them the most threatening to all the interests that are invested in the status quo. If most decisions are made at the state level, what will the Washington lobbyists do? Block grants aren't the only way to loosen the dead hand of the federal bureaucracy. There are other approaches that allow interest groups to maintain what they think they have while at the same time improving the reality in the front lines. States could be provided flexibility to move funds around between groupings or "buckets" of programs—allowing, for example, the local need-based decision to set drug abuse as the number-one priority and the flexibility to redirect funds from other areas to drug treatment. Remembering that no one size fits all, if that is what legislators in Austin, Springfield, or Sacramento decide, knowing what they know about the realities of their state, that should be their choice.

Another form of flexibility would come from adding *waiver authority* to each program. If a state feels it would be more effective marching to a different drummer by linking welfare recipients to a certain job-training program, let it march. Under a waiver authority, accompanied by a careful evaluation of the results, other states can learn from the most successful approaches. The creativity that will be unleashed, especially, as we have seen, the ideas from communities, will stimulate and inform the entire self-sufficiency crusade. No waiver authority will take away the ability of congressional committees to hold hearings on bad choices made by newly empowered states or the potential for journalists to advance their careers by pursuing exposés on bad outcomes. It is a price worth paying.

The waiver idea is making progress. Welfare reauthorization was stalled in Congress for several years, with extensions of the existing (TANF) bill being authorized near the end of each session when agreement could not be reached. Most encouraging, the House-passed version of the TANF reauthorization bill provided waiver authority that included TANF, employment and job training services, food stamps, child care, family services, and public housing. This was hard to do, because it meant powerful committee chairmen giving up some control over some of their programs. As we saw in Figure 12, lots of commitee chairmen are involved. In the Senate, Senator Peter Fitzgerald (IL) and Senator Rick Santorum (PA) have taken a special interest in the waiver/state flexibility idea, and have arranged meetings with most of the relevant Senate committee chairs, and the Senate bill now includes a waiver, though less broad than the House version. With further help from the White House, which has been very supportive, the waiver opportunity has a good chance of becoming law.

I personally have invested considerable time in Washington working on the waiver, and it has been very enlightening. To me, it seemed like a bipartisan issue with overwhelming logic behind it. However, opponents of the waiver either overtly or covertly emerged with several concerns. When I asked one senator, a former governor and waiver supporter who heads one of the committees central to the waiver, why there is opposition he said, gesturing to his colleagues in the cloakroom: "Some of these guys just don't trust governors." The illusion of politicians and staffers that they can do better managing through rules and regulations written in Washington is strong. Many reflexively fear devolution, even with checks, balances, and performance measurements built in. The waivers are carefully circumscribed, revenue neutral, and permission must be obtained from an executive branch interagency waiver board. Others see waivers, perhaps correctly, as the first step down the slippery slope to block grants—more loss of control by D.C. lobbyists and their congressional patrons. Block grants in the human services could get very large, given the huge funding involved, and this could become a target for budget cutters. It is very difficult to get legislation like this passed, since so many committees are involved. The House and the Senate deserve great credit for their accomplishments so far.

These are the kinds of flexibility that can be used to maneuver in areas where the onslaught of opposition from special interest groups is especially intense. Many of these groups will fight tooth and nail in Washington to make sure none of "their" funds get lost in some block grant or flexibility pool. They sometimes are successful in winning battles in Washington they may have lost in the state capitals. The weapon of choice is what I've heard called the "weird hypothetical." The argument might go like this: "Suppose, for political reasons, a governor decides to cut funding, including child care funding, for the western half of the state. Shouldn't we put a "statewideness" requirement in the law to prevent that?" And so the fear of devolution and flexibility is stoked in Washington.

One approach with merit that can be built upon is the idea of creating a *process* where flexibility can be encouraged and allowed on a state-by-state and/or program-by-program basis, avoiding a broad-based political confrontation. This approach minimizes the potency of the hypotheticals and avoids the wholesale taking away of particular restrictions, each of which is near and dear to some group. With a flexibility process, states make known what most needs to be changed as we see which rules are most frequently proposed for waiving. Energy is not wasted in fighting for flexibility in areas that turn out to be less useful. This process would elevate, expand, and institutionalize the waiver process of recent years that so many governors have used effectively.

A House of Representatives committee, headed by Representative Chris Shays, a moderate Republican from Connecticut, has made an interesting start on this idea. I was asked to testify before his wonderfully named Subcommittee on Human Resources and Intergovernmental Relations of the Committee on Government Reform and Oversight of the U.S. House of Representatives. The description of the bill (H.R. 2086) embodies a great vision: "To increase the overall economy and efficiency of government operations and enable more efficient use of federal funding, by enabling local governments and private, nonprofit organizations to use amounts available under federal assistance programs in accordance with local flexibility plans."

Here's how it would work: a state would figure out what it wanted to do and how it would do it and describe it in a plan. The plan would be submitted to Washington, where it would be reviewed as a single proposal, no matter how many federal programs it cut across. After being approved, the state would apply federal funds in the way laid out in the flexibility plan and be held accountable to its plan, not the rules and requirements of the federal programs whose dollars are used to fund the plan.

The nature of some of the questions members of Congress asked me in the hearing on this bill was eye-opening to me. Some Congressmen indicated a real lack of trust that the governors would do the right thing. The need for checks and balances is one thing, a lack of trust is something else, and it leads to gridlock. It's important to remember that governors are elected, too, and if they are irresponsible they will usually be thrown out. One Congressman asked me in the hearings about the problem of consistency: "Won't welfare recipients move from state to state chasing the better benefits?" This would presumably spur governors into the famed "race to the bottom," making sure that their benefits were lower than those in adjacent states. I told him I thought there would always be some movement of people to states with more services, but not enough to worry about. I thought about the fellows in the cafe in the Southern Seven. Many original critics of welfare reform I know have been impressed at how hard the governors worked to make welfare reform successful.

The value of freeing up the fifty creative laboratories that the states represent is enormous. Some will be and have been outstanding, providing potentially valuable examples we would not have had otherwise; most will do fine, and a few problem states are likely to be self-correcting and worth the price for the overall result. For some reason I decided not to respond to the Congressman's consistency query with my usual lecture on the folly of promulgating top-down rules for places as diverse as Detroit and New Mexico. Representative Shays is on the right track, trying to push decision-making to the states, but he needs help from House and Senate leadership and from the White House.

A President who really wants to make a difference for families and children can also start attacking the problem the same way Governor Edgar did in Illinois. He or she could pull together the heads of all the cabinet departments involved, together with some capable and interested outsiders (including businessmen), and form a President's Task Force for Human Services Reform. The task force could be linked to the President's Deputy Chief of Staff for Policy. The name of the group doesn't matter as much as what they would be expected to accomplish—*nothing less than developing a set of recommendations reinventing the federal approach to human services* and reporting back to the president in twelve months. The President's appointments to the group should be people who would work cooperatively to solve problems that cut across departments, and he should make it clear to them that they are expected to create major change and produce results even at the cost of giving up bureaucratic turf.

A parallel effort on block grants and a flexibility/waiver process should be mounted in Congress. President Reagan had a Presidential Task Force on Human Services chaired by a trusted associate from his days as California's governor. Its conclusion: there needed to be more flexibility for states! Observers felt that the cabinet members did all they could. Their biggest problem was that the statutes they administered didn't give them much flexibility to do things differently. The Congress didn't pay much attention to the task force recommendation and the report headed to a shelf. The Reagan task force found that the presidency could create as many reports as it wanted, but the bureaucrats keep on administering the law as it stands until the Congress sends the President a law changing it. This means that the President needs to be working with Congressional leadership from the very beginning in parallel with his task force—moving ahead with some early block grant and flexibility initiatives, looking for the easier wins, or "low hanging fruit," to establish momentum. Pushing for block grants now should be easier than in the past, both because of the success so far of welfare reform, and because the budget is balanced.

The task force should start, of course, with some basic principles.

The principles should include the important ideas of self-sufficiency, integrating services for the whole welfare family, partnering with communities, and accountability for measured outcomes and costs, among other possibilities. There must be a bottom-up focus that starts with families, not with boxes on the many Washington organization charts. As in Illinois, the task force should not see recommending additional spending as part of its job, but rather optimizing the spending of the existing budget. The task force is not the place to fight about budget levels, abortion, or other ideological wedge issues. As in Illinois, if the task force sticks to the basic principles, it can come up with a bipartisan set of recommendations that can be sold to Congress. The appropriate members of Congress should be kept apprised of the task force progress and input solicited so that those recommendations requiring congressional help can get it.

In overhauling human services, the task force would have to continue to work on the process of de-Balkanizing the mess by working with Congress to create block grants to the states with an absolute minimum of strings attached and work with Congress to develop a process for responsibly allowing flexibility to states and in programs.

After the opening block grant and flexibility initiatives, some longer-term problems should be tackled. One is scattershot responsibility in Congress. Each new program has gone to whichever existing committees' jurisdiction seemed closest to the new program. Jurisdiction should be consolidated, ideally into a single committee in each chamber. The executive branch could also do a better job if programs that helped people onto and up the ladder of opportunity were consolidated into one place. The programs that provide funds to states for health and human services programs in the Department of Health and Human Services, the rehabilitation and disability programs in the Department of Education, the job-training programs in the Department of Labor, the food stamp and other food-assistance programs in the Department of Agriculture, and the housing assistance programs in the Department of Housing and Urban Development should be in one department, not five. The logic to this should be unassailably bipartisan. We learned in our tour of Illinois human services the value of integration and working with the whole family, and we learned that it can be a bipartisan cause. It just makes sense. Having said this, I have no doubt that even if the new President, the House speaker, and the Senate majority leader all made it a priority, the tenacity required to make it happen would transcend even Harvey Branigar's imagination. However, rationalizing this river of money would be a gigantic shot in the arm for those of us who are determined to pursue the next phase needed to help the ladies in the backyard and others who need a start.

The executive branch could pull together as many of the pieces as possible into a new Department of Self-Sufficiency, by starting with the Department of Health and Human Services. The Department of Housing and Urban Development could be unwound, sending its assistance programs to the new department and its housing financing responsibilities to the Department of the Treasury. The job-training programs of the Department of Labor would go to the new department. There are other variations—the point is to send integrated flexible programs to the states and administer them in a rational, holistic way with a minimum of paperwork.

Among other challenges, the White House Task Force on Human Services Reform would have to address two extremely important barriers to getting the remaining welfare recipients into the work force—transportation and violence. We learned about the direct connection between these problems and self-sufficiency from Joyce Aldridge and Janice McCrae in Grand Boulevard and our friends in the Southern Seven. Delrice Adams, the self-sufficiency coach we met in Grand Boulevard, and others in the community were essential in helping Joyce and Janice on the violence issues, and for this and other reasons, self-sufficiency coaches need to be built into the process with redeployed funds as we get deeper into the pool of problems. There is no question in my mind or the minds of now-successful longtime welfare recipients that without this support in the early months, they will not last on the job. We have the model, we know the answers, we just need to remove more federal and state funding barriers so that we have flexible funds to pursue what we know works.

Given the large number of convicted felons in the remaining pool of welfare recipients and their non-custodial partners, the task force will have to address this barrier to self-sufficiency, probably by encouraging the Illinois/Safer Foundation ex-offender model tied to job-training and placement funds and communities. Legitimate job training and placement for gang members and other inner-city youth, who we know are a large proportion of the noncustodial parents of welfare children, is a high-potential piece of the puzzle. The federal government is the key to the priorities and flexibility available in the huge flow of job-training and placement funds to the states. The earned income tax credit (EITC), properly managed, should continue to be part of the package that promotes self-sufficiency and an escape from poverty for those who have made the successful transition to work. States still taxing those deep in the poverty pool should be discouraged. Going to work needs to be a meaningful step up the economic ladder in every state.

Communities need to be the centerpiece of the dialogue in the next phase of welfare reform. The majority of the jobs needed to continue moving people to self-sufficiency will not come from the giant corporations (United Airlines, UPS, etc.) that have made the news in connection with the welfare-to-work effort so far. As with the majority of job growth in this country in recent years, most of the jobs will be with small to medium-sized businesses in the community—retail stores, local hospitals, contractors, service firms, etc. Churches are a widespread and important presence in otherwise desolate inner-city communities, and they are often willing to supply transportation, mentoring, and networking to help the client and caseworker fill in some pieces of the puzzle. More important, connections with churches can help fill the moral, ethical, and spiritual voids that underlie so many problems of our country today. Community United Way organizations and local governments can fill in other important gaps.

Congress should be clear that communities are often different than local government, and are *always* different in big cities. As we have seen, in Chicago there are over seventy quite well recognized communities: Garfield Park, Woodlawn, Cabrini Green, Grand Boulevard, Edgewater, Austin, to mention just a few, and though the involvement of city government is important, the real work will get done in the communities. Legislation can call for involvement of community collaboratives such as the ones we met in Grand Boulevard in the planning and decision-making for most programs. Illinois has proven that, with appropriate checks and balances, an effective negotiation process can constructively connect government and communities to the benefit of both. Savings resulting from more effective use of funds can be used to meet other high priority community needs.

The President, his cabinet officers, and members of Congress can use their powerful bully pulpit to push the centrality of communities on our national agenda, and they will find many excellent photo opportunities standing beside community leaders and newly self-sufficient residents in the next stage of welfare reform. A reward system can be set up to give national recognition to communities and governmental units that are effectively collaborating and making good progress. Congressional leaders can ensure that human services legislation is strongly community-centered.

Accountability for actual self-sufficiency results is also a crucial piece of a national bipartisan vision for the new higher ground in welfare reform. It's hard to find anybody against accountability, but we've got a very long way to go to get there. The President should make it clear that he or she is pursuing strong accountability not to "cut needed social spending," but to redeploy dollars from marginal programs to those that are really helping people change their lives for the better. It isn't hard to convince any experienced private sector manager that there is always a least-effective 10 percent of spending in his or her organization that should be changed.

CEOs are perpetually reviewing all parts of a company in the relentless search for cost reduction or improvement. This doesn't get done very often in government, frequently because there is no effective outcome measurement and also because the legislation that created the program doesn't leave much room to do anything about ineffectiveness anyway. These ineffective programs can be an important source of funds to redeploy to fill the gaps we identify as we get deeper into the more difficult segments of our welfare pool. Based on my years spent inside in the human services systems, the amount that can be redeployed when strong outcome measurement is installed will substantially exceed 10 percent. As an added impetus, technology tools available in the new millennium can help make government truly accountable as never before. U.S. industry has led the world in technology and has become the world's most competitive economy. Isn't it about time this know-how found its way into government?

Finally, massive federal spending on job-training and placement programs, especially those at community colleges, needs to be rationalized and effectively connected to the welfare-to-work challenge. Not all federal job-training and placement money should be used on welfare-to-work, but much of it should be. Recent federal legislation provides some improved flexibility and accountability for job training and placement, but there is a long way to go. Traditionally these funds are treated separately from disadvantaged families and communities, focusing on training the workforce at large. However, with low unemployment rates and the huge sums now spent by corporations on worker training, more flexibility in the use of these funds makes sense. Again, there's plenty of money, but congressional leadership should convert a meaningful portion of it into an effective rung on the self-sufficiency ladder. There would also be a huge payoff in both results and redeployable funds if real outcome accountability was implemented in this sprawling, undermanaged area. Legislation should stimulate a direct connection between job-training and placement programs and state human services offices to meet the need of this crucially important population.

The President can pick up the banner of self-sufficiency and lead us to higher ground as we enter the new millennium. We have lots of examples in Illinois and other states of people who had been on welfare most of their adult lives with extremely difficult circumstances who are thrilled to be working and who have been on the job for several years. They will tell you how proud they are to have their children see them go off to work and tell you of their plans to take courses that will prepare them for promotion. As they stand with the President at community events their questions will be: "Why didn't you make these changes a long time ago?" and "What can we do to help my neighbors who aren't working yet?" This is a win, win, win—states and companies need a larger entry-level labor pool to keep growing, poor people need jobs for a better life, and our President needs to show he or she can make a difference. We can take advantage of a great opportunity to keep the momentum going.

Some very good news underlying all of this is that welfare and human services spending can be frozen at existing levels until we're over the hump, and then brought down. Nobody, and I mean nobody, knows if we are spending too much or too little on helping our most disadvantaged citizens until we continue to untangle the bureaucracies and spend our existing dollars wisely. We're also buying insurance against the next Los Angeles riots. We need to keep in mind that the successes to date have been done against the backdrop of a low unemployment rate and a growing economy. We are also buying insurance against much higher costs in the future and against critics like late Senator Moynihan, who famously said that the 1996 welfare law could cause "a huge hidden calamity" in a few years. Some who opposed welfare reform are still waiting to pounce and roll it back. This is a multiyear challenge—an inner-city space program. It is particularly important not to be perceived as taking welfare and human services dollars to fund tax cuts. That can and should come later.

After ensuring national security and keeping the economy growing (the best weapon against poverty), it's hard to come up with a more important national priority than ensuring that the ladder of opportunity is there for all Americans, even those unfortunate enough to be born into multigeneration welfare families. We do, in fact, know the answers, so it won't be nearly as tough as the space program. An overarching vision of self-sufficiency, integration of services, families, communities, and accountability will do it. This vision can be realized with flexibility and devolution, through block grants and waivers, among other possibilities. A President's task force can lay out the road map.

The federal government, states and communities, working with Chambers of Commerce, United Ways, and other non-profits, have the ability to create an America with a seamless array of services that will remove the barriers faced by those remaining on welfare and pave the way to work and self-sufficiency. Employers have shown that they believe it is enlightened self-interest and a reasonable business risk to hire people from the rolls. UPS alone has hired more than 60,000 people from the welfare rolls with good results. It is clear that most people on welfare would rather be working, and as a great nation we owe them this opportunity. It is also clear that just getting an entry-level job doesn't mean immediate sulf-sufficiency and an exit from poverty, but it is a huge and necessary step on that crucially important path.

PRINCIPAL POINTS

1. For the "Next Frontier" of our national effort, the basic common-sense principles underlying self-sufficiency are clear, namely:

   - All of the elements (e.g., welfare checks; transportation; child care; alcohol, substance abuse, and mental health programs; welfare; local employers, church volunteers, and other community members) must come together in a seamless way to provide the ladder of opportunity that the ladies in the backyard will climb.
   - If any one piece of the puzzle is missing, the odds are that self-sufficiency will not happen and money and lives are wasted.
   - Communities must be involved in setting priorities, and self-sufficiency outcomes must be rigorously measured.

2. Presidential and congressional leadership could really *make a difference* if they provided focus and leadership on this major, expensive, dangerous national problem.

3. Block grants devolution, and a congressional-driven waiver/flexibility process are important initiatives that Congress can take to rationalize the many fragmented and dysfunctional programs and funding streams to which states are now subjected. These initiatives should stimulate integration of programs, connections to whole families, involvement of communities, and measured outcomes.

4. Major federally funded programs primarily intended to foster family self-sufficiency should be pulled together into a single congressional committee in the House and in the Senate, and a single, preferably separate, executive branch department, say a Department of Family Self-Sufficiency.

5. As the caseloads continue to come down, programs and funding should be open to including activities that go beyond welfare to work, and include reconnecting and putting to work fathers of children on welfare and also prevention activities. Ex-offender reentry initiatives must be included. All of these activities should have specific measured outcomes and an attractive return on the taxpayer's investment.

6. A properly empowered and effectively led presidential task force on human services reform could dramatically accelerate this now-proven revolutionary process.

Postscript—A Vision

Where there is no vision the people perish.
—Proverbs 29:18

I am convinced that in this country we are surrounded by good people and organizations we can call upon—a huge, untapped potential to help us responsibly deal with the challenge of the disadvantaged among us. Because no one, even a governor or the President, is really in charge of all of the pieces of the problem of poverty and disadvantaged people, we *all* are—and we are all in a position to make a difference. The chance for every American to have a chance is within our reach. Each citizen only needs to find an opportunity where they are convinced they can help.

A businessperson can:
Inquire of the local community organization, human services office, or call the governor's office and arrange for hiring a disadvantaged person, making sure that the supports are in place to ensure success on the job. A businessperson can also help the local United Way or nonprofits start to connect with local human services offices to help people become self-sufficient.

A homemaker can:

Start or become active in a community collaborative, working to connect government services to the churches, schools, businesses, and local government. Volunteer for mentoring—become that badly needed caring and connected adult. Set up a church child care activity linked to the local human services office.

A journalist can:

Call attention to the fact that we *know* the answers to the challenge of helping most of even the most deeply disadvantaged people become self-sufficient, and help convey to the public what is needed to make it happen. Feature articles celebrating people who are making a difference and articles about people who have moved from welfare to self-sufficiency will show the way to others. Research and explain to readers ways to get involved with the community. This would be a public service as well as being interesting to readers.

A welfare recipient can:

Accept the new changes in the system as the first steps to a better life and encourage family and friends to move ahead. Within the boundaries of safety, a welfare recipient can work with the government to reattach a father to his family.

A federal or state legislator can:

Visit families on welfare and some communities, then go back and pass laws that focus on self-sufficiency and that move us away from the Balkanization of services toward a seamless, integrated system. Eliminate policies that create barriers or disincentives to self-sufficiency. Insist that any human services legislation provide for flexibility and community collaboration. Only authorize funding that includes incentives for success on measured outcomes.

Board members or management staff of United Way, Junior League, or other charity organizations can:

Identify the other helping organizations in the community and start working to address community priorities together. Help form a community collaborative. Persuade your state to work toward seamlessly integrated services and community involvement.

A church leader can:

Reach out and connect the helping activities of the church to the rest of the community, and government. For example, church volunteers willing to mentor first-time workers can be connected to these workers by the community collaborative or local human services office. If there is no broad-based inclusive community collaborative, help form one.

A governor can:

Pull together the heads of the human services departments, some capable outsiders from business, academia, and elsewhere and charge them with developing and implementing a seamless, integrated, family-focused system that deeply involves communities and that has strong outcome measurement accountability. Install postemployment self-sufficiency coaches in the human services organization and ensure that contracts with providers are performance based. Incorporate the new system in legislation, if possible.

A talk-show host can:

On the national level: invite and interview guests familiar with the bizarre way the federal government is illogically fragmenting taxpayers' well-intended investments in poor people, illustrating with community level anecdotes the unintended consequences of top-down decision making ("Lock your daughter out, then we can help you"; empowerment zone disasters such as Atlanta, etc.). At the local level: identify total state spending on poor people, get a Rube Goldberg chart for the state and city, then interview some ladies in the backyard and caseworkers. Highlight the need for seamless integration of services focused on the whole family, community involvement, and measuring outcomes. Interview political leaders and ask them about specific measurable results.

The President of the United States can:

Initiate with Congress legislation for human services block grants and a waiver/flexibility process. Pull the members of the cabinet with responsibility for major human services programs and other leaders into a President's Task Force for Human Services Reform. Charge them with developing a plan for reinventing human services to provide integration for whole families, connections with communities, and measured outcomes.

A school principal can:

Join or form a local community collaborative and work to connect schools to human services. Drop by the local human services office and talk with the office manager about ways to work together. Help reconnect welfare recipients and the fathers of their children with your school. Call on local employers and help find jobs for students at risk of becoming dependent on welfare.

A college student can:

Volunteer to help a local community collaborative or human services office. Seek an intern position helping state government carry out human services reform. Upon graduation, consider a two-year self-designed Peace Corps–type assignment helping on reform. If the state doesn't have such a program, help the governor set one up.

A retiree can:

Work with the local human service office, calling on businesses in the community to persuade them to hire a welfare recipient—then stay with it long enough to make sure the placement is successful. Be a mentor.

A foundation executive can:

Direct grants to projects that have broad community involvement and that foster connections with state human services systems. Work with the state to ensure that there is a good chance a project will be replicated if it is successful.

A policeman can:

Join a local community group and look for ways that the police department can help on the safety challenges many welfare-to-work participants face.

An official in the justice system can:

Work with the people who are being discharged from confinement to connect them with the communities to which they are going to return. Encourage education and training in prison. For selected cases, modify the length of the sentence to reflect educational accomplishment while in confinement.

A union leader can:

Be flexible about job changes in the state human services systems as the systems are reorganized to produce results. Outside state systems, work with employers to give this new source of labor a chance, even if it means starting out with lower wages and benefits than normal. This approach is likely to produce more new union members in the long run.

A caseworker can:

Get excited about making a difference. Help is on its way. Encourage union leaders to welcome change, since some psychic income should, at long last, come with the job in addition to the paycheck. Don't be bashful about identifying useless paperwork or coming up with ideas to connect services more strongly. Ring doorbells in the community to find job opportunities for the clients. Write me a note.

An academic can:

Consider some ethnographic research that sheds light on the cracks in the not-yet-seamless system of helping people become self-sufficient. Make a point to get out and meet the people that are part of this process.

· · ·

My personal journey, though already over ten years long, remains incomplete. I feel passionately that we *have most of the answers,* so the challenge now is mobilizing the key people in the leadership of the states, with important additional help in the form of flexibility from Washington, to complete the job we started. I've changed from someone looking for a way to help others and enjoy an intellectual challenge to someone who wants to generate a nationwide crusade. Our great country could be that much greater.

On a deeper, personal level, more than ever before, I am convinced that most (but clearly not all) of the ladies in the backyard around the state and around the nation were dealt some bad cards in life and that they *can* be self-sufficient and *want* to be self-sufficient. We could have been one of them. I'll never really know what it is like to live in the ghetto with black skin, but I believe I have learned a great deal, and this knowledge, energetically and thoughtfully applied, can make a difference in welfare reform at all levels. And all levels *must* be engaged if change is to happen.

Victor Hugo said, "There is nothing more powerful than an idea whose time has come." We know what we need to know to give all Americans access to America's opportunities. This is finally a big and realistic idea whose time has come.

I plan to dedicate myself to traveling to any state where I have a chance to persuade a governor to go beyond changing the rules and regulations (a top-down fix) and engage in fundamental community-based reform. As a volunteer, I'll help the governor's team get started—returning, in effect, to my earlier career as a consultant.

We can now see a path that, without spending additional taxpayer dollars, can allow us to be as proud of our country as we would like to be—and we can offer equal opportunity (not equal outcomes) to all. I can hear Harvey telling me we've got great momentum now—to give anything less than maximum effort to get to the finish line would be a big mistake!

Appendix A—

Welfare-to-Work Job Training
and Placement

MISSION AND PRINCIPLES

I. MISSION: Develop a strategy and plan to move those remaining on welfare assistance to work.

II. PRINCIPLES:

1. Community level efforts and networks of employers are essential in each community for an effective welfare-to-work effort. Local solutions are the key.

2. Human services must be closely connected to job training/placement/retraining and retention efforts in order to effectively service most elements of the welfare populations.

3. Single points of entry to all relevant services are essential for effective resource utilization and results.

4. Public and private resources, both human services and job training/placement, must geographically match the welfare population needs.

5. The state should oversee the system, but parts of it may be operated by community providers, other government and/or private sector organizations, or by the state, depending upon the strengths of the community. Accountability/measured outcomes are essential.

6. Community efforts should be focused on problem solving to achieve measurable outcomes, with sufficient flexibility to be effective.

7. Utilize market-driven strategies to create a situation where hiring employees from welfare is in the employers' self-interest, and each employee expects that work will improve his/her life.

Appendix B—

Essential Elements and
Lessons Learned

1. Commitment of the governor and his/her top staff persons is essential.

2. Establishment of a broad-based collaborative at the state level is essential with membership from the governor's office (human services and budget), agency heads, business, academia, and community leaders.

3. One of the first tasks of a state collaborative is to gain broad-based agreement on a set of principles that include integrating services for the whole family at the local level, deeply involving communities in the priority setting, service delivery and reform process, and measuring outcomes. Principles should be bipartisan.

4. Careful selection of sufficient community test sites (probably three to five) is essential, and should reflect a *cross-section* of major state demographics.

5. It can be assumed that an effective, broadly representative community group, perceived by the community as representative, can be created. It can be created in eighteen to twenty-four months, either from scratch or by building upon an existing organization.

6. These community organizations must be pushed to ensure openness and inclusiveness, so that empowerment by the state can be perceived as legitimate. Membership should include school leadership, business, churches/synagogues/mosques, clients/users of systems, links to local government, public housing, other leading community organizations, police (especially in a city), and the justice system. Provider's participation is important but problematic, and should normally be kept to a minority or be represented by a separate but related provider advisory group. Community liaisons from each involved state department should be appointed.

7. Early in the process a high-level position must be created in the governor's office (such as Assistant to the Governor for Human Services Reform) with the sole agenda of pursuing reform and managing the test-site relationships. The person in this position should work primarily by involving state employees at all levels, but should be supported by a small staff—say three to five full-time, and consultants as needed.

8. Early in the process a management information systems team should be created, preferably headed by an outsider, working for the state collaborative. This team must evaluate what is required to link disparate state systems in a multiple location, single point of entry, PC-based system that makes available all demographic information on a client family, and all services available, both public and private.

9. Without an extensive needs assessment and without the necessity of a comprehensive overall strategy, each community should, early on, pick a specific, tangible initiative that addresses important perceived problems. This initiative should cross-cut several state programs or departments and require the state to redeploy workers, redeploy funds, or otherwise change the way of delivering services. The odds are this initiative will involve some variation of paving the way for welfare clients to obtain and hold jobs (transportation, self-sufficiency coaching, child care, etc.).

10. Employers must become involved and play a crucial role *at the community level,* providing jobs necessary for systems exits and self-sufficiency. Properly approached, employers will usually willingly become involved.

11. To achieve necessary redeployment at the local level in the test sites, state negotiators (with a lead negotiator) representing each involved state agency need to sit down with community representatives selected by the community group. State negotiators must be at a high-enough level to speak for the agency directors.

12. After success of the first initiative (e.g., former welfare recipients are on the job and staying there), attention can be turned to a broader community strategy for capacity-building and service delivery—the odds are that the community will need considerable help in this area.

13. After the value of working with these communities has been established, and demand from other communities that wish to work in this way with the state has been created, the next big step into statewide system reform can be taken by the governor and the legislature. Other preconditions include broad-based understanding of the value and desirability of integrating services (public and private) at the local level and understanding the value of working with the whole family. In addition, the desirability of outcome measurement should have been established.

14. Statewide organization redesign/reform can be greatly facilitated/enhanced with the assistance of an analytical and objective third-party organization.

15. The statewide organization redesign should be consistent with the reform-effort principles, have broad-based involvement of multiple stakeholders, and institutionalize the community/geographic approach, integration of services (one-stop), focus on the whole family, and measurement of outcomes.

Endnotes

Introduction

1. *Statistical Abstract of the United States,* U.S. Bureau of the Census (Washington: Government Printing Office, 2004–2005), Table 524, p. 347 (1996 inflation adjusted)—Federal $373 billion; state and local $151 billion.
2. *Income, Poverty and Health Insurance Coverage in the U.S.: 2003,* U.S. Bureau of the Census (Washington: Government Printing Office, 2003).
3. *Federal Register,* vol. 69, no. 30 (Washington: February 13, 2004, 7336–7338), 13428–13430.
4. Department of Health and Human Services (http://www.acf.dhhs.gov/news/stats).
5. *Tracking the Dollars: State Social Service Spending in One Low Income Community* (Chicago: Woodstock Institute, January 1996), 19. *Community Budget Analysis of (Human Services) Dollars* (Chicago: Governor's Task Force, 1994), 2–8. Also: Budget Office, State of Illinois. McKinsey & Company, GB 2000-Maximizing the Impact of Human Services Funding for the Grand Boulevard Community. Chicago (October 2000), 42. Note: The numbers from these sources vary somewhat, but "more than 240 million" is conservative, includes them all, and makes the point. Also see page 157.

6. Figure 3, page 125, this book.
7. Department of Health and Human Services (http://www.acf.dhhs.gov/news/stats).
8. Ibid.
9. Katherine S. Newman (interview), *Russell Sage Foundation News,* (New York: Russell Sage, 1999), Issue no. 4.
10. Department of Health and Human Services, Administration for Children and Families, "Changes in Caseloads Since Welfare Reform" (Washington: 2003).

Chapter 1

1. Evans E. Crawford, *The Hum: Call and Response in African American Preaching* (Nashville TN: Abington Press, 1995), 13.
2. Matt O'Connor, "Firm Beating Raiders to the Punch," *Chicago Tribune,* August 24, 1987, C1. Jerry Flint, "Know When to Fold Them," *Forbes,* December 28, 1987.
3. Michael L. Gillette, *Presidential Election Study: Oral History, 1998 Bush Campaign* (Lyndon B. Johnson School of Public Affairs, University of Texas at Austin, June 12, 1990).
4. Paul A. Gigot, "Perils of Tokenism Loom over Bush's Domestic Agenda," *Wall Street Journal,* New York, December 23, 1988.

Chapter 2

1. *1998 Green Book,* "Background Material and Data on Programs within the Jurisdiction of the Committee on Ways and Means" (Washington: Government Printing Office, May 1998), 524.
2. Rebecca Blank, *It Takes a Nation* (Princeton, NJ: Princeton University Press, 1997), 43.
3. *Summary of Federal and State Job Training Programs,* Springfield, IL (Governor's Office, State of Illinois, 1997).
4. *State of Illinois Budget FY 1996,* Office of the Budget (Springfield, IL).
5. *Poverty in the U.S.: 1997,* U. S. Bureau of the Census, 1998.
6. Agency Overview, Illinois Department of Public Aid, Springfield, IL, July 1998.
7. *1998 Green Book,* Tables 8–18, 642–643.
8. *Welfare to Work Outcomes and Performance Management,* Illinois Department of Human Services (Springfield, IL, October 1998).

9. Illinois Department of Human Services, Springfield, IL, 1999.
10. *Green Book,* 931.
11. See Alex Kotlowitz, *There Are No Children Here* (New York: Double-day, 1991) for a vivid description of the life of African American males in Chicago's tough neighborhoods.
12. *State of Illinois Budget—FY 1999,* Office of the Budget, Springfield, IL.
13. Chicago Housing Authority Web site *(http://www.thecha.org).*

Chapter 3

1. Lutheran Child and Family Services, *Annual Report* (River Forest, IL, 1998), 11.

Chapter 4

1. Jane Mayer and Jill Abramson, *Strange Justice: The Selling of Clarence Thomas* (New York: Houghton Mifflin, 1994), 208.
2. Joseph Kirby and Susan Kuzka, "Edgar Claims Netsch Plan Is His," *Chicago Tribune,* September 8, 1994.
3. Gary MacDougal, "Communities Key to Human Services," *Chicago Tribune,* October 2, 1994, sec. 4, pg. 2.
4. Rebecca Blank, *It Takes a Nation* (Princeton: Princeton University Press), 294, fig. 1–8.

Chapter 5

1. Catholic Charities of Illinois, *Annual Report* (Chicago, 1997).
2. Daniel T. Oliver and Vernon L. Kirby, "Catholic Charities—Mired in the Great Society?" *Alternatives in Philanthropy* (Washington: Washington Capital Research Center, February 1998).
3. Hull House, *Annual Report* (Chicago, 1997), 14.
4. Abraham Lincoln Centre, *Annual Report* (Chicago, 1996), 21.
5. Chuck Neubauer, Tim Novak, and Dave McKinney, "Cellini: State Capitol's Quiet Captain of Clout," *Chicago Sun-Times,* October 6, 1996, 16.
6. James P. Pinkerton, *What Comes Next?* (New York: Hyperion, 1995), chapter 6.
7. Daniel T. Oliver and Vernon L. Kirby, "Catholic Charities—Mired in the Great Society?" *Alternatives in Philanthropy* (Washington: Washington Capital Research Center), 4.

8. Louise Kiernan, "Oprah's Poverty Program Stalls," *Chicago Tribune,* August 27, 1996.

Chapter 6

1. Governor's Task Force on Human Services Reform, *Proposal to the Annie Casey Foundation* (Chicago, February 14, 1994), 37.
2. McKinsey & Company, *GB 2000—Maximizing the Impact of Human Services Funding for the Grand Boulevard Community.* Chicago (October 2000), pg. 42.
3. *Tracking the Dollars: State Social Service Spending in One Low Income Community* (Chicago: Woodstock Institute, January 1996), 19. *Community Budget Analysis of (Human Services) Dollars* (Chicago: Governor's Task Force, 1994), 2–8. Also: Budget Office, State of Illinois.
4. Governor's Task Force on Human Services Reform, *Proposal to the Annie Casey Foundation* (Chicago, February 14, 1994), Appendix P, Table 3.1.
5. *Federal Register,* vol. 69, no. 30, February 13, 2004, 7336–7338.
6. Interview: Jared Diamond, Professor U.C.L.A. School of Medicine, expert on New Guinea and author of *Guns, Germs and Steel* (New York: Norton, 1997).
7. Governor's Task Force on Human Services Reform, *Proposal to the Annie Casey Foundation* (Chicago, February 14, 1994), Appendix M.
8. Ibid, 37 and Appendix D.
9. Ibid, Appendix S.
10. Ibid, Appendix M.
11. Ibid, Appendix R.
12. Dr. Steven Preister, *Some Initial Reflections: Lessons Learned in Illinois* (Baltimore: Casey Foundation, May 3, 1996), 16.
13. Dr. Richard Sherman, *Evaluation of Community Federation Projects* (Chicago: IOTA, November 1997).
14. Nicholas Lemann, *The Promised Land* (New York: Knopf, 1991).

Chapter 7

1. Voices for Illinois Children, *Kid's Count* (Chicago, October 1998).
2. *Administration on Children and Families, Change in TANF Caseloads, (http:www.acf.ddhs.gov/news/stats/caseload.htm).*
3. Danziger, et al., *Barriers to the Employment of Welfare Mothers* (Ann Arbor: University of Michigan Poverty Research and Training Center, September 28, 1998), 4.

4. James Ricco, Daniel Freelander, and Stephen Freeman, *Gain: Benefits, Costs, and Three-Year Impacts of a Welfare to Work Program* (New York: Manpower Demonstration Research Corporation, 1994).
5. Katherine S. Newman (interview), *Russell Sage Foundation News,* Issue no. 4, 1999.
6. Danziger, et al., 5.
7. Ibid, 6.
8. "2005 Social Security Changes" (http://www.ssa.gov/pressoffice/factsheets/colafacts2005.htm).
9. *Statistical Abstract of the United States* (Washington: Bureau of the Census, 2004–2005), Table 524, 347.
10. Danziger, et al., 12.

Chapter 8

1. Interview: Larry Singer, President, Public Policy Breakthroughs, Arlington, VA, 1999.
2. Gary MacDougal, "The Missing Half of the Welfare Debate," *Wall Street Journal,* September 6, 1995.
3. Dr. Steven Preister, ibid.
4. Illinois Department of Human Services, *Overview* (Springfield, 1999).
5. *Are States Improving the Lives of Poor Children: A Scale Measure,* Tufts University Center on Hunger and Poverty, February 24, 1998.
6. Clint Bolick, *Transformation: The Promise and Power of Empowerment* (Oakland, CA: Institute for Contemporary Studies Press, 1996).
7. Administration on Children and Families, ibid.
8. Rob Karwath, "State's Troubled Families May Get 1-Stop Welfare," *Chicago Tribune,* March 23, 1994, 1.
9. Gary MacDougal, "A Better Way for Children in Need," *Chicago Tribune,* October 22, 1997, 13.
10. Clarence Page, "Important Ray of Hope in Reforming Welfare," *Chicago Tribune,* October 22, 1997, 13.

Chapter 9

1. Center for Public Integrity Web site *(www.opensecrets.org/cpi/504224.htm).*
2. *Chicago Tribune,* January 7, 1999.
3. *Senate Transcript,* State of Illinois 89th General Assembly (Springfield), May 1, 1996.

4. *House of Representatives Transcript,* State of Illinois 89th General Asembly (Springfield), May 24, 1996.
5. Dr. Steven Priester, ibid.
6. *Designing the Department of Human Services* (Chicago: McKinsey & Co., March 1997).

Chapter 10

1. Department of Human Services, *Overview,* Springfield, IL. 1999.
2. Rebecca Blank, *It Takes a Nation* (Princeton: Princeton University Press, 1997), 76.
3. Kathryn Edin and Laura Lein, *Making Ends Meet* (New York: Russell Sage Foundation, 1997).
4. *Green Book* and Author's Calculations.
5. Rebecca Blank, 113.
6. Edin and Lein, ibid.

Chapter 11

1. Hearing Transcript, Subcommittee on Oversight and Investigations of the Committee on Economic and Educational Opportunities, U.S. House of Representatives (Washington, March 27, 1995).
2. Ibid.
3. Margaret C. Dunkle, *Who Controls Major Programs for Children and Families* (The Institute for Educational Leadership, Washington, 1995).
4. *Statistical Abstract of the United States. Green Book,* 61.
5. Margaret C. Dunkle, ibid.

Acknowledgments

I owe thanks to many people involved in the complicated systems and situations important to this story. I am particularly grateful to the "ladies in the backyard" and others on welfare, some of whose names were changed, for their willingness to be candid with me about some of the most intimate aspects of their lives. There is also a long list of caseworkers, employees of the human services systems, and community leaders who were very, very helpful, and to name some will undoubtedly get me in trouble with the others—you know who you are, and I extend my sincerest thanks.

The route from the conception of this book to St. Martin's Press was an interesting one, and not at all direct. I picked out bestselling author Sam Freedman as a role model, based on my enjoyment of his inspirational book *Upon This Rock,* the story of an inner-city African American minister who led the revitalization of a tough New York City neighborhood. Sam was not only kind enough to meet with me, he devoted valuable time to leading me through four iterations of what turned out to be a lengthy book proposal. I started out referring to myself in the third person, and with each version he pushed me to reveal more of myself. He was determined to help me in my quest to make social policy interesting, and I thank him for his invaluable mentoring.

A former McKinsey partner, Carter Bales, put me in touch with Bill Matassoni, a communications professional, who got excited about the proposal and passed it on to his good friend Carol Franco, director of the Harvard Business School Press. Carol called me and said she thought the book deserved a broader audience than a business press would provide, adding that she had cried when she read the proposal, a reaction I did not at all expect but which touched me deeply. Carol took the proposal to the big annual Frankfurt Book Fair, where she gave it to the well-known New York agent Doris Michaels. When Doris returned from Frankfurt, she called me in Chicago saying that she loved the proposal and that she had read it right away because Carol had tears in her eyes as she described it. Doris went on to say that she was also moved to tears when she read it. All of this puzzled and excited me and gave rise to a lot of interest in the book. Ultimately the trail led to St. Martin's Press and a great relationship with the legendary Truman Talley, my editor and publisher, and his terrific assistant, Jill Sieracki. I give full credit and blame to Mac Talley for the original subtitle. He insisted that "How One Man Helped Solve America's Poverty Problem" would cause more people to pick up the book, and this was more important than my discomfort with its egocentricity. My candidate, "Breakthroughs in the Fight to End America's Poverty Problem," was dismissed as too policy-wonkish. As can be seen, I ended up changing to a more modest subtitle in the second (paperback) edition.

Hanns Kuttner, a real expert on national human services policies, was immensely helpful critiquing every chapter and in fact-gathering. Linda Mills contributed greatly, especially in areas relating to state policy issues and research. Hanns is a conservative and Linda is a liberal, and the seamless working relationship with both of them validated my conviction that welfare reform and poverty can be approached in a bipartisan way.

Eric Wanner, the wonderful president of the Russell Sage Foundation, graciously responded to my numerous requests for research materials. Jim Pinkerton, the noted columnist and commentator, gets thanks for urging me to write this book. Thanks also go to Rene Scherr for his critique and Julio Rodriguez, Greg Washington, and Linda Bixler for research help. Peter Osnos of *Public Affairs*, Alfred Regnery of Regnery Publishing, and Larry Mone of the Manhattan Institute, and my longtime friend Carl Kaysen, former head of the Institute for Advanced Study in Princeton, provided ideas and encouragement. Doug Nelson, president of the Annie E. Casey Foundation, deserves special mention. Doug invested valuable time serving as a sounding board for my ideas, a number of which grew out of our work together at Casey.

I am humbly grateful and indebted to all of the terrific people who shepherded me along this new path.

The University of California at Los Angeles positively transformed my life. To give others this opportunity, all profits from this book will be added to a fund I have established to provide scholarships to UCLA for students from the eight most disadvantaged high schools in Los Angeles.

My loving wife, ballerina-medievalist Charlene Gehm, was wonderful, as always, providing the first critique of every chapter, making sure I didn't sound like a policy wonk, and providing the peaceful, supportive environment needed to write this. I am a lucky guy.

Gary MacDougal

Index

Index

Index

Index